Exploring Introductory

and

A GRAPHING APPROACH

Intermediate Algebra

**Student
Solutions
Manual**

Christine S. Verity

**Student
Activity
Manual**

Laurie Boswell

FOR MATH 107

Special Edition for Lansing Community College

Richard N. Aufmann, Palomar College
Joanne S. Lockwood, Plymouth State College
Laurie Boswell, Plymouth State Collge

D1158913

Houghton Mifflin Company   Boston

EXPLORING INTRODUCTORY AND INTERMEDIATE ALGEBRA: A GRAPHING APPROACH, STUDENT SOLUTIONS MANUAL
by Richard N. Aufmann, Joanne S. Lockwood, and Laurie Boswell, and Christine S. Verity
Copyright © 2004 by Houghton Mifflin Company. All rights reserved.

Senior Sponsoring Editor: Lynn Cox
Senior Development Editor: Dawn Nuttall
Assistant Editor: Lisa Pettinato
Manufacturing Manager: Florence Cadran
Senior Marketing Manager: Ben Rivera

EXPLORING INTRODUCTORY AND INTERMEDIATE ALGEBRA: A GRAPHING APPROACH, STUDENT ACTIVITY MANUAL
by Richard N. Aufmann, Joanne S. Lockwood, and Laurie Boswell
Copyright © 2004 Houghton Mifflin Company. All rights reserved.

Senior Sponsoring Editor: Lynn Cox
Senior Development Editor: Dawn Nuttall
Assistant Editor: Lisa Pettinato
Manufacturing Manager: Florence Cadran
Senior Marketing Manager: Ben Rivera

Custom Publishing Editor: Jan Scipio
Custom Publishing Production Manager: Tina Kozik
Project Coordinator: Kim Gavrilles

Cover Design: Amy Files

ISBN: 0-618-67276-1
N-05336

1 2 3 4 5 6 7 8 9 – BKM – 07 06 05

Houghton Mifflin
Custom Publishing

222 Berkeley Street • Boston, MA 02116

Address all correspondence and order information to the above address.

Exploring Introductory

A GRAPHING APPROACH

and Intermediate Algebra

Student Solutions Manual   Chapters 1–6

Table of Contents

Chapter 1: Fundamental Concepts

Prep Test

1. $875 + 49 = 924$

2. $1602 - 358 = 1244$

3. $39(407) = 15,873$

4. $456 \div 19 = 24$

5. 127.16

6. $-6 > -8$
   $-10 < -8$
   $0 > -8$
   $8 > -8$

   a, c, d are greater than -8.

7. $\dfrac{1}{2} = 0.5$

   $\dfrac{7}{10} = 0.7$

   $\dfrac{3}{4} = 0.75$

   $\dfrac{89}{100} = 0.89$

   a and **C**, **b** and **D**, **c** and **A**, **d** and **B**.

8. 24 is the smallest number that both 8 and 12 divide evenly.

9. 4 is the greatest number that divides both 16 and 20 evenly.

10. $21 = 3 \cdot 7$

Go Figure

Since $\boxed{5} = 4$, then $\boxed{x}$ or $\boxed{y}$ would give a smaller value. Because $\enclose{circle}{5} = 6$, then $\enclose{circle}{x}$ or $\enclose{circle}{y}$ would give a larger value. Finally if $y = x - 1$, then $x > y$. So the largest value is $\enclose{circle}{x}$.

Section 1.1

1. Understand the problem and state the goal, devise a strategy to solve the problem, solve the problem, and review the solution and check your work.

3. Answers may vary. For example, if the writing is not neat, a number might easily be misread.

5. Deductive reasoning involves drawing a conclusion, that is based on given facts. Examples will vary.

7. Notice from the diagram that there are two black tiles in each row, except the middle row where the two diagonals cross and there is only one black tile. If there are a total of 101 black tiles and 1 is in the middle row, 100 black tiles are used in rows having two black tiles each. That means there are $100 \div 2 = 50$ rows with two black tiles and one row with one black tile. There are a total of $50 + 1 = 51$ rows of tiles in the square floor. Because the floor is a square, there are also 51 columns of tiles. The total number of tiles on the floor is $51 \times 51 = 2601$ tiles.

9. If a number is divisible by 2, 3, 4, and 5, these numbers should be included among the factors. First notice that 2 is a factor of 4, so if a number is divisible by 4 it is also divisible by 2. Therefore, the smallest number divisible by 2, 3, 4, and 5 is the product of 3, 4, and 5: $3 \cdot 4 \cdot 5 = 60$. The next largest number divisible by all four numbers is $2 \cdot 3 \cdot 4 \cdot 5 = 120$. Therefore, there is only 1 positive integer in the first one hundred positive integers that is divisible by all of the numbers 2, 3, 4, and 5.

11. Following the pattern A, B skipping C and D. Then E,F, skipping G and H. Then I, J, skipping K and L. So the next two letters are M and N.

13. The number of students, out of the 100 interviewed, who read *at least one* of the newspapers is:
    $63 + 41 - 10 = 94$.
    Therefore, the number of students who read neither newspaper is:
    $100 - 94 = 6$.
    Of the 100 hundred students, 6 students read neither newspaper.

15. One strategy for this problem is to look for a pattern and then guess and check. Start with 11:

Integer	Reversed	Difference
11	11	$11 - 11 = 0$
12	21	$21 - 12 = 9$
13	31	$31 - 13 = 18$
14	41	$41 - 14 = 27$
15	51	$51 - 15 = 36$
16	61	$61 - 16 = 45$
17	71	$71 - 17 = 54$
18	81	$81 - 18 = 63$
19	91	$91 - 19 = 72$
20	02	$02 - 20 = -18$
21	12	$12 - 21 = -9$
22	22	$22 - 22 = 0$
23	32	$32 - 23 = 9$

Notice that 12 and 23 are such numbers, and that in each the second digit is one more than the first. Using this pattern, 34, 45, 56, 67, 78, and 89 would also be such numbers.

Integer	Reversed	Difference
34	43	$43 - 34 = 9$
45	54	$54 - 45 = 9$
56	65	$65 - 56 = 9$
67	76	$76 - 67 = 9$
78	87	$87 - 78 = 9$
89	98	$98 - 89 = 9$

Therefore, there are 8 integers greater than 10 and less than 100 that are increased by 9 when their digits are reversed.

17. Strategy
One strategy is using guess and check to find the next largest palindrome and then writing an equation to find the speed of the car.

Solution
The next largest palindrome would begin and end in 1. Here are successively larger numbers beginning and ending with 1:
15,961 not a palindrome
15,971 not a palindrome
15,981 not a palindrome
15,991 not a palindrome
16,001 not a palindrome
16,011 not a palindrome
16,021 not a palindrome
16,031 not a palindrome
16,041 not a palindrome
16,051 not a palindrome
16,061 not a palindrome
The next largest palindrome is 16,061. The car was driven $16,061 - 15,951 = 110$ miles during the two hours. Rate, time, and distance are related as $r \times t = d$

$r \times 2 = 110$

$r = \dfrac{110}{2}$

$r = 55$

The car was being driven at a speed of 55 miles per hour during these two hours.

19. First, find the total number of squares in the grid. Because it is a 100-by-100 grid, there are $100(100) = 10,000$ squares total.
Next, find the number of shaded squares. Because there are 100 squares shaded in the top row, 99 shaded in the second row, 98 in the third row, and so on, this is the sum:
$100 + 99 + 98 + 97 + \cdots + 3 + 2 + 1$, or the sum of the first 100 integers. The sum of the first n integers is given by the formula $\dfrac{n(n+1)}{2}$. So this sum is $\dfrac{100(100+1)}{2} = \dfrac{100(101)}{2} = \dfrac{10,100}{2} = 5050$.
Now find the number of unshaded squares—this is the difference between the total number of squares and the number of shaded squares:
$10,000 - 5050 = 4950$
The ratio of the squares shaded to the squares not shaded is $\dfrac{5050}{4950} = \dfrac{50(101)}{50(99)} = \dfrac{101}{99}$.

21. Suppose there is one girl and one boy. Then the girl has no sisters and 1 brother. This doesn't fit the conditions of the problem.

Now suppose there are 2 girls and 1 boy in the family. Then each girl has 1 sister and 1 brother, which satisfies the condition that each girl has the same number of brothers as sisters. The boy has 2 sisters but no brothers. This doesn't fit the conditions of the problem.

Now suppose there are 2 girls and 2 boys. Then each girl has 1 sister and 2 brothers, which does not satisfy the condition that each girl has the same number of brothers as sisters.

Now suppose there are 3 girls and 2 boys. Then each girl has 2 sisters and 2 brothers, which satisfies the condition that each girl has the same number of brothers as sisters. Each boy has 3 sisters and 1 brother, which doesn't satisfy the condition that each boy has twice as many sisters as brothers.

Now suppose that there are 3 girls and 3 boys. Then each girl has 2 sisters and 3 brothers, which does not satisfy the condition that each girl has the same number of brothers as sisters.

Now suppose that there are 4 girls and 3 boys. Then each girl has 3 sisters and 3 brothers, which satisfies the condition that each girl has the same number of brothers as sisters. Each boy has 4 sisters and 2 brothers, which satisfies the condition that each boy has twice as many sisters as brothers.

With both conditions met, there are 4 girls and 3 boys in the family, or a total of $4 + 3 = 7$ children.

23. The LCD of 2, 4, 6, 8, 10, and 12 is 120.
The sum becomes:

$$\frac{60}{120} + \frac{30}{120} + \frac{20}{120} + \frac{15}{120} + \frac{12}{120} + \frac{10}{120}$$

Therefore, eliminating $\frac{15}{120}$ and $\frac{12}{120}$ from the

sum we obtain: $\frac{60}{120} + \frac{30}{120} + \frac{20}{120} + \frac{10}{120} = \frac{120}{120} = 1$

Thus, if we eliminate $\frac{1}{8}$ and $\frac{1}{10}$ from the

original sum, the sum of the remaining terms is equal to 1.

25. If it takes one loaf 30 minutes to fill the oven, doubling in volume each minute, then at 29 minutes, the oven would be half filled. At 28 minutes, the oven would be one quarter filled with one loaf. So for the oven to be half filled with two loaves of bread, would be at the 28-minute mark.

27. 5, 11, 17, 23, 29, 35, . . .
The pattern of the sequence is that each term is 6 more than the previous term. Six more than the last term of the sequence is $35 + 6 = 41$. The next term in the sequence is 41.

29. 1, 8, 27, 64, 125, . . .
This is a sequence of consecutive perfect cubes: 1^3, 2^3, 3^3, 4^3, and 5^3. The next term in the sequence would be 6 cubed, or $6^3 = 216$.

31. 2, 3, 7, 16, 32, 57, . . .
The differences between successive terms follows the pattern 1, 4, 9, 16, 25, the sequence of consecutive perfect squares. The next term in this pattern would be the next perfect square 36, so the next term in the original sequence is 36 more than the previous: $57 + 36 = 93$
The next term in the sequence is 93.

33. a, b, f, g, k, l, p, q, . . .
The pattern of the sequence is that two consecutive letters of the alphabet are listed and then the next 3 consecutive letters are omitted, and so on. Therefore, after p and q are listed, the next three letters (r, s, and t) are omitted, and then the next letter listed in the sequence would be u.

35. $12,345,679 \cdot 9 = 111,111,111$
$12,345,679 \cdot 18 = 222,222,222$
$12,345,679 \cdot 27 = 333,333,333$
$12,345,679 \cdot 36 = 444,444,444$
$12,345,679 \cdot 45 = 555,555,555$
Answers will vary; for example, multiplying a multiple of 9 times 12, 345,679 results in a nine-digit number with repeating digits.
$12,345,679 \cdot 54 = 666,666,666$
$12,345,679 \cdot 63 = 777,777,777$

37. The first figure in the sequence shows a line pointing straight down. In the next figure, the line has been rotated counter-clockwise 90 degrees. In the third figure, the line has been rotated another 90 degrees counterclockwise. In the last figure, the line has been rotated yet another 90 degrees counterclockwise. We would expect the next figure in the sequence to have the line rotated another 90 degrees counterclockwise. The next figure in the sequence is

39. We are given that $\nabla\nabla = \oplus\oplus\oplus$ and $\oplus\oplus\oplus = \Lambda\ \Lambda\ \Lambda\ \Lambda$.
These are the same

$\nabla\nabla = \oplus\oplus\oplus$ and $\oplus\oplus\oplus = \Lambda\ \Lambda\ \Lambda\ \Lambda$

Therefore, these are equal.

Since 2 ∇'s = 4 Λ's, 6 ∇'s = 12 Λ's. That is,
$\nabla\nabla\nabla\nabla\nabla\nabla = \Lambda\ \Lambda\ \Lambda\ \Lambda\ \Lambda\ \Lambda\ \Lambda\ \Lambda\ \Lambda\ \Lambda\ \Lambda\ \Lambda$

41. We are given that ♦♦♦ = ♣♣. Then we know that ♦♦♦♦♦♦ = ♣♣♣♣. Furthermore, ♠♠ = ♦♦♦♦♦♦. Thus, ♠♠ = ♣♣♣♣. Also, ♣♣♣♣ = ♥. So, ♠♠ = ♥. We are asked how many ♥'s equal ♠♠♠♠♠♠. Since ♠♠ = ♥, ♠♠♠♠♠♠ = ♥♥♥. Therefore, 3 ♥'s equal ♠♠♠♠♠♠.

43. The difference is always 3087.

45. February and March, since there are 28 days in February.

47. The conclusion is based on a principle. Therefore, it is an example of deductive reasoning.

49. The conclusion is based on observation of a pattern. Therefore, it is an example of inductive reasoning.

51. From statement (a), neither Tony nor Anita owns the utility stock or the automotive stock.

From statement (b), Maria does not own the automotive stock. There are now Xs for 3 of the 4 siblings in the automotive stock column; therefore, Jose must own the automotive stock. Place a √ in that box. Since Jose owns the automotive stock, he cannot own any of the other stocks. Write Xb for these conditions.

From statement (c), Tony does not own the technology stock. There are now Xs for 3 of the 4 stocks in Tony's row; therefore, Tony must own the oil stock. Place a √ in that box. Since Tony owns the oil stock, none of the other siblings can own it. Write Xc for these conditions. Since there are now 3 Xs in Anita's row, Anita must own the technology stock. Place a √ in that box.

	Utility	Auto	Tech	Oil
Anita	Xa	Xa	√	Xc
Tony	Xa	Xa	Xc	√
Maria	√	Xb	Xb	Xb
Jose	Xb	√	Xb	Xb

Anita owns the technology stock; Tony owns the oil stock; Maria owns the utility stock, and Jose owns the automotive stock.

53. From statement (a), Chicago did not host the comic book convention.

From statement (b), Philadelphia did not host the baseball card convention. Neither Seattle nor Chicago hosted the coin convention.

From statement (c), Atlanta did not host the coin convention. There are now Xs for 3 of the 4 cities in the coin column; therefore, Philadelphia hosted the coin convention. Place a √ in that box. Since Philadelphia hosted the coin convention, it cannot host any of the other conventions. Write Xc for these conditions.

From statement (d), Chicago did not host the stamp convention. There are now Xs in 3 of the 4 conventions in the Chicago row. Therefore, Chicago hosted the baseball card convention. Place a √ in that box. Since Chicago hosted the baseball card convention, none of the other cities can host the baseball card convention. Write Xd for these conditions.

Going back over the statements, notice that in (a) the comic book convention was in August and that in (c) the Atlanta convention was in July. Therefore, Atlanta did not host the comic book convention. Write Xc for this condition. There are now Xs in 3 of the 4 conventions in the Atlanta row. Therefore, Atlanta hosted the stamp convention. Place a √ in that box. That means that Seattle did not host the stamp convention. Write Xc for this condition. There are now Xs in 3 of the 4 conventions in the Seattle row. Therefore, Seattle hosted the comic book convention. Place a √ in that box.

	Coin	Stamp	Comic	B cards
Atlanta	Xc	√	Xc	Xd
Chicago	Xb	Xd	Xa	√
Philly.	√	Xc	Xc	Xb
Seattle	Xb	Xc	√	Xd

Atlanta hosted the stamp convention; Chicago hosted the baseball card convention; Philadelphia hosted the coin convention; Seattle hosted the comic book convention.

Applying Concepts 1.1

55. No, you cannot make that conclusion. Not all numbers ending in a 1, 5, or 6 is a fourth power of a number. For example, 1331 ends in a 1, but is the third power of 11.

57. Solve by using guess and check. Start by listing each possible 6-digit number fitting the description and then checking to see if the number is a multiple of 12 but not a multiple of 9.

	1*K*31*K*4	÷ 12	÷ 9
K = 0	103104	yes	yes
K = 1	113114	no	no
K = 2	123124	no	no
K = 3	133134	no	no
K = 4	143144	no	no
K = 5	153154	no	no
K = 6	163164	yes	no

We find that when $K = 6$ we have the 6-digit number 163164, which is divisible by 12 but not divisible by 9. Therefore, $K = 6$.

59. Solve using guess and check.
Let $a = b = c = 1$:
$1^2 + 1^2 + 1^2 = 3$, not a perfect square
Let $a = b = 1$ and $c = 2$:
$1^2 + 1^2 + 2^2 = 1 + 1 + 4 = 6$, not a perfect square
Let $a = 1$ and $b = c = 2$:
$1^2 + 2^2 + 2^2 = 1 + 4 + 4 = 9$, a perfect square
Since $9 = 3^2$, $d = 3$.

Section 1.2

1. Explanations will vary.

3. $\{x \mid x < 5\}$ does not include the element 5, whereas $\{x \mid x \le 5\}$ does include the element 5.

5. a. No. Explanations will vary.

b. Yes. Explanations will vary.

7. a. Natural numbers: 31, 8600

b. Whole numbers: 31, 8600

c. Integers: 31, –45, –2, 8600

d. Positive integers: 31, 8600

e. Negative integers: –45, –2

f. Prime numbers: 31

9. a. Integers: –17

b. Rational numbers: $-17, 0.3412, \dfrac{27}{91}, 6.\overline{12}$

c. Irrational numbers: $\dfrac{3}{\pi}, -1.010010001 \ldots$

d. Real numbers: all

11. The integers between –4 and 0:
$\{-3, -2, -1\}$

13. The odd natural numbers less than 15:
$\{1, 3, 5, 7, 9, 11, 13\}$

15. The letters in the word *banana:*
$\{a, b, n\}$

17. The natural numbers less than 0: $\varnothing$

19. The integers less than –5:
$\{x \mid x < -5, x \in \text{integers}\}$

21. The real numbers greater than or equal to –4:
$\{x \mid x \ge -4\}$

23. The real numbers between –2 and 5:
$\{x \mid -2 < x < 5\}$

25. $4 \notin \{-8, -4, 0, 4, 8\}$
False because 4 is an element of the set.

27. $\{a\} \in \{a, b, c, d, e\}$
False because the *set* consisting of the element a is not an *element* of the given set.

29. $0 \in \varnothing$
False because the empty set contains no elements.

31. $\{x \mid x < -1\}$
The set is the real numbers less than –1. Draw a right parenthesis at –1 and darken the number line to the left of –1. The graph is shown below.

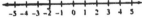

33. $\{x \mid x \le -2\}$
The set is the real numbers less than or equal to –2. Draw a right bracket at –2 and darken the number line to the left of –2. The graph is shown below.

35. $A = \{2, 3, 5, 8\}$ and $B = \{9, 10\}$
$A \cup B = \{2, 3, 5, 8, 9, 10\}$

37. $A = \{x \mid x \in \text{rational numbers}\}$ and $B = \{x \mid x \in \text{real numbers}\}$
$A \cup B = \{x \mid x \in \text{real numbers}\}$ because all rational numbers are real numbers.

39. $A = \{2, 4, 6, 8, 10\}$ and $B = \{4, 6\}$
$A \cap B = \{4, 6\}$

41. $A = \{x \mid x \in \text{rational numbers}\}$ and $B = \{x \mid x \in \text{irrational numbers}\}$
$A \cap B = \varnothing$ because there are not rational numbers that are also irrational numbers.

43. $M = \{1, 4, 6, 8, 9, 10\}$ and $C = \{2, 3, 5, 7\}$
$M \cup C = \{1, 2, 3, 4, 5, 6, 7, 8, 9, 10\}$
$M \cap C = \varnothing$

45. $\{\,x\,|\,x \le 2\,\} \cup \{\,x\,|\,x > 4\,\}$
The set is the set of real numbers either less than or equal to 2 or greater than 4. The graph is shown below.

47. $\{\,x\,|\,x > -1\,\} \cap \{\,x\,|\,x \le 4\,\}$
The set is the set of real numbers both greater than −1 and less than or equal to 4. The set is $\{\,x\,|\,-1 < x \le 4\,\}$.

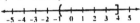

49. The graph of $\{\,x\,|\,-1 < x < 5\,\}$ is shown below.

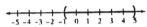

51. The graph of $\{\,x\,|\,-1 \le x \le 1\,\}$ is shown below.

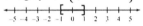

53. $\{\,x\,|\,x < -2\,\} \cup \{\,x\,|\,x < -4\,\}$
The set is the set of real numbers either less than −2 or less than −4. The set is $\{\,x\,|\,x < -2\,\}$.

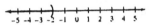

55. $[-5, 7]$ The set is the real numbers greater than or equal to −5 and less than or equal to 7. $\{\,x\,|\,-5 \le x \le 7\,\}$

57. $(-9, 5]$ The set is the real numbers greater than −9 and less than or equal to 5. $\{\,x\,|\,-9 < x \le 5\,\}$

59. $[-2, \infty)$ The set is the real numbers greater than or equal to −2. $\{\,x\,|\,x \ge -2\,\}$

61. $\{\,x\,|\,0 \le x \le 3\,\}$ The set is the real numbers greater than or equal to 0 and less than or equal to 3. $[0, 3]$

63. $\{\,x\,|\,-2 \le x < 7\,\}$ The set is the real numbers greater than or equal to −2 and less than 7. $[-2, 7)$

65. $\{\,x\,|\,x \le -5\,\}$ The set is the real numbers less than or equal to −5. $(-\infty, -5]$

67. $\{\,x\,|\,x > 23\,\}$ The set is the real numbers greater than 23. $(23, \infty)$

69. $[0, 3]$
This is the set of real numbers greater than or equal to 0 and less than or equal to 3. The graph is shown below.

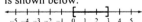

71. $(1, \infty)$
This is the set of real numbers greater than 1. The graph is shown below.

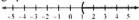

73. $(-3, 4] \cup [-1, 5)$
This is the set of real numbers greater than −3 and less than 5. The graph is shown below.

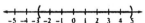

75. $[-5, 4) \cap (-2, \infty)$
This is the set of real numbers greater than −2 and less than 4. The graph is shown below.

77. $(-\infty, 2] \cup (4, \infty)$
This is the set of real numbers less than or equal to 2 or greater than 4. The graph is shown below.

Applying Concepts 1.2

79. Explanations will vary.

81. A set is well defined if it is possible to determine whether any given item is an element of the set. Examples will vary. For example, the set of great songs is not a well defined set.

Section 1.3

1. Sometimes true
The opposite of 0 is 0.

3. Never true.
The natural numbers do not include 0. The integers include 0.

5. Sometimes true
For instance, if a negative integer is subtracted from a positive integer, the difference is greater than either of the two integers.
$-1 - (-5) = 4$

7. Explanations will vary.

9. a. Add the absolute values of the numbers. Then attach the sign of the addends.

   b. Find the absolute value of each number. Then subtract the lesser of these absolute values from the greater one. Attach the sign of the number with the greater absolute value.

11. a. Multiply the absolute values of the numbers. The product is positive.

   b. Multiply the absolute values of the numbers. The product is negative.

13. The opposite of 25 is −25.

15. The opposite of −34 is 34.

17. The opposite of 0 is 0.

19. The opposite of 12 is −12.

21. $-(-16) = 16$

23. $-(49) = -49$

25. $|\,16\,| = 16$

27. $|\,-32\,| = 32$

29. $-|\,86\,| = -86$

31. $-|\,-54\,| = -54$

33.

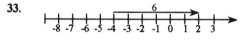

2 is 6 units to the right of –4.

35.

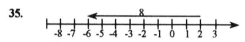

–6 is 8 units to the left of 2.

37.

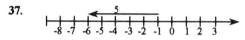

–6 is 5 units to the left of –1.

39. $|\,-6\,| = 6,\ |\,15\,| = 15$
$15 - 6 = 9$
$-6 + 15 = 9$

41. $|\,-23\,| = 23,\ |\,-17\,| = 17$
$23 + 17 = 40$
$(-23) + (-17) = -40$

43. $|\,17\,| = 17,\ |\,-3\,| = 3,\ |\,29\,| = 29$
$17 - 3 = 14 \quad 17 + (-3) = 14$
$14 + 29 = 43$
$17 + (-3) + 29 = 43$

45. $|\,13\,| = 13,\ |\,62\,| = 62,\ |\,-38\,| = 38$
$13 + 62 = 75$
$75 - 38 = 37$
$13 + 62 + (-38) = 37$

47. $13 + (-22) + 4 + (-5) = -9 + 4 + (-5)$
$\qquad\qquad\qquad\qquad\ = -5 + (-5)$
$\qquad\qquad\qquad\qquad\ = -10$

49. $-6 - 8 = -6 + (-8) = -14$

51. $-12 - 16 = -12 + (-16) = -28$

53. $-12 - (-3) - (-15) = -12 + 3 + 15$
$\qquad\qquad\qquad\qquad = -9 + 15$
$\qquad\qquad\qquad\qquad = 6$

55. $4 - 12 - (-8) = 4 + (-12) + 8$
$\qquad\qquad\qquad = -8 + 8$
$\qquad\qquad\qquad = 0$

57. $13 - 7 - (-15) - 9 = 13 + (-7) + 15 + (-9)$
$\qquad\qquad\qquad\qquad = 6 + 15 + (-9)$
$\qquad\qquad\qquad\qquad = 21 + (-9)$
$\qquad\qquad\qquad\qquad = 12$

59. $-16 - 47 - 63 - 12$
$= -16 + (-47) + (-63) + (-12)$
$= -63 + (-63) + (-12)$
$= -126 + (-12)$
$= -138$

61. The sum of –8 and 11 is $-8 + 11$.
$|\,-8\,| = 8,\ |\,11\,| = 11$
$11 - 8 = 3$
$-8 + 11 = 3$

63. –9 added to –11 is $-11 + (-9)$.
$|\,-11\,| = 11,\ |\,-9\,| = 9$
$11 + 9 = 20$
$-11 + (-9) = -20$

65. The sum of –16, –8, and 14 is
$-16 + (-8) + 14 = -24 + 14$
$\qquad\qquad\qquad\ = -10$

67. The difference between 7 and 14 is
$7 - 14 = 7 + (-14) = -7$

69. –4 minus –12 is
$-4 - (-12) = -4 + 12 = 8$

71. 24 minus –24 is
$24 - (-24) = 24 + 24 = 48$

73. a. For Calcavecchia,
$$0 + (-6) + (-4) + 0 = -10$$
For Duval,
$$-1 + (-6) + (-2) + (-5)$$
$$= -7 + (-2) + (-5)$$
$$= -9 + (-5)$$
$$= -14$$
For Els,
$$-1 + (-4) + (-4) + 0$$
$$= -5 + (-4)$$
$$= -9$$
For Furyk,
$$-3 + (-1) + (-2) + (-3)$$
$$= -4 + (-2) + (-3)$$
$$= -6 + (-3)$$
$$= -9$$
For Izawa,
$$-1 + (-6) + 2 + (-5)$$
$$= -7 + 2 + (-5)$$
$$= -5 + (-5)$$
$$= -10$$
For Langer,
$$1 + (-3) + (-4) + (-3)$$
$$= -2 + (-4) + (-3)$$
$$= -6 + (-3)$$
$$= -9$$
For Michelson,
$$-5 + (-3) + (-3) + (-2)$$
$$= -8 + (-3) + (-2)$$
$$= -11 + (-2)$$
$$= -13$$
For Triplett,
$$-4 + (-2) + (-2) + (-1)$$
$$= -6 + (-2) + (-1)$$
$$= -8 + (-1)$$
$$= -9$$
For Woods,
$$-2 + (-6) + (-4) + (-4)$$
$$= -8 + (-4) + (-4)$$
$$= -12 + (-4)$$
$$= -16$$

b. The order from lowest score to highest score is: Woods, Duval, Michelson, Calcavecchia, Izawa, Els, Furyk, Langer, and Triplett.

75. For Kansas,
$$29,676 + (-1860) = \$27,816$$
For Minnesota,
$$29,676 + 2425 = \$32,101$$
For Missouri,
$$29,676 + (-2231) = \$27,445$$
For Nebraska,
$$29,676 + (-1847) = \$27,829$$
For North Dakota,
$$29,676 + (-4761) = \$25,068$$
For South Dakota,
$$29,676 + (-3561) = \$26,115$$

77.

-6 is three 2-unit steps to the left of 0.

79. $-8 \cdot 12 = -96$

81. $24(-14) = -336$

83. $0(-41) = 0$

85. $6(-7)(4) = -42(4) = -168$

87. $-4(-3)(-7) = 12(-7) = -84$

89. $-4(-4)(-3)(-5) = 16(-3)(-5)$
$$= -48(-5)$$
$$= 240$$

91. $-56 \div (7) = -8$

93. $(-48) \div (-8) = 6$

95. $\dfrac{0}{-17} = 0$

97. $\dfrac{-63}{9} = -7$

99. $12(-7) = -84$

101. $10(-11) = -110$

103. $21(-4)(-3) = -84(-3) = 252$

105. $\dfrac{64}{-8} = -8$

107. $\dfrac{98}{-14} = -7$

109. $\dfrac{-168}{-7} = 24$

111. $-4 \div 1 = -4$
$$-4(16) = -64$$
$$-64(-4) = 256$$
$$256(-4) = -1024$$
The next three terms are -64, 256, and -1024.

113. $-6 \div (-1) = 6$
$$-36(6) = -216$$
$$-216(6) = -1296$$
$$-1296(6) = -7776$$
The next three terms are -216, -1296 and -7776.

115. $-27,992,000(4) = -111,968,000$
The annual net income for Tickets.com would be $-\$111,968,000$.

117. $-12,300,000 \div 3 = -4,100,000$
The average monthly net income was $-\$4,100,000$.

119. $2^5 = 2 \cdot 2 \cdot 2 \cdot 2 \cdot 2$
$= 4 \cdot 2 \cdot 2 \cdot 2$
$= 8 \cdot 2 \cdot 2$
$= 16 \cdot 2$
$= 32$

121. $0^{17} = 0 \cdot 0 \cdot 0 \cdot 0 \cdot 0 \cdot 0 \cdot 0 \cdot 0 \cdot 0$
$\cdot 0 \cdot 0 \cdot 0 \cdot 0 \cdot 0 \cdot 0 \cdot 0 \cdot 0 = 0$

123. $7^4 = 7 \cdot 7 \cdot 7 \cdot 7$
$= 49 \cdot 7 \cdot 7$
$= 343 \cdot 7$
$= 2401$

125. $9^3 = 9 \cdot 9 \cdot 9$
$= 81 \cdot 9$
$= 729$

127. $-4^3 = -(4 \cdot 4 \cdot 4) = -64$

129. $(-3)^4 = (-3)(-3)(-3)(-3) = 81$

131. $2^2 \cdot 3^2 = 2 \cdot 2 \cdot 3 \cdot 3 = 4 \cdot 9 = 36$

133. $(-3) \cdot 2^2 = (-3) \cdot 2 \cdot 2 = -3 \cdot 4 = -12$

135. $(-4) \cdot (-2)^3 = -4 \cdot (-2)(-2)(-2) = (-4)(-8) = 32$

137. $2^3 \cdot 3^3 \cdot (-4) = 2 \cdot 2 \cdot 2 \cdot 3 \cdot 3 \cdot 3 \cdot (-4)$
$= 8 \cdot 27 \cdot (-4)$
$= 216 \cdot (-4)$
$= -864$

139. $(-7) \cdot 4^2 \cdot 3^2 = (-7) \cdot 4 \cdot 4 \cdot 3 \cdot 3$
$= (-7) \cdot 16 \cdot 9$
$= -112 \cdot 9$
$= -1008$

141. $8^2 \cdot (-3)^3 \cdot 5 = 8 \cdot 8 \cdot (-3)(-3)(-3) \cdot 5$
$= 64 \cdot (-27) \cdot 5$
$= -1728 \cdot 5$
$= -8640$

143. $37 - 6 \cdot 5 = 37 - 30 = 7$

145. $2^2 \cdot 3 - 3 = 4 \cdot 3 - 3$
$= 12 - 3$
$= 9$

147. $3^4 + \dfrac{15}{5} = 3 \cdot 3 \cdot 3 \cdot 3 + 3$
$= 81 + 3$
$= 84$

149. $12 + 4 \cdot 2^3 = 12 + 4 \cdot 8$
$= 12 + 32$
$= 44$

151. $2^2(3^2) - 2 \cdot 3 = 4(9) - 6$
$= 36 - 6$
$= 30$

153. $(8-2)^2 - 3 \cdot 4 + 6 = 6^2 - 12 + 6$
$= 36 - 12 + 6$
$= 24 + 6$
$= 30$

155. $2(8-5)^3 + 6(1+3)^3 - 9^2 = 2(3)^3 + 6(4)^3 - 81$
$= 2(27) + 6(64) - 81$
$= 54 + 384 - 81$
$= 438 - 81$
$= 357$

157. $8 - 2(3)^2 = 8 - 2(9)$
$= 8 - 18$
$= -10$

159. $27 - 18 \div (-3^2) = 27 - 18 \div (-3 \cdot 3)$
$= 27 - 18 \div (-9)$
$= 27 - (-2)$
$= 27 + 2$
$= 29$

161. $14 - 2^2 - (4-7) = 14 - 4 - (-3)$
$= 10 + 3$
$= 13$

163. $24 \div \dfrac{3^2}{5-8} - (-5) = 24 \div \dfrac{3 \cdot 3}{5-8} + 5$
$= 24 \div \dfrac{9}{-3} + 5$
$= 24 \div (-3) + 5$
$= -8 + 5$
$= -3$

165. $18 \div (2^3 - 9) + (-3) = 18 \div (8-9) + (-3)$
$= 18 \div (-1) + (-3)$
$= -18 + (-3)$
$= -21$

167. $4(-8) \div [2(7-3)^2] = (-32) \div [2(4)^2]$
$= -32 \div [2(16)]$
$= -32 \div [32]$
$= -1$

169. Strategy
To find the average temperature, divide the sum of the temperatures by seven.

Solution
$$\frac{-4 + 2 + 7 + (-5) + (-4) + (-2) + (-1)}{7} = \frac{-7}{7} = -1$$
The average daily low temperature was $-1°C$.

171. Strategy
To find the score, find the sum of the product of each score and value.

Solution
$28(8) + 5(-2) + 7(0) = 224 + (-10) + 0 = 214$
The score is 214 points.

173. Strategy
To determine if the distance is more or less than a football field, evaluate the expression and compare it to the length of a football field (300 ft).

Solution
$16 \cdot 5^2 = 16 \cdot 25 = 400$
The distance is 400ft. It is more than the length of a football field since the length of a football field is 300 ft.

175. Strategy
To find the average temperature, divide the sum of the temperatures by six.

Solution
$$\frac{-46 + -42 + -25 + -10 + 7 + 20}{6} = \frac{-96}{6} = -16$$
The average daily low temperature was $-16°F$.

177. Strategy
To find the difference in average temperatures, first find the average temperature of the first three months in Chicago. Then find the average temperature of the first three months in Minneapolis. Finally find the difference between the two averages.

Solution
For the first three months in Chicago,
$$\frac{-24 + -12 + 0}{3} = \frac{-36}{3} = -12$$
For the first three months in Minneapolis,
$$\frac{-34 + -33 + -32}{3} = \frac{-99}{3} = -33$$
$-12 - (-33) = 21$
The difference is $21°F$.

Applying Concepts 1.3

179. **a.** $1 + (-5) = -4$
$\quad 1 + 5 = 6$

b. $2 + (-6) = -4$
$\quad 2 + 6 = 8$

181. **a.** negative 7

b. the opposite of negative 10

c. the opposite of the absolute value of 9

d. the opposite of the absolute value of negative 24

183. Answers will vary. For example, row 1: $-3, 2, 1$; row 2: $4, 0, -4$; row 3: $-1, -2, 3$.

185. **a.** Possible products include:
$(-17)(-1) = 17$
$(-16)(-2) = 32$
$(-15)(-3) = 45$
$(-14)(-4) = 56$
$(-13)(-5) = 65$
$(-12)(-6) = 72$
$(-11)(-7) = 77$
$(-10)(-8) = 80$
$(-9)(-9) = 81$
The greatest product is 81.

b. Possible sums include:
$-16 + -1 = -17$
$-8 + -2 = -10$
$-4 + -4 = -8$
The least sum is -17.

Section 1.4

1. Never true
To add fractions, write each fraction with a common denominator. Then, add the numerators and place over the common denominator.

3. Never true
The rule for multiplying fractions is to multiply the numerators and multiply the denominators.

5. Always true

7. Always true

9. **a.** No

b. Yes

11. Answers will vary.

13. $\dfrac{1}{9} - \dfrac{5}{27} = \dfrac{3}{27} - \dfrac{5}{27} = \dfrac{3}{27} + \dfrac{-5}{27}$
$\qquad = \dfrac{3 + (-5)}{27} = \dfrac{-2}{27} = -\dfrac{2}{27}$

15. $-\dfrac{5}{6} - \dfrac{5}{9} = -\dfrac{15}{18} - \dfrac{10}{18} = \dfrac{-15}{18} + \dfrac{-10}{18}$
$\qquad = \dfrac{-15 + (-10)}{18} = \dfrac{-25}{18} = -\dfrac{25}{18}$

17. $-\dfrac{7}{12} + \dfrac{5}{8} = -\dfrac{14}{24} + \dfrac{15}{24} = \dfrac{-14}{24} + \dfrac{15}{24}$
$\qquad = \dfrac{-14 + 15}{24} = \dfrac{1}{24}$

19. $-\dfrac{5}{8} - \left(-\dfrac{11}{12}\right) = -\dfrac{5}{8} + \dfrac{11}{12} = -\dfrac{15}{24} + \dfrac{22}{24}$
$\qquad = \dfrac{-15}{24} + \dfrac{22}{24} = \dfrac{-15 + 22}{24} = \dfrac{7}{24}$

21. $-\dfrac{5}{16}+\dfrac{3}{4}-\dfrac{7}{8}=-\dfrac{5}{16}+\dfrac{12}{16}-\dfrac{14}{16}$

$\qquad =\dfrac{-5}{16}+\dfrac{12}{16}+\dfrac{-14}{16}=\dfrac{-5+12+(-14)}{16}$

$\qquad =\dfrac{-7}{16}=-\dfrac{7}{16}$

23. $\dfrac{3}{4}-\left(-\dfrac{7}{12}\right)-\dfrac{7}{8}=\dfrac{3}{4}+\dfrac{7}{12}-\dfrac{7}{8}$

$\qquad =\dfrac{18}{24}+\dfrac{14}{24}-\dfrac{21}{24}=\dfrac{18}{24}+\dfrac{14}{24}+\dfrac{-21}{24}$

$\qquad =\dfrac{18+14+(-21)}{24}=\dfrac{11}{24}$

25. $\dfrac{5}{16}+\dfrac{1}{8}-\dfrac{1}{2}=\dfrac{5}{16}+\dfrac{2}{16}-\dfrac{8}{16}$

$\qquad =\dfrac{5}{16}+\dfrac{2}{16}+\dfrac{-8}{16}$

$\qquad =\dfrac{5+2+(-8)}{16}=\dfrac{-1}{16}=-\dfrac{1}{16}$

27. $-16.92-6.925=-23.845$

29. $2.54-3.6=-1.06$

31. $-3.87+8.546=4.676$

33. $-18.39+4.9-23.7=-37.19$

35. $-3.09-4.6+27.3=19.61$

37. $\dfrac{2}{3}-\dfrac{1}{2}+\dfrac{5}{6}=\dfrac{4}{6}-\dfrac{3}{6}+\dfrac{5}{6}$

$\qquad =\dfrac{4}{6}+\dfrac{-3}{6}+\dfrac{5}{6}$

$\qquad =\dfrac{4+(-3)+5}{6}=\dfrac{6}{6}=1$

39.
$\quad 17.6920$
$\underline{\;-\;6.9027}$
$\quad 10.7893$
$6.9027-17.692=-10.7893$

41. $\dfrac{11}{12}-\left(-\dfrac{1}{4}\right)$, because $\dfrac{11}{12}-\left(-\dfrac{1}{4}\right)=\dfrac{11}{12}+\dfrac{1}{4}$, so the

difference is positive, whereas the difference

$-\dfrac{1}{8}-\dfrac{3}{4}$ is negative.

43. $-\dfrac{2}{9}\left(-\dfrac{3}{14}\right)=\dfrac{2}{9}\cdot\dfrac{3}{14}=\dfrac{2\cdot3}{9\cdot14}$

$\qquad =\dfrac{2\cdot\overset{1}{\cancel{3}}}{\cancel{3}\cdot3\cdot\cancel{2}\cdot7}=\dfrac{1}{21}$

45. $\left(-\dfrac{3}{4}\right)\left(-\dfrac{8}{27}\right)=\dfrac{3}{4}\cdot\dfrac{8}{27}=\dfrac{3\cdot8}{4\cdot27}$

$\qquad =\dfrac{\overset{1}{\cancel{3}}\cdot\overset{1}{\cancel{2}}\cdot\overset{1}{\cancel{2}}\cdot2}{\cancel{2}\cdot\cancel{2}\cdot\cancel{3}\cdot3\cdot3\cdot3}=\dfrac{2}{9}$

47. $\dfrac{5}{8}\left(-\dfrac{7}{12}\right)\dfrac{16}{25}=-\left(\dfrac{5}{8}\cdot\dfrac{7}{12}\cdot\dfrac{16}{25}\right)$

$\qquad =-\dfrac{5\cdot7\cdot16}{8\cdot12\cdot25}=-\dfrac{\overset{1}{\cancel{5}}\cdot7\cdot\overset{1}{\cancel{2}}\cdot\overset{1}{\cancel{2}}\cdot\overset{1}{\cancel{2}}\cdot2}{\cancel{2}\cdot\cancel{2}\cdot\cancel{2}\cdot2\cdot3\cdot\cancel{5}\cdot5}$

$\qquad =-\dfrac{7}{30}$

49. $\dfrac{5}{6}\div\left(-\dfrac{3}{4}\right)=-\left(\dfrac{5}{6}\div\dfrac{3}{4}\right)=-\left(\dfrac{5}{6}\cdot\dfrac{4}{3}\right)$

$\qquad =-\left(\dfrac{5\cdot4}{6\cdot3}\right)=-\left(\dfrac{5\cdot\overset{1}{\cancel{2}}\cdot2}{2\cdot3\cdot3}\right)=-\dfrac{10}{9}$

51. $-\dfrac{7}{10}\div\dfrac{2}{5}=-\left(\dfrac{7}{10}\div\dfrac{2}{5}\right)=-\left(\dfrac{7}{10}\cdot\dfrac{5}{2}\right)$

$\qquad =-\left(\dfrac{7\cdot5}{10\cdot2}\right)=-\left(\dfrac{\overset{1}{\cancel{5}}\cdot7}{2\cdot2\cdot\cancel{5}}\right)=-\dfrac{7}{4}$

53. $-\dfrac{4}{9}\div\left(-\dfrac{2}{3}\right)=\dfrac{4}{9}\div\dfrac{2}{3}=\dfrac{4}{9}\cdot\dfrac{3}{2}$

$\qquad =\dfrac{4\cdot3}{9\cdot2}=\dfrac{\overset{1}{\cancel{2}}\cdot2\cdot\overset{1}{\cancel{3}}}{\cancel{3}\cdot3\cdot\cancel{2}}=\dfrac{2}{3}$

55. $1.06(-3.8)=-4.028$

57. $-2.4(6.1)(0.9)=-13.176$

59. $-3.4(-22.1)(-0.5)=-37.57$

61. $\dfrac{-1.27}{-1.7}=0.75$

63. $\dfrac{-6.904}{1.35}=-5.11$

65. $-\dfrac{1}{2}\cdot\dfrac{8}{9}=-\dfrac{1\cdot8}{2\cdot9}=\dfrac{1\cdot\overset{1}{\cancel{2}}\cdot2\cdot2}{\cancel{2}\cdot3\cdot3}=-\dfrac{4}{9}$

67. $-\dfrac{3}{8}\div\dfrac{1}{4}=-\dfrac{3}{8}\cdot\dfrac{4}{1}=-\dfrac{3\cdot4}{8\cdot1}$

$\qquad =-\dfrac{3\cdot\overset{1}{\cancel{2}}\cdot\overset{1}{\cancel{2}}}{2\cdot\cancel{2}\cdot\cancel{2}}=-\dfrac{3}{2}$

69. $\left(-\dfrac{8}{9}\right)\left(-\dfrac{3}{4}\right)$, because the product is positive,

while the quotient $-\dfrac{5}{16}\div\dfrac{3}{8}$ is negative.

71. Strategy
To find the annual losses, multiply Midway's first-quarter losses by the number of quarters per year.

Solution
$-25.852 \cdot 4 = -\$103.408$ million

73. Strategy
To find monthly loss, divide Six Flags' first-quarter losses by the number of months per quarter.

Solution
$\dfrac{-103.752}{3} = -\$43.584$ million

75. Strategy
To find difference, subtract Midway Games' first-quarter net income from Fox Entertainment's first-quarter net income.

Solution
$19.0 - (-11.481) = \$30.481$ million

77. The trade balance was lowest in 2000 at –$369.7 billion and highest in 1975 at $12.4 billion.

79. Strategy
To find the difference in trade balances, subtract the trade balance in 1990 (–81.1) from the trade balance in 2000 (–369.7).

Solution
$(-369.7) - (-81.1) = -372$
The difference is $372 billion.

81. The greatest difference in trade balances was between 1999-2000.

83. Strategy
To find the per quarter trade balance, divide the trade balance in 2000 (–369.7 billion) by 4.

Solution
$\dfrac{-369.7}{4} = -92.425$ billion

The average trade balance per quarter in 2000 was –$92.425 billion.

85. $(0.2)^2 \cdot (-0.5) + 1.72 = (0.04)(-0.5) + 1.72$
$\qquad\qquad\qquad\qquad = -0.02 + 1.72 = 1.7$

87. $(-1.6)^2 - 2.52 \div (1.8) = 2.56 - 1.4 = 1.16$

89. $-\dfrac{7}{12} + \dfrac{5}{6}\left(\dfrac{1}{6} - \dfrac{2}{3}\right) = -\dfrac{7}{12} + \dfrac{5}{6}\left(\dfrac{1}{6} - \dfrac{4}{6}\right)$

$\qquad = -\dfrac{7}{12} + \dfrac{5}{6}\left(-\dfrac{3}{6}\right)$

$\qquad = -\dfrac{7}{12} + \dfrac{5}{6}\left(-\dfrac{1}{2}\right)$

$\qquad = -\dfrac{7}{12} - \dfrac{5}{12}$

$\qquad = -\dfrac{12}{12}$

$\qquad = -1$

91. $\dfrac{11}{16} - \left(-\dfrac{3}{4}\right)^2 + \dfrac{7}{8} = \dfrac{11}{16} - \dfrac{9}{16} + \dfrac{7}{8}$

$\qquad = \dfrac{11}{16} - \dfrac{9}{16} + \dfrac{14}{16} = \dfrac{16}{16} = 1$

93. $\left(-\dfrac{1}{3}\right)^2 \cdot \left(-\dfrac{9}{4}\right) + \dfrac{3}{4} = \dfrac{1}{9}\left(-\dfrac{9}{4}\right) + \dfrac{3}{4}$

$\qquad = -\dfrac{1}{4} + \dfrac{3}{4} = \dfrac{2}{4} = \dfrac{1}{2}$

95. $\left(\dfrac{1}{3} - \dfrac{5}{6}\right) + \dfrac{7}{8} \div \left(-\dfrac{1}{2}\right)^3 = \left(\dfrac{1}{3} - \dfrac{5}{6}\right) + \dfrac{7}{8} \div \left(-\dfrac{1}{8}\right)$

$\qquad = \left(\dfrac{1}{3} - \dfrac{5}{6}\right) + \dfrac{7}{8} \cdot \dfrac{-8}{1}$

$\qquad = \left(\dfrac{2}{6} - \dfrac{5}{6}\right) - 7$

$\qquad = \dfrac{-3}{6} - 7$

$\qquad = \dfrac{-1}{2} + \dfrac{-14}{2}$

$\qquad = -\dfrac{15}{2}$

97. Strategy
To find the difference in low temperatures in March in Anchorage, subtract the record in March (–24) from the average in March (18).

Solution
$18 - (-24) = 42$
The difference is 42°F.

99. Strategy
To find the difference in average low temperatures in December, subtract the average in Fairbanks (–14) from the average in Anchorage (10).

Solution
$10 - (-14) = 24$
The difference is 24°F.

101. Strategy
To find the average for the year, divide the sum of all the record low temperatures for Fairbanks by 12 (the total number of months).

Solution
$$
\begin{array}{r}
-61 \\
-58 \\
-49 \\
-24 \\
-1 \\
30 \\
35 \\
27 \\
3 \\
-27 \\
-46 \\
\underline{-62} \\
-233
\end{array}
\qquad
\frac{-233}{12} = -19.4
$$

The average of the record low monthly temperatures is $-19.4°F$

103. Strategy
To find the difference in deficits, subtract the deficit in 1980 (-73.835) from the deficit in 1985 (-212.334).

Solution
$(-212.334) - (-73.835) = -138.499$
The difference is $138.499 billion.

105. Strategy
To find how many times greater the deficit was, divide the deficit in 1985 (-212.334) by the deficit in 1975 (-53.242).

Solution
$$\frac{-212.334}{-53.242} = 3.988 \approx 4$$
It was 4 times greater.

107. Strategy
To find the per quarter deficit, divide the deficit in 1970 (-2.842 billion) by 4.

Solution
$$\frac{-2.842}{4} = -0.7105 \text{ billion} = -710.5 \text{ million}$$
The deficit per quarter was $-$710.5 million.

109. Strategy
To find the average, add the values of each year and divide by 5.

Solution
$$
\begin{array}{r}
-107.450 \\
-21.940 \\
69.246 \\
79.263 \\
\underline{+117.305} \\
136.424
\end{array}
$$
$$\frac{136.424}{5} = 27.2848$$
The average was $27.2848 billion.

Applying Concepts 1.4

111. Strategy
To find the average, add the fractions and divide the sum by 2.

Solution
$$
\left(\frac{5}{6} + \frac{3}{4}\right) \div 2 = \left(\frac{10}{12} + \frac{9}{12}\right) \div \frac{2}{1}
$$
$$
= \frac{19}{12} \cdot \frac{1}{2} = \frac{19}{24}
$$
The average is $\frac{19}{24}$

113. No. In Step 2, addition was performed before multiplication.

115. Yes. Add the two numbers and then divide the sum by 2.

117. Answers will vary.

Section 1.5

1. A variable is a letter that is used to stand for an unknown quantity or for a quantity that can change or vary.

3. It means to replace the variables in a variable expression with numbers and then simplify the resulting numerical expression.

5. Answers will vary. For example, an input/output table for an equation (showing the relationship between two variables) lists values of one variable in the first column and the corresponding values of the other variable (after simplifying the resulting numerical expression) in the second column.

7. Always true

9. $-3a + 4b$
$-3(2) + 4(3) = -6 + 12$
$= 6$

11. $-3c + 4$
$-3(-4) + 4 = 12 + 4$
$= 16$

13. $6b \div (-a)$

$6(3) \div (-2) = 18 \div (-2)$

$\quad = -9$

15. $(b-a)^2 + 4c$

$(3-2)^2 + 4(-4) = 1^2 + 4(-4)$

$\quad = 1 + (-16)$

$\quad = -15$

17. $\dfrac{b+c}{d}$

$\dfrac{4+(-1)}{3} = \dfrac{3}{3}$

$\quad = 1$

19. $\dfrac{2d+b}{-a}$

$\dfrac{2(3)+4}{-(-2)} = \dfrac{6+4}{2}$

$\quad = \dfrac{10}{2}$

$\quad = 5$

21. $2(b+c) - 2a$

$2[4+(-1)] - 2(-2) = 2(3) - 2(-2)$

$\quad = 6 - (-4)$

$\quad = 6 + 4$

$\quad = 10$

23. $\dfrac{-4bc}{2a-b}$

$\dfrac{-4(4)(-1)}{2(-2)-4} = \dfrac{16}{-4-4}$

$\quad = \dfrac{16}{-8}$

$\quad = -2$

25. $(b-a)^2 - (d-c)^2$

$[4-(-2)]^2 - [3-(-1)]^2 = [4+2]^2 - [3+1]^2$

$\quad = 6^2 - 4^2$

$\quad = 36 - 16$

$\quad = 20$

27. $4ac + (2a)^2$

$4(-2)(-1) + [2(-2)]^2 = 4(-2)(-1) + (-4)^2$

$\quad = 4(-2)(-1) + 16$

$\quad = 8 + 16$

$\quad = 24$

29. $c^2 - ab$

$(-0.8)^2 - (2.7)(-1.6) = 0.64 - (-4.32)$

$\quad = 0.64 + 4.32$

$\quad = 4.96$

31. $\dfrac{b^3}{c} - 4a$

$\dfrac{(-1.6)^3}{-0.8} - 4(2.7) = \dfrac{-4.096}{-0.8} - 4(2.7)$

$\quad = 5.12 - 10.8$

$\quad = -5.68$

33. $\left| -4ab \right|$

$\left| -4(-2)(-3) \right| = \left| -24 \right|$

$\quad = 24$

35. Let $L = 70$ cm and $W = 40$ cm:

$P = 2L + 2W$

$\quad = 2(70) + 2(40)$

$\quad = 140 + 80$

$\quad = 220$

The perimeter of the rectangle is 220 cm.

37. Let $L = 70$ cm and $W = 40$ cm:

$A = LW$

$\quad = 70(40)$

$\quad = 2800$

The area of the rectangle is 2800 cm^2.

39. Let $h = 2$ m and $b = 3$ m:

$A = \dfrac{1}{2}hb$

$\quad = \dfrac{1}{2}(2)(3)$

$\quad = 1(3)$

$\quad = 3$

The area of the triangle is 3 m^2.

41. Let $t = 4$ and $C = \$70{,}000$:

$V = C - 5500t$

$\quad = 70{,}000 - 5500(4)$

$\quad = 70{,}000 - 22{,}000$

$\quad = 48{,}000$

The depreciated value is \$48,000.

43. Let $C = -11°C$:

$D = 4C + 180$

$\quad = 4(-11) + 180$

$\quad = -44 + 180$

$\quad = 136$

The car will slide 136 ft.

45. Typical graphing calculator screens are shown below.

a. To find the value of y when $x = 3$, read the output from the table when the input is 3. The value of y is 11.

b. To find the value of x when $y = 5$, read the input from the table when the output is 5. The value of x is 1.

47. Typical graphing calculator screens are shown below.

Plot1 Plot2 Plot3		X	Y1	
\Y1■X²		1	1	
\Y2=		1.5	2.25	
\Y3=		2	4	
\Y4=		2.5	6.25	
\Y5=		3	9	
\Y6=		3.5	12.25	
\Y7=		4	16	
		Y1■X²		

a. To find the value of y when $x = 2$, read the output from the table when the input is 2. The value of y is 4.

b. To find the value of x when $y = 12.25$, read the input from the table when the output is 12.25. The value of x is 3.5.

49. Typical graphing calculator screens are shown below.

Plot1 Plot2 Plot3		X	Y1	
\Y1■2X²+1		1.5	5.5	
\Y2=		1.75	7.125	
\Y3=		2	9	
\Y4=		2.25	11.125	
\Y5=		2.5	13.5	
\Y6=		2.75	16.125	
\Y7=		3	19	
		Y1■2X²+1		

a. To find the value of y when $x = 1.75$, read the output from the table when the input is 1.75. The value of y is 7.125.

b. To find the value of x when $y = 16.125$, read the input from the table when the output is 16.125. The value of x is 2.75.

51. Typical graphing calculator screens are shown below.

Plot1 Plot2 Plot3		X	Y1	
\Y1■X^2+3X+1		0	1	
\Y2=		1	5	
\Y3=		2	11	
\Y4=		3	19	
\Y5=		4	29	
\Y6=		5	41	
\Y7=		6	55	
		Y1■X^2+3X+1		

a. To find the value of y when $x = 3$, read the output from the table when the input is 3. The value of y is 19.

b. To find the value of x when $y = 29$, read the input from the table when the output is 29. The value of x is 4.

53. The architect charges a fee of \$4740 to design a 1600-square foot house.

55. A typical graphing calculator screen is shown below. Note that the temperature is given by Y1 and the elevation is given by X.

X	Y1	
2450	101	
2950	98.5	
3450	96	
3950	93.5	
4450	91	
4950	88.5	
5450	86	
Y1■-.005X+113.25		

a. To find the temperature (Y1) when the elevation (X) is 4450 feet, read the output from the table when the input is 4450. The temperature is 91°F.

b. To find the elevation when the temperature is 101°F, read the input from the table when the output is 101. The elevation of Inner Gorge is 2450 feet.

57. A typical graphing calculator screen is shown below. Note that the time to the next eruption is given by Y1 and the length of the last eruption is given by X.

X	Y1	
2	56.8	
2.5	63	
3	69.2	
3.5	75.4	
4	81.6	
4.5	87.8	
5	94	
Y1■12.4X+32		

a. To find how long until the next eruption (Y1) when the last eruption (X) lasted 3.5 minutes, read the output from the table when the input is 3.5. The next eruption will be in 75.4 minutes.

b. To find length of the last eruption when the time between the two eruptions was 63 minutes, read the input from the table when the output is 63. The length of the last eruption was 2.5 minutes.

59. A typical graphing calculator screen is shown below. Note that height of the baseball is given by Y1 and the time after it has been released is given by X.

X	Y1	
.5	33	
1	53	
1.5	65	
2	69	
2.5	65	
3	53	
3.5	33	

Y1 ☐ -16X^2+64X+5

a. To find the height (Y1) 2 seconds after its release (X), read the output from the table when the input is 2. The height is 69 feet.

b. To find the number of seconds after release when the height is 65 feet, read the input from the table when the output is 65. The time is 1.5 and 2.5 seconds after release.

61. a. A typical graphing calculator screen is shown below. Note that the perimeter is given by Y1 and the length of one side is given by X.

X	Y1	
2	8	
4	16	
6	24	
8	32	
10	40	
12	48	
14	56	

Y1 ☐ 4X

b. When the length of a side of a square is 12 in., the perimeter is 48 in.

63. a. A typical graphing calculator screen is shown below. Note that the volume is given by Y1 and the length of one side is given by X.

X	Y1	
1	1	
2	8	
3	27	
4	64	
5	125	
6	216	
7	343	

Y1 ☐ X^3

b. When the length of a side of a cube is 3 m, the volume of the cube is 27 m^3.

Applying Concepts 1.5

65. $\dfrac{1}{3}a^5b^6$

$$\dfrac{1}{3}\left(\dfrac{2}{3}\right)^5\left(-\dfrac{3}{2}\right)^6 = \dfrac{1}{3}\left(\dfrac{32}{243}\right)\left(\dfrac{729}{64}\right)$$
$$= \dfrac{32}{729}\left(\dfrac{729}{64}\right)$$
$$= \dfrac{1}{2}$$

67. $\left|5ab - 8a^2b^2\right|$

$$\left|5\cdot\dfrac{2}{3}\left(-\dfrac{3}{2}\right) - 8\left(\dfrac{2}{3}\right)^2\left(-\dfrac{3}{2}\right)^2\right| = \left|-5 - 8\right|$$
$$= \left|-13\right|$$
$$= 13$$

69. $2^y - y^2 = 2^3 - 3^2$
$$= 8 - 9$$
$$= -1$$

71. $z^x = (-2)^2 = 4$

73. $y^{(x^2)} = 3^{2^2}$
$$= 3^4$$
$$= 81$$

Section 1.6

1. Always true

3. Always true

5. Sometimes true
Like terms must have the same variables and the same variable parts.

7. Always true

9. Sometimes true
Any real number could be substituted for x.

11. Never true
The other number is represented by $15 - x$.

13. The Commutative Property says that two numbers can be added in either order. The Associate Property states that when three numbers are added together, the numbers can be grouped in any order.

15. $2\cdot 5 = 5\cdot ?$
$2\cdot 5 = 5\cdot 2$

17. $9 + 17 = ? + 9$
$9 + 17 = 17 + 9$

19. $4(5x) = (?\cdot 5)x$
$4(5x) = (4\cdot 5)x$

21. $(4 + 5) + 6 = ? + (5 + 6)$
$(4 + 5) + 6 = 4 + (5 + 6)$

23. $y \cdot ? = 0$
$y \cdot 0 = 0$

25. The Multiplication Property of One

27. The Addition Property of Zero

29. The Inverse Property of Multiplication

31. The Associative Property of Addition

33. The Commutative Property of Multiplication

35. $2x^2$, $5x$, $\underline{-8}$

37. $\underline{6}, -n^4$

39. $7\underline{x^2y}$, $6\underline{xy^2}$

41. coefficient of x^2: 1
coefficient of $-9x$: -9

43. coefficient of n^3: 1
coefficient of $-4n^2$: -4
coefficient of $-n$: -1

45. $12y + 9y = (12+9)y$
$= 21y$

47. $4y - 10y = (4-10)y$
$= -6y$

49. $x + y$ is already in simplest form because the terms do not have the same variable parts.

51. $-12xy + 17xy = (-12+17)xy$
$= 5xy$

53. $-5x^2 - 12x^2 + 3x^2 = (-5x^2 - 12x^2) + 3x^2$
$= (-5-12)x^2 + 3x^2$
$= -17x^2 + 3x^2$
$= (-17+3)x^2$
$= -14x^2$

55. $3x - 8y - 10x + 4x = 3x - 10x + 4x - 8y$
$= (3x - 10x) + 4x - 8y$
$= (3-10)x + 4x - 8y$
$= -7x + 4x - 8y$
$= (-7x + 4x) - 8y$
$= (-7+4)x - 8y$
$= -3x - 8y$

57. $-5x + 7x - 4x = (-5x + 7x) - 4x$
$= (-5+7)x - 4x$
$= 2x - 4x$
$= (2-4)x$
$= -2x$

59. $12y^2 + 10y^2 = (12+10)y^2$
$= 22y^2$

61. $9z^2 - 9z^2 = 0$

63. $\dfrac{2}{5}y - \dfrac{3}{4}y = \left(\dfrac{2}{5} - \dfrac{3}{4}\right)y$
$= \left(\dfrac{8}{20} - \dfrac{15}{20}\right)y$
$= -\dfrac{7}{20}y$

65. $4(3x) = (4\cdot 3)x = 12x$

67. $(3a)(-2) = (-2)(3a)$
$= (-2\cdot 3)a$
$= -6a$

69. $\dfrac{1}{8}(8x) = \left(\dfrac{1}{8}\cdot 8\right)x$
$= 1x$
$= x$

71. $\dfrac{1}{7}(14x) = \left(\dfrac{1}{7}\cdot 14\right)x$
$= \dfrac{14}{7}x$
$= 2x$

73. $(33y)\left(\dfrac{1}{11}\right) = \left(\dfrac{1}{11}\right)(33y)$
$= \left(\dfrac{1}{11}\cdot 33\right)y$
$= \dfrac{33}{11}y$
$= 3y$

75. $-2(a+7) = -2(a) + (-2)(7)$
$= -2a - 14$

77. $3(5x^2 + 2x) = 3(5x^2) + 3(2x)$
$= 15x^2 + 6x$

79. $-3(2y^2 - 7) = -3(2y^2) - (-3)(7)$
$= -6y^2 + 21$

81. $4(-3a^2 - 5a + 7)$
$= 4(-3a^2) - 4(5a) + 4(7)$
$= -12a^2 - 20a + 28$

83. $6a - (5a+7) = 6a - 1(5a+7)$
$= 6a + (-1)(5a+7)$
$= 6a + (-1)(5a) + (-1)(7)$
$= 6a - 5a - 7$
$= (6-5)a - 7$
$= 1a - 7$
$= a - 7$

85. $6(2y-7)-3(3-2y)$
$= 6(2y-7)+(-3)(3-2y)$
$= 6(2y)-6(7)+(-3)(3)-(-3)(2y)$
$= 12y-42-9+6y$
$= 12y+6y-42-9$
$= (12+6)y-51$
$= 18y-51$

87. $-2[3x-(5x-2)] = -2[3x-5x+2]$
$\qquad\qquad\qquad\quad = -2[-2x+2]$
$\qquad\qquad\qquad\quad = 4x-4$

89. Difference between p and 6: $p-6$
$\dfrac{4}{p-6}$

91. Sum of t and 15: $t+15$
$\dfrac{3}{8}(t+15)$

93. $13-x$

95. $\dfrac{3}{7}n$

97. Product of five and a number: $5x$
$5x-8$

99. Product of seven and a number: $7x$
$7x+14$

101. Cube of a number: x^3
Total of a number and the cube of a number:
$x+x^3$
$(x+x^3)-6$

103. One-half of a number: $\dfrac{1}{2}x$
$11+\dfrac{1}{2}x$

105. Product of thirteen and a number: $13x$
$80-13x$

107. Square of a number: x^2
Seven times the square of a number: $7x^2$
$7x^2-4$

109. the unknown number: x
the total of the number and ten: $x+10$
$x+(x+10) = x+x+10$
$\qquad\qquad\quad = 2x+10$

111. the unknown number: x
the difference between nine and the number:
$9-x$
$x-(9-x) = x-9+x$
$\qquad\qquad\quad = 2x-9$

113. the unknown number: x
one-fifth of the number: $\dfrac{1}{5}x$
three-eighths of the number: $\dfrac{3}{8}x$
$\dfrac{1}{5}x-\dfrac{3}{8}x = \dfrac{8}{40}x-\dfrac{15}{40}x$
$\qquad\qquad\quad = -\dfrac{7}{40}x$

115. the unknown number: x
the total of the number and nine: $x+9$
$(x+9)+4 = x+9+4$
$\qquad\qquad\quad = x+13$

117. the unknown number: x
three times the number: $3x$
the sum of three times the number and 40:
$3x+40$
$2(3x+40) = 6x+80$

119. the unknown number: x
one-fourth of the number: $\dfrac{1}{4}x$
$16\left(\dfrac{1}{4}x\right) = 4x$

121. the unknown number: x
nine times the number: $9x$
twice the number: $2x$
$9x-2x = 7x$

123. the unknown number: x
the difference between the number and five:
$x-5$
$(x-5)+19 = x-5+19$
$\qquad\qquad\quad = x+14$

125. the cruising speed of a propeller-driven plane: p
Twice the cruising speed of a propeller-driven plane: $2p$.

127. the amount of cashews: c
Four times as many cashews: $4c$.

129. the age of the 8¢ stamp: a
25 years older than an 8¢ stamp: $a+25$.

131. measure of the largest angle: L
measure of the smallest angle: $\dfrac{1}{2}L-10$

133. number of nickels: x
number of dimes: $35-x$

135. number of hours of overtime worked: h
employee's weekly pay: $640+24h$

Applying Concepts 1.6

137. $C - 0.7C = (1 - 0.7)C = 0.3C$

139.
$$-\frac{1}{4}[2x + 2(y - 6y)] = -\frac{1}{4}[2x + 2y - 12y]$$
$$= -\frac{1}{4}[2x - 10y]$$
$$= -\frac{1}{4}2x + \frac{1}{4}10y$$
$$= -\frac{1}{2}x + \frac{5}{2}y$$

141. For example, four less than five times a number

143. For example, the product of five and four less than a number

145. number of nickels in the bank: n
Value of the nickels in the bank (in cents): $5n$
number of dimes in the bank: d
Value of the dimes in the bank (in cents): $10d$
Total value of the coins in the bank (in cents): $5n + 10d$

147. number of oxygen atoms: x
number of hydrogen atoms: $2x$

Chapter Review Exercises

1. Since I have one brother and two sisters, there are 4 children in my family. On my mother's side, there are 10 grandchildren. There are $10 - 4 = 6$ grandchildren, other than the 4 of us, on my mother's side. That means that we have 6 first cousins on this side of the family. On my father's side, there are 11 grandchildren. There are $11 - 4 = 7$ grandchildren, other than the 4 of us, on my father's side. That means that we have 7 first cousins on this side of the family. In all, we have $6 + 7 = 13$ first cousins.

2. 1, 2, 4, 7, 11, 16, . . .
The differences between successive terms follow the pattern 1, 2, 3, 4, 5. The next term in this pattern would be 6, so the next term in the original sequence is 6 more than the previous: $16 + 6 = 22$
The next term in the sequence is 22.

3. We are given that ♠♠♠♠ = ♦♦, ♦♦♦♦ = ♣♣, and ♣♣♣ = ♥♥♥♥♥♥.
So, if ♣♣♣ = ♥♥♥♥♥♥, then ♣♣ = ♥♥♥♥. And because ♦♦♦♦ = ♣♣, then ♦♦♦♦ = ♥♥♥♥, or equivalently, ♦♦ = ♥♥.
Then ♠♠♠♠ = ♥♥. Therefore, 4 ♠'s are equal to 2 ♥'s.

4. The integers between −9 and −2:
$\{-8, -7, -6, -5, -4, -3\}$

5. $\{x \mid x \le -10\}$

6. $C \cap D = \{2, 3\}$

7. $\{x \mid -2 \le x \le 3\}$

8. $(-\infty, -44)$

9. $(-2, 4]$

10. $\{x \mid x \le 3\} \cup \{x \mid x < -2\}$
$\{x \mid x \le 3\}$.

11. $\{x \mid x < 3\} \cap \{x \mid x > -2\}$
$\{x \mid -2 < x < 3\}$

12. $\left(-\frac{1}{3}\right)\left(\frac{3}{7}\right) = -\frac{1}{7}$

13. $-6.8 \div 47.92 = \dfrac{-6.8}{47.92} \approx -0.1$

14. $-247.8 + -193.4 = -441.2$

15. $\dfrac{7}{8} - \dfrac{5}{6} = \dfrac{21}{24} + \dfrac{20}{24} = \dfrac{41}{24}$

16. $\dfrac{5}{9} \div \left(-\dfrac{2}{3}\right) = \dfrac{5}{9} \cdot \dfrac{-3}{2} = -\dfrac{5}{6}$

17.
$$3 - (8 - 10) \div 2 = 3 - (-2) \div 2$$
$$= 3 - (-1)$$
$$= 3 + 1$$
$$= 4$$

18.
$$4 + 2|3 - 6| = 4 + 2|-3|$$
$$= 4 + 2(3)$$
$$= 4 + 6$$
$$= 10$$

19. Strategy
To find the temperature, add the rise in temperature (5°) to the original temperature (−8°).

Solution
$-8°C + 5°C = -3°C$
The temperature was −3°C.

20. Strategy
To find the difference, subtract the temperature at which mercury freezes (−38.87°C) from the temperature at which mercury boils (356.58°C).

Solution
$$356.58 - (-38.87) = 356.58 + 38.87$$
$$= 395.45$$
The difference is 395.45°C.

21. Let $L = 12.5$ cm and $W = 6.25$ cm:

$$P = 2L + 2W$$
$$= 2(12.5) + 2(6.25)$$
$$= 25 + 12.5$$
$$= 37.5$$

The perimeter is 37.5 cm.

22. a. A typical graphing calculator screen is shown below. Note that the pressure is given by Y1 and the depth is given by X.

X	Y1
2	16
4	17
6	18
8	19
10	20
12	21
14	22

Y₁■15+0.5X

b. At a depth of 6 ft, the pressure is 18 lb/in^2.

23. $a - b(c + d)$

$6 - 2(1 + -7) = 6 - 2(-6) = 6 + 12 = 18$

24. $ab^2 - c$

$$4\left(-\frac{1}{2}\right)^2 - \frac{5}{7} = 4\left(\frac{1}{4}\right) - \frac{5}{7} = 1 - \frac{5}{7} = \frac{7}{7} - \frac{5}{7} = \frac{2}{7}$$

25. The Commutative Property of Multiplication

26. $(-6d)(-4) = 24d$

27. $7a^2 + 10a - 4a^2 = 7a^2 - 4a^2 + 10a$
$$= 3a^2 + 10a$$

28. $4(6a - 3) - (5a + 1) = 24a - 12 - 5a - 1$
$$= 24a - 5a - 12 - 1$$
$$= 19a - 13$$

29. Twice a number: $2x$

Quotient of twice a number and 16: $\dfrac{2x}{16}$

Eight times the quotient of twice a number and 16: $8\left(\dfrac{2x}{16}\right)$

30. The distance from Earth to the sun: d
The distance from Neptune to the sun: $30d$

Chapter Test

1. Strategy: make a list.
211 is prime
212 is composite (divisible by 2)
213 is composite (divisible by 3)
214 is composite (divisible by 2)
215 is composite (divisible by 5)
216 is composite (divisible by 2)
217 is composite (divisible by 7)
218 is composite (divisible by 2)
219 is composite (divisible by 3)
The largest prime number between 210 and 220 is 211.

2. The integers between -7 and 1.
$\{-6, -5, -4, -3, -2, -1, 0\}$

3. $\{x \mid x \geq -2\}$

4. $A \cap B = \{-1, 0, 1\}$

5. $\{x \mid -4 \leq x \leq 6\}$

6. $[-20, \infty)$

7. $(-\infty, -1]$

8. $\{x \mid x \leq -3\} \cup \{x \mid x > 0\}$

9. $12 - 4(3 - 5)^2 \div (-1) = 12 - 4(-2)^2 \div (-1)$
$$= 12 - 4(4) \div (-1)$$
$$= 12 - 16 \div (-1)$$
$$= 12 + 16$$
$$= 28$$

10. $\left(-\dfrac{3}{8}\right)\left(-\dfrac{4}{15}\right) = \dfrac{\overset{1}{\cancel{3}} \cdot \overset{1}{\cancel{4}}}{\underset{2}{\cancel{8}} \cdot \underset{5}{\cancel{15}}} = \dfrac{1}{10}$

11. $\dfrac{3}{4} - \dfrac{2}{3} = \dfrac{9}{12} - \dfrac{8}{12}$
$$= \dfrac{9 - 8}{12}$$
$$= \dfrac{1}{12}$$

12. $-3.597 - (-4.826) = -3.597 + 4.826 = 1.229$

13. $x \div y$

$$\dfrac{1}{8} \div \left(-\dfrac{5}{12}\right) = \dfrac{1}{8} \cdot \dfrac{-12}{5} = -\dfrac{3}{10}$$

14. $m + n(p - q)^2$

$$-3 + 4(2 - -1)^2 = -3 + 4(2 + 1)^2$$
$$= -3 + 4(3)^2$$
$$= -3 + 4(9)$$
$$= -3 + 36$$
$$= 33$$

15. Let $U = 127$, $N = 147$, and $F = 20,000$.

$$T = UN + F$$
$$= (127)(147) + 20,000$$
$$= 18,669 + 20,000$$
$$= 38,669$$

The total cost is \$38,669.

16. a. $d = 50 - 16t^2$
$$= 50 - 16(0.25)^2$$
$$= 50 - 16(0.0625)$$
$$= 50 - 1$$
$$= 49$$

The diver is 49 ft above the water after 0.25 s.

b. A typical graphing calculator screen is shown below. Note that the pressure is given by Y1 and the depth is given by X.

X	Y1	
0	50	
.25	49	
.5	46	
.75	41	
1	34	
1.25	25	
1.5	14	

Y1■50−16X^2

From information in the table, when Y1 = 25 ft, X = 1.25 s.

17. $-3y^2 + 9y - 5y^2 = -8y^2 + 9y$

18. $3(4w - 1) - 7(w + 2) = 12w - 3 - 7w - 14$
$$= 5w - 17$$

19. two more than a number: $x + 2$
difference between the number and three $x - 3$
two more than a number added to the difference between the number and three:
$(x - 3) + (x + 2) = 2x - 1$

20. The speed of the second car: s
The speed of the first car: $s + 15$

Chapter 2: Introduction to Functions and Relations

Prep Test

1. $-\dfrac{6}{3} + 4 = -2 + 4 = 2$

2. $-2x + 5$
$-2(-3) + 5 = 6 + 5 = 11$

3. $\dfrac{2r}{r-1}$
$\dfrac{2(5)}{5-1} = \dfrac{10}{4}$
$\qquad = 2.5$

4. $2p^3 - 3p + 4$
$2(-1)^3 - 3(-1) + 4 = 2(-1) + 3 + 4$
$\qquad\qquad\qquad = -2 + 7$
$\qquad\qquad\qquad = 5$

5. $x = 0$

6. $y = 6x - 5$
$y = 6\left(-\dfrac{1}{3}\right) - 5 = -2 - 5 = -7$

Go Figure

Arrange all the guesses on a number line.

215 217 219 220 221 223

Visually, we can see that the difference between 215 and 219 is 4, and the difference between 223 and 219 is also 4. The difference between 217 and 219 is 2, and the difference between 221 and 219 is also 2. The difference between 219 and 220 is 1.
So, the correct number was 219.

Section 2.1

1. Answers will vary.

3. A solution of an equation in two variables is an ordered pair that makes the equation a true statement.

5. The input variable is t. The output variable is s.

7.

9. The x-coordinate for A is -2.
The x-coordinate for B is 0.
The y-coordinate for C is 0.
The y-coordinate for D is -3.

11. $y = 2x - 10$

-4	$2(3) - 10$
	$6 - 10$
	-4

$-4 = -4$
Yes, $(3, -4)$ is a solution of $y = 2x - 10$.

13. $y = \dfrac{3}{2}x + 7$

5	$\frac{3}{2}(-2) + 7$
	$-3 + 7$
	4

$5 \neq 4$
No, $(-2, 5)$ is not a solution of $y = \dfrac{3}{2}x + 7$.

15.

Input, x	$-2x + 1$	Output
-3	$-2(-3) + 1$	7
-2	$-2(-2) + 1$	5
-1	$-2(-1) + 1$	3
0	$-2(0) + 1$	1
1	$-2(1) + 1$	-1
2	$-2(2) + 1$	-3
3	$-2(3) + 1$	-5

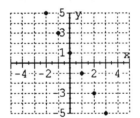

17.

Input, x	$\frac{3}{4}x+1$	Output
-8	$\frac{3}{4}(-8)+1$	-5
-4	$\frac{3}{4}(-4)+1$	-2
0	$\frac{3}{4}(0)+1$	1
4	$\frac{3}{4}(4)+1$	4
8	$\frac{3}{4}(8)+1$	7

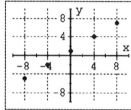

19.

Input, x	x^2+1	Output
-3	$(-3)^2+1$	10
-2	$(-2)^2+1$	5
-1	$(-1)^2+1$	2
0	$(0)^2+1$	1
1	$(1)^2+1$	2
2	$(2)^2+1$	5
3	$(3)^2+1$	10

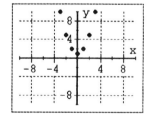

21.

Input, x	x^2+4x-3	Output
-5	$(-5)^2+4(-5)-3$	2
-4	$(-4)^2+4(-4)-3$	-3
-3	$(-3)^2+4(-3)-3$	-6
-2	$(-2)^2+4(-2)-3$	-7
-1	$(-1)^2+4(-1)-3$	-6
0	$(0)^2+4(0)-3$	-3
1	$(1)^2+4(1)-3$	2

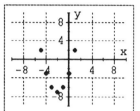

23. a. Evaluate $d=11t$ for each value of t. The input/output table is shown below.

Input, t	$11t$	Output, d
0	$11(0)$	0
5	$11(5)$	55
10	$11(10)$	110
15	$11(15)$	165
20	$11(20)$	220
25	$11(25)$	275
30	$11(30)$	330

b. The ordered pair $(20, 220)$ means that in 20 s, the jogger runs 220 ft.

25. a. Evaluate $d=16t^2$ for each value of t. The input/output table is shown below.

Input, t	$16t^2$	Output, d
0	$16(0)^2$	0
0.5	$16(0.5)^2$	4
1	$16(1)^2$	16
1.5	$16(1.5)^2$	36
2	$16(2)^2$	64
2.5	$16(2.5)^2$	100
3	$16(3)^2$	144

b. The ordered pair $(1.5, 36)$ means that in 1.5 s, the object will fall 36 ft.

27. a. Evaluate $Q = 0.75w$ for each value of w. The input/output table is shown below.

Input, w	$0.75w$	Output, Q
0	0.75(0)	0
5	0.75(5)	3.75
10	0.75(10)	7.5
15	0.75(15)	11.25
20	0.75(20)	15
25	0.75(25)	18.75
30	0.75(30)	22.5

b. The ordered pair (15, 11.25) means that in a 15-gram piece of 18-carat gold jewelry, there are 11.25 g of gold.

29. a. Evaluate $h = -16t^2 + 70t + 5$ for each value of t. The input/output table is shown below.

t	$-16t^2 + 70t + 5$	h
0	$-16(0)^2 + 70(0) + 5$	5
0.5	$-16(0.5)^2 + 70(0.5) + 5$	36
1	$-16(1)^2 + 70(1) + 5$	59
1.5	$-16(1.5)^2 + 70(1.5) + 5$	74
2	$-16(2)^2 + 70(2) + 5$	81
2.5	$-16(2.5)^2 + 70(2.5) + 5$	80
3	$-16(3)^2 + 70(3) + 5$	71

b. The ordered pair (2.5, 80) means that the ball is 80 ft above the ground 2.5 s after it is released.

31.

Input, x	$2x - 4$	Output
-2	2(-2) - 4	-8
-1	2(-1) - 4	-6
0	2(0) - 4	-4
1	2(1) - 4	-2
2	2(2) - 4	0

Using a [-10, 10] window,

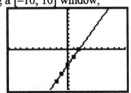

33.

Input, x	$\dfrac{x}{2}+1$	Output
-4	$\dfrac{-4}{2}+1$	-1
-2	$\dfrac{-2}{2}+1$	0
0	$\dfrac{0}{2}+1$	1
2	$\dfrac{2}{2}+1$	2
4	$\dfrac{4}{2}+1$	3

Using a [-5, 5] window,

35.

Input, x	$\dfrac{-5x}{4}$	Output
-8	$\dfrac{-5(-8)}{4}$	10
-4	$\dfrac{-5(-4)}{4}$	5
0	$\dfrac{-5(0)}{4}$	0
4	$\dfrac{-5(4)}{4}$	-5
8	$\dfrac{-5(8)}{4}$	-10

Using a [-10, 10] window,

37.

Input, x	$\dfrac{3x}{4} - 4$	Output
−8	$\dfrac{3(-8)}{4} - 4$	−10
−4	$\dfrac{3(-4)}{4} - 4$	−7
0	$\dfrac{3(0)}{4} - 4$	−4
4	$\dfrac{3(4)}{4} - 4$	−1
8	$\dfrac{3(8)}{4} - 4$	2

Using a [−12, 12] window,

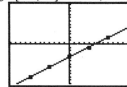

39. Using a [−5, 5] window,

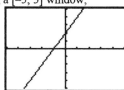

41. Using a [−5, 5] window,

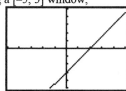

43. Using a [−5, 5] window,

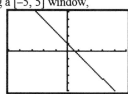

45. a. When $x = 4$, $y = 10$.

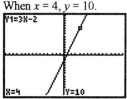

b. When $y = 13$, $x = 5$.

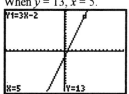

47. a. When $x = 10$, $y = 0$.

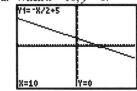

b. When $y = -6$, $x = 22$.

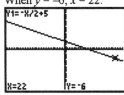

49. a. When $x = -8$, $y = 19$.

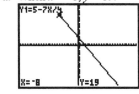

b. When $y = -9$, $x = 8$.

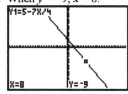

51. a. When $x = 24$, $y = -11$.

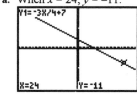

b. When $y = -14$, $x = 28$.

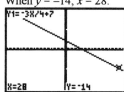

53. a. When $x = 0$, $y = 10$.

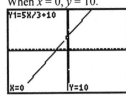

b. When $y = 0$, $x = -6$.

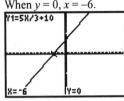

55. $y = 2x + 5$
$y = 2(7.5) + 5 = 15 + 5 = 20$
$(7.5, 20)$

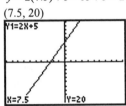

57. $y = 2 - 3x$
$y = 2 - 3(-6.3) = 2 + 18.9 = 20.9$
$(-6.3, 20.9)$

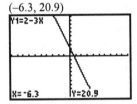

59. $y = \dfrac{3}{4}x + 3$
$y = \dfrac{3}{4}\left(-\dfrac{16}{3}\right) + 3 = -4 + 3 = -1$
$\left(-\dfrac{16}{3}, -1\right)$

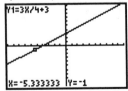

61. $y = \dfrac{5}{3}x + 5$
$y = \dfrac{5}{3}\left(-\dfrac{57}{10}\right) + 5 = -\dfrac{19}{2} + 5 = -\dfrac{9}{2}$
$\left(-\dfrac{57}{19}, -\dfrac{9}{2}\right)$

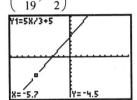

63. $y = -2.3x + 4.8$
$y = -2.3(12.1) + 4.8 = -27.83 + 4.8 = -23.03$
$(12.1, -23.03)$

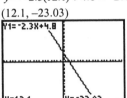

Applying Concepts 2.1

65. The y-coordinate is 0.

67. Answers will vary. For example, $(-3, 2)$ and $(5, 2)$.

69. $(5, 4)$ and $(-3, -1)$

71. a. The distance to the x-axis from $(3, 5)$ is 5.

b. The distance to the y-axis from $(3, 5)$ is 3.

73. a. The distance to the x-axis from $(7, -4)$ is 4.

b. The distance to the y-axis from $(7, -4)$ is 7.

75. a. The distance to the x-axis from $(-2, 0)$ is 0.

b. The distance to the y-axis from $(-2, 0)$ is 2.

77.

79.

81.

Section 2.2

1. A relation is a set of ordered pairs. A function is a relation in which no two ordered pairs have the same first coordinate and different second coordinates.

3. The domain is the set of first coordinates of the function; the range is the set of second coordinates of the function.

5. To evaluate a function means to replace the independent variable by a given number and simplify the resulting expression.

7. No. By definition, a function cannot have different second coordinates with the same first coordinate.

9. Domain: $\{-3, -2, -1, 0, 1\}$
Range: $\{-13, -11, -9, -7, -5\}$
Yes

11. Domain: $\{-4, -2, 0, 2\}$
Range: $\{6, 8, 10, 12\}$
No, the relation is not a function because there are two ordered pairs with the same first coordinate but different second coordinates.

13. Domain: $\{2, 3, 4, 5, 6\}$
Range: $\{-6, -3, 6\}$
Yes

15. Domain: $\{-4, -2, 0, 3, 5\}$
Range: $\{0\}$
Yes

17. $y(x) = 1 - 3x$
$y(-4) = 1 - 3(-4) = 1 + 12 = 13$

19. $P(n) = n^2 - 4n - 7$
$P(-3) = (-3)^2 - 4(-3) - 7$
$ = 9 + 12 - 7$
$ = 14$

21. $f(x) = 3x^3 - 4x^2 + 7$
$f(2) = 3(2)^3 - 4(2)^2 + 7$
$ = 24 - 16 + 7$
$ = 15$

23. $s(t) = \dfrac{4t}{t^2 + 2}$
$s(2) = \dfrac{4(2)}{(2)^2 + 2} = \dfrac{8}{4 + 4} = 1$

25. $ABS(x) = |2x - 7|$
$ABS(-3) = |2(-3) - 7| = |-6 - 7| = |-13| = 13$

27.

Input, x	$2 - 2x$	Output
-2	$2 - 2(-2)$	6
-1	$2 - 2(-1)$	4
0	$2 - 2(0)$	2
1	$2 - 2(1)$	0
2	$2 - 2(2)$	2

Using a $[-10, 10]$ window,

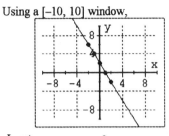

29.

Input, x	$-\dfrac{2}{3}x + 4$	Output
-6	$-\dfrac{2}{3}(-6) + 4$	8
-3	$-\dfrac{2}{3}(-3) + 4$	6
0	$-\dfrac{2}{3}(0) + 4$	4
3	$-\dfrac{2}{3}(3) + 4$	2
6	$-\dfrac{2}{3}(6) + 4$	0

Using a $[-10, 10]$ window,

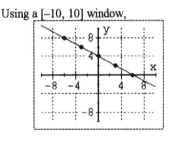

31.

Input, x	$x^2 - 2$	Output
-3	$(-3)^2 - 2$	7
-2	$(-2)^2 - 2$	2
-1	$(-1)^2 - 2$	-1
0	$(0)^2 - 2$	-2
1	$(1)^2 - 2$	-1
2	$(2)^2 - 2$	2
3	$(3)^2 - 2$	7

Using a $[-10, 10]$ window,

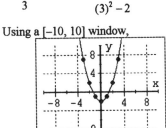

33.

Input, x	$-x^2 + 2x - 1$	Output
-2	$-(-2)^2 + 2(-2) - 1$	-9
-1	$-(-1)^2 + 2(-1) - 1$	-4
0	$-(0)^2 + 2(0) - 1$	-1
1	$-(1)^2 + 2(1) - 1$	0
2	$-(2)^2 + 2(2) - 1$	-1
3	$-(3)^2 + 2(3) - 1$	-4
4	$-(4)^2 + 2(4) - 1$	-9

Using a $[-10, 10]$ window,

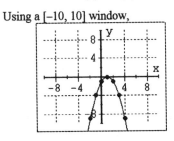

35.

Input, x	-2	Output
-2	-2	-2
-1	-2	-2
0	-2	-2
1	-2	-2
2	-2	-2
3	-2	-2
4	-2	-2

Using a $[-10, 10]$ window,

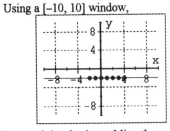

37. The graph is a horizontal line through $(0, 1)$.

39. $f(x) = 2x - 7$
$f(10) = 2(10) - 7 = 20 - 7 = 13$

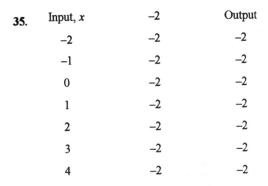

41. $g(x) = \dfrac{2}{3}x + 8$

$g(-27) = \dfrac{2}{3}(-27) + 8 = -18 + 8 = -10$

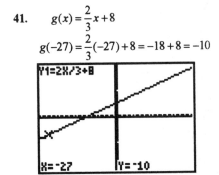

43. $y(x) = 9 - \dfrac{15}{8}x$

$y(8) = 9 - \dfrac{15}{8}(8) = 9 - 15 = -6$

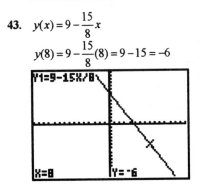

45. $f(x) = x^2 + 2x - 5$
$f(3) = (3)^2 + 2(3) - 5$
$= 9 + 6 - 5 = 10$

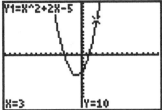

47. $g(x) = x^3 + 4x^2 - 2$
$g(-3) = (-3)^3 + 4(-3)^2 - 2$
$= -27 + 36 - 2 = 7$

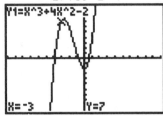

49. $F(x) = x^3 + 4x^2 - x - 3$
$F\left(-\dfrac{5}{2}\right) = \left(-\dfrac{5}{2}\right)^3 + 4\left(-\dfrac{5}{2}\right)^2 - \left(-\dfrac{5}{2}\right) - 3$
$= -\dfrac{125}{8} + 25 + \dfrac{5}{2} - 3 = \dfrac{71}{8}$

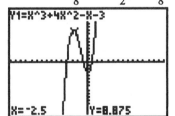

51. $g(x) = 10 - x^2$
$g(-4) = 10 - (-4)^2 = 10 - 16 = -6$
$g(-3) = 10 - (-3)^2 = 10 - 9 = 1$
$g(-2) = 10 - (-2)^2 = 10 - 4 = 6$
$g(-1) = 10 - (-1)^2 = 10 - 1 = 9$
$g(0) = 10 - (0)^2 = 10 - 0 = 10$
$g(1) = 10 - (1)^2 = 10 - 1 = 9$
$g(2) = 10 - (2)^2 = 10 - 4 = 6$
$g(3) = 10 - (3)^2 = 10 - 9 = 1$
$g(4) = 10 - (4)^2 = 10 - 16 = -6$

Range = {–6, 1, 6, 9, 10}

53. $P(n) = \dfrac{n(n+1)}{2}$
$P(1) = \dfrac{1(1+1)}{2} = \dfrac{2}{2} = 1$
$P(2) = \dfrac{2(2+1)}{2} = \dfrac{2(3)}{2} = 3$
$P(3) = \dfrac{3(3+1)}{2} = \dfrac{3(4)}{2} = 6$
$P(4) = \dfrac{4(4+1)}{2} = \dfrac{4(5)}{2} = 10$
$P(5) = \dfrac{5(5+1)}{2} = \dfrac{5(6)}{2} = 15$
$P(6) = \dfrac{6(6+1)}{2} = \dfrac{6(7)}{2} = 21$
$P(7) = \dfrac{7(7+1)}{2} = \dfrac{7(8)}{2} = 28$

Range = {1, 3, 6, 10, 15, 21, 28}

55. $v(s) = \dfrac{s}{s^2 + 1}$
$v(-3) = \dfrac{-3}{(-3)^2 + 1} = \dfrac{-3}{9+1} = -\dfrac{3}{10}$
$v(-2) = \dfrac{-2}{(-2)^2 + 1} = \dfrac{-2}{4+1} = -\dfrac{2}{5}$
$v(-1) = \dfrac{-1}{(-1)^2 + 1} = \dfrac{-1}{1+1} = -\dfrac{1}{2}$
$v(0) = \dfrac{0}{(0)^2 + 1} = 0$
$v(1) = \dfrac{1}{(1)^2 + 1} = \dfrac{1}{1+1} = \dfrac{1}{2}$
$v(2) = \dfrac{2}{(2)^2 + 1} = \dfrac{2}{4+1} = \dfrac{2}{5}$
$v(3) = \dfrac{3}{(3)^2 + 1} = \dfrac{3}{9+1} = \dfrac{3}{10}$

Range = $\left\{ -\dfrac{3}{10}, -\dfrac{2}{5}, -\dfrac{1}{2}, 0, \dfrac{1}{2}, \dfrac{2}{5}, \dfrac{3}{10} \right\}$

57. $f(t) = 2t - 4$
$f(-1) = 2(-1) - 4 = -2 - 4 = -6$
$f(0) = 2(0) - 4 = 0 - 4 = -4$
$f(2) = 2(2) - 4 = 4 - 4 = 0$
No values are excluded.

59. $f(x) = \dfrac{x}{x+5}$
$f(-5) = \dfrac{-5}{-5+5} = \dfrac{-5}{0}$ undefined
$f(0) = \dfrac{0}{0+5} = 0$
$f(2) = \dfrac{2}{2+5} = \dfrac{2}{7}$
–5 is excluded

61. $F(x) = \dfrac{x-1}{x^2 - 2x - 3}$

$F(-1) = \dfrac{-1-1}{(-1)^2 - 2(-1) - 3}$

$\quad = \dfrac{-2}{1+2-3} = \dfrac{-2}{0}$ undefined

$F(1) = \dfrac{1-1}{(1)^2 - 2(1) - 3} = \dfrac{0}{1-2-3} = 0$

$F(3) = \dfrac{3-1}{(3)^2 - 2(3) - 3}$

$\quad = \dfrac{2}{9-6-3} = \dfrac{2}{0}$ undefined

−1 and 3 are excluded

63. $f(t) = 3t + 1$

$f(-6) = 3(-6) + 1 = -18 + 1 = -17$

$f(0) = 3(0) + 1 = 1$

$f(5) = 3(5) + 1 = 15 + 1 = 16$

No values are excluded.

65. $g(v) = \dfrac{v+1}{v+4}$

$g(-4) = \dfrac{-4+1}{-4+4} = \dfrac{-3}{0}$ undefined

$g(-1) = \dfrac{-1+1}{-1+4} = 0$

$g(0) = \dfrac{0+1}{0+4} = \dfrac{1}{4}$

−4 is excluded

67. $F(x) = \dfrac{2x-4}{x+2}$

$F(-2) = \dfrac{2(-2)-4}{-2+2} = \dfrac{-4-4}{0}$ undefined

$F(0) = \dfrac{2(0)-4}{0+2} = \dfrac{-4}{2} = -2$

$F(2) = \dfrac{2(2)-4}{2+2} = \dfrac{4-4}{4} = 0$

−2 is excluded

69. $z(t) = \dfrac{t}{t^2 + 1}$

$z(-1) = \dfrac{-1}{(-1)^2 + 1} = \dfrac{-1}{1+1} = \dfrac{-1}{2}$

$z(0) = \dfrac{0}{(0)^2 + 1} = 0$

$z(2) = \dfrac{2}{(2)^2 + 1} = \dfrac{2}{4+1} = \dfrac{2}{5}$

No values are excluded.

71. $f(x) = \dfrac{2}{x-1}$

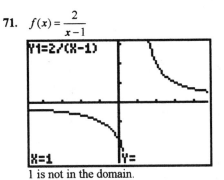

1 is not in the domain.

73. $g(x) = \dfrac{x}{x+3}$

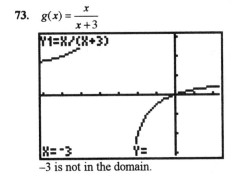

−3 is not in the domain.

75. $F(x) = \dfrac{x}{2x-3}$

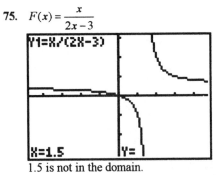

1.5 is not in the domain.

77. $f(x) = \dfrac{1}{x^2 - 1}$

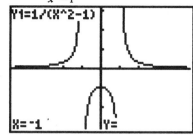

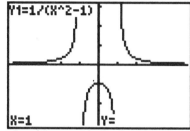

−1 and 1 are not in the domain.

79. $g(x) = \dfrac{x}{x^2 - 2x - 3}$

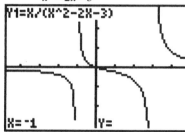

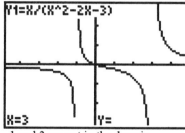

−1 and 3 are not in the domain.

81. $F(x) = \dfrac{1}{2x^2 - x - 1}$

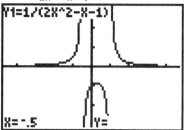

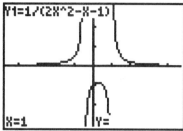

−0.5 and 1 are not in the domain.

83. a. Let $s = 4$:
$$P(s) = 4s$$
$$P(4) = 4(4)$$
$$= 16$$
The perimeter is 16 m.

b. Let $s = 5$:
$$P(s) = 4s$$
$$P(5) = 4(5)$$
$$= 20$$
The perimeter is 20 ft.

85. a. Let $t = 2$:
$$h(t) = -16t^2 + 80t + 4$$
$$h(2) = -16(2)^2 + 80(2) + 4$$
$$= -64 + 160 + 4$$
$$= 100$$
The height of the ball above the ground after 2 s is 100 ft.

b. Let $t = 4$:
$$h(t) = -16t^2 + 80t + 4$$
$$h(4) = -16(4)^2 + 80(4) + 4$$
$$= -256 + 320 + 4$$
$$= 68$$
The height of the ball above the ground after 4 s is 68 ft.

87. a. Let $t = 25$:
$$s(t) = \frac{1087\sqrt{t+273}}{16.52}$$
$$s(25) = \frac{1087\sqrt{25+273}}{16.52}$$
$$= \frac{1087\sqrt{298}}{16.52}$$
$$\approx 1136$$

When the temperature is 25°C, the speed of sound in air is approximately 1136 ft/s.

b. Let $t = 30$: (a temperature greater than 25)
$$s(t) = \frac{1087\sqrt{t+273}}{16.52}$$
$$s(30) = \frac{1087\sqrt{30+273}}{16.52}$$
$$= \frac{1087\sqrt{303}}{16.52}$$
$$\approx 1145$$

Since $1145 > 1138$, then it can be said that when the temperature increases, the speed of sound in air also increases.

89. a. Let $n = 5$:
$$N(n) = \frac{3}{2}n^2 - \frac{3}{2}n$$
$$N(5) = \frac{3}{2}(5)^2 - \frac{3}{2}(5)$$
$$= \frac{75}{2} - \frac{15}{2}$$
$$= \frac{60}{2} = 30$$

A league that has 5 teams must schedule 30 games.

b. Let $n = 6$:
$$N(n) = \frac{3}{2}n^2 - \frac{3}{2}n$$
$$N(6) = \frac{3}{2}(6)^2 - \frac{3}{2}(6)$$
$$= \frac{3}{2}(36) - \frac{18}{2}$$
$$= \frac{108}{2} - \frac{18}{2}$$
$$= 45$$

A league that has 6 teams must schedule 45 games.

91. a. Let $L = 3$:
$$T(L) = 2\pi\sqrt{\frac{L}{32}}$$
$$T(3) = 2\pi\sqrt{\frac{3}{32}}$$
$$\approx 1.92$$

It takes approximately 1.92 s for a 3-foot long pendulum to make one swing.

b. Let $L = 9/12 = 0.75$:
$$T(L) = 2\pi\sqrt{\frac{L}{32}}$$
$$T(0.75) = 2\pi\sqrt{\frac{0.75}{32}}$$
$$\approx 0.96$$

It takes approximately 0.96 s for a 9-inch long pendulum to make one swing.

Applying Concepts 2.2

93. Answers will vary. Possibilities:
a. $\{(1, 2), (4, 7), (6, 9)\}$
b. $\{(1, 4), (2, 4), (3, 4)\}$

95. Answers will vary. One possibility is
$$f(x) = \frac{1}{x-5}.$$

Section 2.3

1. If every vertical line intersects a graph at most once, then the graph is the graph of a function.

3. a. The value of the x-coordinate is 0.
b. The value of the y-coordinate is 0.

5. a. The domain of a function is the set of all values of the independent variable. The range of a function is the set of all values of the dependent variable.
b. The domain of a function is the set of all input values. The range of a function is the set of all output values.

7. This graph passes the vertical line test: every vertical line intersects the graph at most once. So, yes, this is the graph of a function.

9. This graph does not pass the vertical line test: there are some vertical lines that intersect the graph at more than one point. So, no, this is not the graph of a function.

11. This graph passes the vertical line test: every vertical line intersects the graph at most once. So, yes, this is the graph of a function.

13. $f(x) = 3x + 6$
$f(0) = 3(0) + 6 = 6$

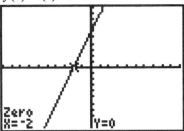

The x-intercept is $(-2, 0)$. The y-intercept is $(0, 6)$.

15. $h(x) = x^2 - x - 6$
$h(0) = (0)^2 - 0 - 6 = -6$

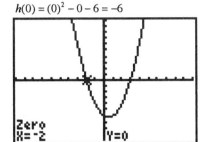

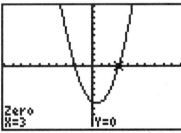

The x-intercepts are $(-2, 0)$ and $(3, 0)$.
The y-intercept is $(0, -6)$.

17. $G(x) = 2x^2 + 5x - 3$
$G(0) = 2(0)^2 + 5(0) - 3 = -3$

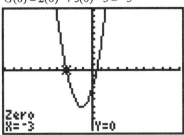

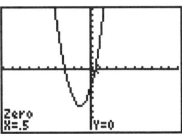

The x-intercepts are $(-3, 0)$ and $(0.5, 0)$.
The y-intercept is $(0, -3)$.

19. $s(x) = -x^2 + 4x + 5$
$s(0) = -(0)^2 + 4(0) + 5 = 5$

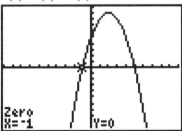

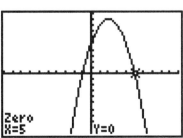

The x-intercepts are $(-1, 0)$ and $(5, 0)$.
The y-intercept is $(0, 5)$.

21. $g(x) = x^3 - 4x^2 - 7x + 10$
$g(0) = (0)^3 - 4(0)^2 - 7(0) + 10 = 10$

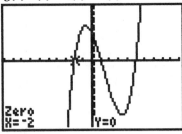

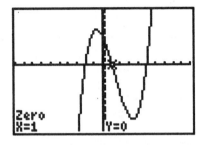

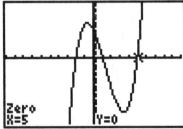

The x-intercepts are $(-2, 0)$, $(1, 0)$ and $(5, 0)$.
The y-intercept is $(0, 10)$.

23. $P(x) = x^3 - x^2 - 12x$
$P(0) = (0)^3 - (0)^2 - 12(0) = 0$

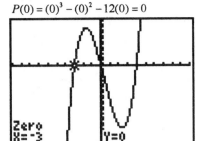

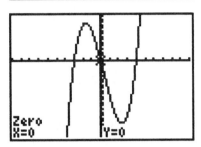

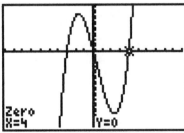

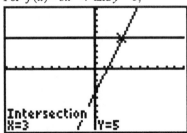

The x-intercepts are $(-3, 0)$, $(0, 0)$ and $(4, 0)$.
The y-intercept is $(0, 0)$.

25. For $f(x) = 3x - 4$ and $y = 5$,

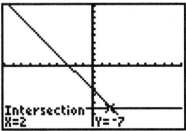

The number is 3.

27. For $h(x) = -\dfrac{3}{2}x - 4$ and $y = -7$,

The number is 2.

29. For $f(x) = \dfrac{5}{2}x - 2$ and $y = 2$,

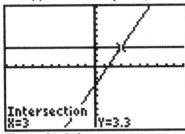

The number is 1.6.

31. For $h(t) = 2.1t - 3$ and $y = -1$,

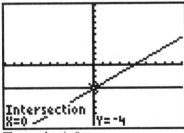

The number is 3.

33. For $f(x) = \dfrac{6}{7}x - 4$ and $y = -4$,

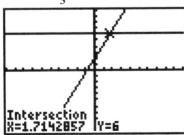

The number is 0.

35. For $f(x) = \dfrac{7}{3}x + 2$ and $y = 6$,

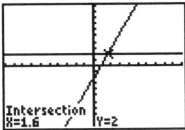

The number is 1.71.

37. For $f(x) = \dfrac{8}{x+1}$ and $y = 2$,

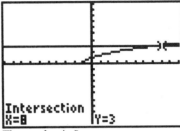

The number is 3.

39. For $h(x) = \sqrt{x+1}$ and $y = 3$,

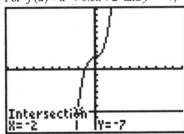

The number is 8.

41. For $f(x) = x^3 + 0.5x + 2$ and $y = -7$,

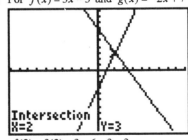

The number is -2.

43. For $f(x) = 3x - 3$ and $g(x) = -2x + 7$

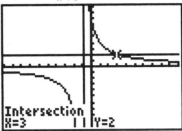

$f(2) = 3(2) - 3 = 6 - 3 = 3$

$g(2) = -2(2) + 7 = -4 + 7 = 3$

The input value is 2.

45. For $f(x) = 2x + 8$ and $g(x) = -3x - 2$

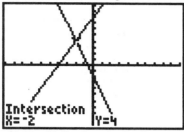

$f(-2) = 2(-2) + 8 = -4 + 8 = 4$

$g(-2) = -3(-2) - 2 = 6 - 2 = 4$

The input value is –2.

47. For $f(x) = \frac{3}{2}x + 2$ and $g(x) = -3x - 7$

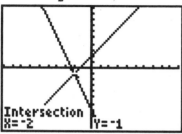

$f(-2) = \frac{3}{2}(-2) + 2 = -3 + 2 = -1$

$g(-2) = -3(-2) - 7 = 6 - 7 = -1$

The input value is –2.

49. For $f(x) = 2x - 2$ and $g(x) = -2x + 8$

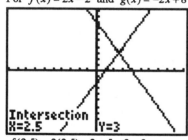

$f(2.5) = 2(2.5) - 2 = 5 - 2 = 3$

$g(2.5) = -2(2.5) + 8 = -5 + 8 = 3$

The input value is 2.5.

51. For $f(x) = -2x - 3.25$ and $g(x) = 3x + 8.5$

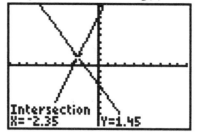

$f(-2.35) = -2(-2.35) - 3.25 = 4.7 - 3.25 = 1.45$

$g(-2.35) = 3(-2.35) + 8.5 = -7.05 + 8.5 = 1.45$

The input value is –2.35.

53. For $f(x) = 1.6x - 6$ and $g(x) = -2.4x + 2.4$

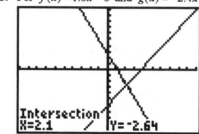

$f(2.1) = 1.6(2.1) - 6 = 3.36 - 6 = -2.64$

$g(2.1) = -2.4(2.1) + 2.4 = -5.04 + 2.4 = -2.64$

The input value is 2.1.

55. a. $h(x) = 4x - 1$

$h(-2) = 4(-2) - 1 = -8 - 1 = -9$

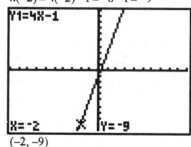

$(-2, -9)$

b. $h(x) = 4x - 1$

$h(1) = 4(1) - 1 = 3$

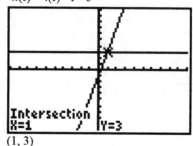

$(1, 3)$

57. **a.** $F(x) = -\dfrac{x}{3} + 2$

$F(-6) = \dfrac{-6}{3} + 2 = 2 + 2 = 4$

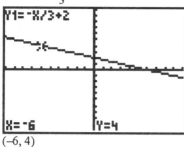

$(-6, 4)$

b. $F(x) = -\dfrac{x}{3} + 2$

$F(9) = -\dfrac{9}{3} + 2 = -3 + 2 = -1$

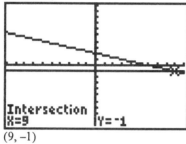

$(9, -1)$

59.   For $Q(w) = 0.75w$ on [0, 50] and [0. 40],

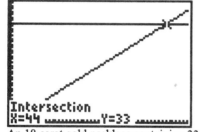

An 18-carat gold necklace containing 33 g of pure gold would weigh 44 g.

61. **a.**   For $s(t) = 175 - 16t^2$ on [−10, 10] and [−175, 175]

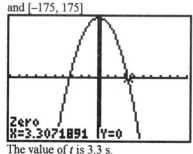

The value of t is 3.3 s.

b.   The rock hits the bottom of the ravine in 3.3 s.

63.   For $P(t) = 50 - \dfrac{30}{t+1}$ on [0, 10] and [0, 50],

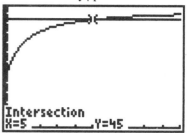

The population will be 45,000 in 5 years.

65.   For $D(p) = \dfrac{250{,}000}{80 + 4p}$ on [0, 50] and [0, 2000],

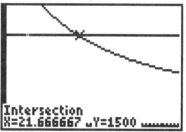

The 1500 games can be sold at $22 per game.

67.   For $g(t) = 3t + 3$ and $f(t) = 4.5t$ on [0, 4] and [0, 20],

Emily will catch up to Ramona in 2 h.

69.   For $P(t) = 53{,}000 + 1000t$ and $R(t) = 42{,}000 + 2000t$ on [0, 15] and [0, 75 000],

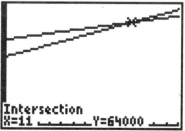

The populations of the two cities will be equal in $2000 + 11 = 2011$.

Applying Concepts 2.3

71. For $g(x) = -2x - 1$ and $g(a) = -5$

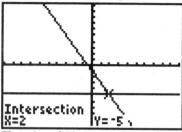

Intersection
X=2   Y=-5

The value of a is 2.

73. For $F(x) = -\dfrac{5}{4}x - 1$ and $F(a) = 9$

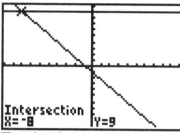

Intersection
X=-8   Y=9

The value of a is −8.

75. For $f(x) = 0.01(x^4 - 49x^2 + 36x + 252)$ and $f(a) = 1$

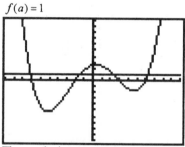

The graphs intersect 4 times.

77. For $f(x) = x^2 - x - 1$ and $g(x) = -3x + 2$

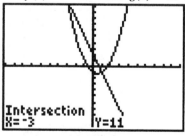

Intersection
X=-3   Y=11

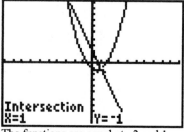

Intersection
X=1   Y=-1

The functions are equal at −3 and 1.

79. For $f(x) = x + 4$ and $g(x) = x^2 + 3x - 4$,

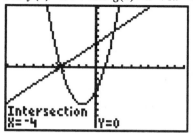

Intersection
X=-4   Y=0

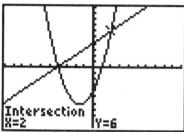

Intersection
X=2   Y=6

The functions are equal at −4 and 2.

Chapter Review Exercises

1.

Input, x	$\dfrac{1}{2}x - 3$	Output
−6	$\dfrac{1}{2}(-6) - 3$	−6
−4	$\dfrac{1}{2}(-4) - 3$	−5
−2	$\dfrac{1}{2}(-2) - 3$	−4
0	$\dfrac{1}{2}(0) - 3$	−3
2	$\dfrac{1}{2}(2) - 3$	−2
4	$\dfrac{1}{2}(4) - 3$	−1

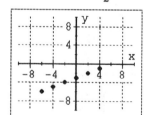

2.

Input, x	$x^2 + x - 3$	Output
-3	$(-3)^2 + (-3) - 3$	3
-2	$(-2)^2 + (-2) - 3$	-1
-1	$(-1)^2 + (-1) - 3$	-3
0	$(0)^2 + (0) - 3$	-3
1	$(1)^2 + (1) - 3$	-1
2	$(2)^2 + (2) - 3$	3
3	$(3)^2 + (3) - 3$	9

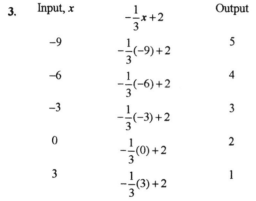

3.

Input, x	$-\dfrac{1}{3}x + 2$	Output
-9	$-\dfrac{1}{3}(-9) + 2$	5
-6	$-\dfrac{1}{3}(-6) + 2$	4
-3	$-\dfrac{1}{3}(-3) + 2$	3
0	$-\dfrac{1}{3}(0) + 2$	2
3	$-\dfrac{1}{3}(3) + 2$	1

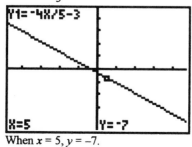

4. a. For $y = -\dfrac{4}{5}x - 3$,

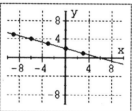

When $x = 5$, $y = -7$.

b. For $y = -\dfrac{4}{5}x - 3$,

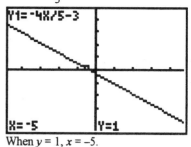

When $y = 1$, $x = -5$.

5. a. For $y = \dfrac{5}{3}x - 1$,

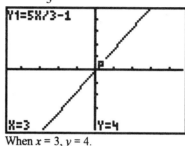

When $x = 3$, $y = 4$.

b. For $y = \dfrac{5}{3}x - 1$,

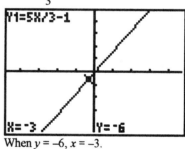

When $y = -6$, $x = -3$.

6. Domain: $\{-1, 0, 1, 2, 3, 4\}$
Range: $\{-1, 1, 3, 5\}$
Yes, the relation is a function.

7. For $h(t) = -2t^2 + 5$

$h(-4) = -2(-4)^2 + 5$
$= -2(16) + 5 = -32 + 5 = -27$
$h(-3) = -2(-3)^2 + 5$
$= -2(9) + 5 = -18 + 5 = -13$
$h(-2) = -2(-2)^2 + 5$
$= -2(4) + 5 = -8 + 5 = -3$
$h(-1) = -2(-1)^2 + 5$
$= -2(1) + 5 = -2 + 5 = 3$
$h(0) = -2(0)^2 + 5$
$= 0 + 5 = 5$
$h(1) = -2(1)^2 + 5$
$= -2(1) + 5 = -2 + 5 = 3$
$h(2) = -2(2)^2 + 5$
$= -2(4) + 5 = -8 + 5 = -3$
$h(3) = -2(3)^2 + 5$
$= -2(9) + 5 = -18 + 5 = -13$
$h(4) = -2(4)^2 + 5$
$= -2(16) + 5 = -32 + 5 = -27$

The range is $\{-27, -13, -3, 3, 5\}$.

8. $F(x) = \dfrac{3x - 6}{x + 2}$

$F(-2) = \dfrac{3(-2) - 6}{-2 + 2} = \dfrac{-6 - 6}{0}$ undefined

$F(0) = \dfrac{3(0) - 6}{0 + 2} = \dfrac{-6}{2} = -3$

$F(2) = \dfrac{3(2) - 6}{2 + 2} = \dfrac{6 - 6}{4} = 0$

-2 is excluded.

9. $G(x) = \dfrac{x}{x^2 - 9}$

$G(-3) = \dfrac{-3}{(-3)^2 - 9} = \dfrac{-3}{9 - 9} = \dfrac{-3}{0}$ undefined

$G(0) = \dfrac{0}{(0)^2 - 9} = \dfrac{0}{-9} = 0$

$G(3) = \dfrac{3}{(3)^2 - 9} = \dfrac{3}{9 - 9} = \dfrac{3}{0}$ undefined

-3 and 3 are excluded.

10.

Input, x	$-2x + 3$	Output
-3	$-2(-3) + 3$	9
-2	$-2(-2) + 3$	7
-1	$-2(-1) + 3$	5
0	$-2(0) + 3$	3
1	$-2(1) + 3$	1

Using a $[-10, 10]$ window,

11.

Input, x	$-x^2 + 4x - 1$	Output
-1	$-(-1)^2 + 4(-1) - 1$	-6
0	$-(0)^2 + 4(0) - 1$	-1
1	$-(1)^2 + 4(1) - 1$	2
2	$-(2)^2 + 4(2) - 1$	3
3	$-(3)^2 + 4(3) - 1$	2
4	$-(4)^2 + 4(4) - 1$	-1
5	$-(5)^2 + 4(5) - 1$	-6

Using a $[-10, 10]$ window,

12.

Input, x	-4	Output
-2	-4	-4
-1	-4	-4
0	-4	-4
1	-4	-4
2	-4	-4

Using a $[-10, 10]$ window,

13. For $f(x) = -\dfrac{5}{4}x + 5$,

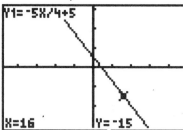

For $y = -15$, $x = 16$.

$$f(16) = -\frac{5}{4}(16) + 5 = -20 + 5 = -15$$

14. For $g(x) = 3 - \dfrac{9}{5}x$,

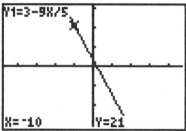

For $y = 21$, $x = -10$.

$$g(-10) = 3 - \frac{9}{5}(-10) = 3 + 18 = 21$$

15. For $f(x) = -x^3 - 4x^2 + 2$,

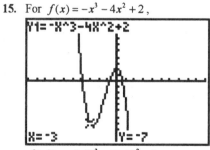

$$\begin{aligned}
f(-3) &= -(-3)^3 - 4(-3)^2 + 2 \\
&= 27 - 4(9) + 2 \\
&= 27 - 36 + 2 \\
&= -7
\end{aligned}$$

16. For $F(x) = x^3 - x^2 + 2x - 2$,

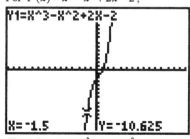

$$\begin{aligned}
F(-1.5) &= (-1.5)^3 - (-1.5)^2 + 2(-1.5) - 2 \\
&= -3.375 - 2.25 - 3 - 2 \\
&= -10.625
\end{aligned}$$

17. $G(x) = \dfrac{-2}{x+1}$

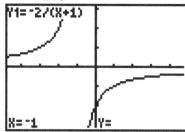

−1 is not in the domain.

18. $F(x) = \dfrac{x}{2x - 4}$

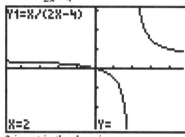

2 is not in the domain.

19. This graph passes the vertical line test: every vertical line intersects the graph at most once. So, yes, this is the graph of a function.

20. $F(x) = \dfrac{1}{2}x - 3$

$$F(0) = \frac{1}{2}(0) - 3 = -3$$

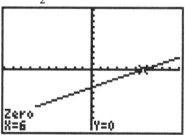

The x-intercept is $(6, 0)$. The y-intercept is $(0, -3)$.

21. $H(x) = x^2 + 2x - 8$

$H(0) = (0)^2 + 2(0) - 8 = -8$

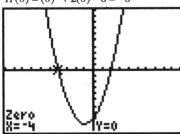

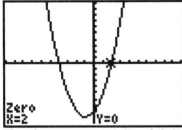

The x-intercepts are $(-4, 0)$ and $(2, 0)$.
The y-intercept is $(0, -8)$.

22. For $f(x) = \dfrac{1}{2}x - 3$ and $y = -\dfrac{5}{4}$,

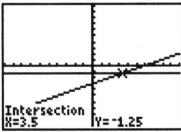

The number is 3.5.

23. For $f(x) = -2x + 4$ and $g(x) = \dfrac{3}{2}x + 11$,

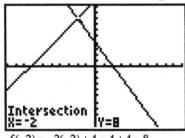

$f(-2) = -2(-2) + 4 = 4 + 4 = 8$

$g(-2) = \dfrac{3}{2}(-2) + 11 = -3 + 11 = 8$

The input value is -2.

24. a. For $h(t) = 75t + 300$ on $[0, 10]$
and $[0, 1000]$

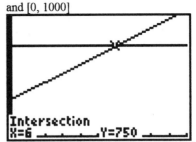

The plane will be 750 ft above sea level in 6 min.

b. For $h(t) = 75t + 300$ on $[0, 10]$
and $[0, 1000]$

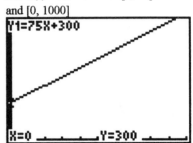

The airport is 300 ft above sea level.

25. For $V(x) = 400 + 24x$ and $W(x) = 350 + 34x$ on $[0, 20]$ and $[0, 1000]$,

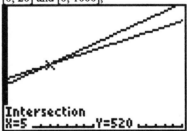

The values of the two investments will be equal in $2000 + 5 = 2005$.

Chapter Test

1.

Input, x	$-x^2 + 4x + 5$	Output
−2	$-(-2)^2 + 4(-2) + 5$	−7
−1	$-(-1)^2 + 4(-1) + 5$	0
0	$-(0)^2 + 4(0) + 5$	5
1	$-(1)^2 + 4(1) + 5$	8
2	$-(2)^2 + 4(2) + 5$	9
3	$-(3)^2 + 4(3) + 5$	8
4	$-(4)^2 + 4(4) + 5$	5
5	$-(5)^2 + 4(5) + 5$	0
6	$-(6)^2 + 4(6) + 5$	−7

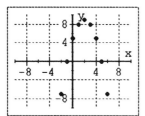

2.

Input, x	$\frac{2}{3}x - 2$	Output
−6	$\frac{2}{3}(-6) - 2$	−6
−3	$\frac{2}{3}(-3) - 2$	−4
0	$\frac{2}{3}(0) - 2$	2
3	$\frac{2}{3}(3) - 2$	0
6	$\frac{2}{3}(6) - 2$	2
9	$\frac{2}{3}(9) - 2$	4

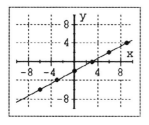

3. For $y = -\frac{4}{5}x - 3$,

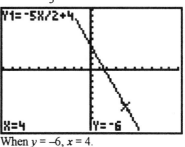

When $y = -6$, $x = 4$.

4. Domain: $\{-4, -2, 0, 2, 4\}$
Range: $\{-2, -1, 0\}$
Yes, the relation is a function.

5. For $P(x) = x^2 - 3x - 1$
$$P(-2) = (-2)^2 - 3(-2) - 1$$
$$= 4 + 6 - 1 = 9$$
$$P(-1) = (-1)^2 - 3(-1) - 1$$
$$= 1 + 3 - 1 = 3$$
$$P(0) = (0)^2 - 3(0) - 1 = -1$$
$$P(1) = (1)^2 - 3(1) - 1$$
$$= 1 - 3 - 1 = -3$$
$$P(2) = (2)^2 - 3(2) - 1$$
$$= 4 - 6 - 1 = -3$$
$$P(3) = (3)^2 - 3(3) - 1$$
$$= 9 - 9 - 1 = -1$$
The range is $\{-3, -1, 3, 9\}$.

6. a. $f(x) = \frac{2x+4}{x-2}$
$$f(-2) = \frac{2(-2)+4}{-2-2} = \frac{-4+4}{-4} = 0$$

b. $f(x) = \frac{2x+4}{x-2}$
$$f(0) = \frac{2(0)+4}{0-2} = \frac{4}{-2} = -2$$

c. $f(x) = \frac{2x+4}{x-2}$
$$f(2) = \frac{2(2)+4}{2-2} = \frac{4+4}{0} \text{ undefined}$$

7.

Input, x	$-\dfrac{3}{2}x+4$	Output
–2	$-\dfrac{3}{2}(-2)+4$	7
0	$-\dfrac{3}{2}(0)+4$	4
2	$-\dfrac{3}{2}(2)+4$	1
4	$-\dfrac{3}{2}(4)+4$	–2
6	$-\dfrac{3}{2}(6)+4$	–5

Using a [–10, 10] window,

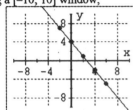

8.

Input, x	$-x^2-2x+3$	Output
–4	$-(-4)^2-2(-4)+3$	–5
–3	$-(-3)^2-2(-3)+3$	0
–2	$-(-2)^2-2(-2)+3$	3
–1	$-(-1)^2-2(-1)+3$	4
0	$-(0)^2-2(0)+3$	3
1	$-(1)^2-2(1)+3$	0
2	$-(2)^2-2(2)+3$	–5

Using a [–10, 10] window,

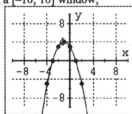

9. For $f(x)=-\dfrac{4}{3}x+3$,

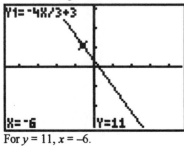

For $y = 11$, $x = -6$.

$$f(-6)=-\dfrac{4}{3}(-6)+3=8+3=11$$

10. For $g(x)=\dfrac{x}{2}-5$,

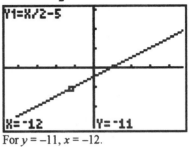

For $y = -11$, $x = -12$.

$$g(-12)=\dfrac{-12}{2}-5=-6-5=-11$$

11. $f(x)=\dfrac{-2}{x^2-9}$

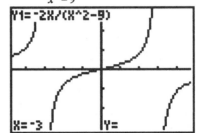

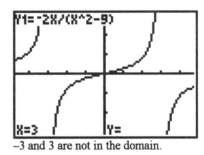

–3 and 3 are not in the domain.

12. Answers will vary.

13. $G(x)=3+\dfrac{3}{4}x$

$$G(0)=3+\dfrac{3}{4}(0)=3$$

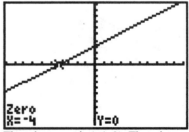

The x-intercept is (–4, 0). The y-intercept is (0, 3).

14. $p(x) = x^2 - 2x - 3$

$p(0) = (0)^2 - 2(0) - 3 = -3$

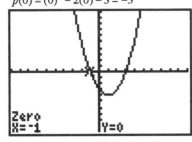

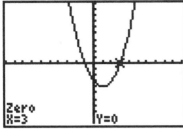

The x-intercepts are $(-1, 0)$ and $(3, 0)$.
The y-intercept is $(0, -3)$.

15. For $f(x) = 2 + \dfrac{5}{4}x$ and $y = -3$,

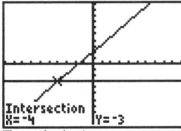

The number is -4.

16. For $f(x) = -\dfrac{5}{2}x + 4$ and $g(x) = \dfrac{3}{4}x - 9$,

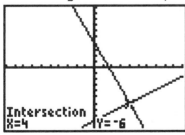

$f(4) = -\dfrac{5}{2}4 + 4 = -10 + 4 = -6$

$g(4) = \dfrac{3}{4}(4) - 9 = 3 - 9 = -6$

The number is 4.

17. a. For $P(x) = \dfrac{100x + 100}{x + 5}$ on $[0, 10]$

and $[0, 100]$

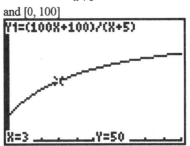

After adding an additional 3 g of acid, the concentration of acid is 50%.

b. For $P(x) = \dfrac{100x + 100}{x + 5}$ on $[0, 10]$

and $[0, 100]$

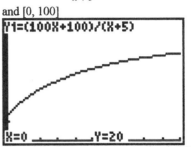

The original percent concentration is 20%.

18. For $H(t) = 2t + 40$ on $[0, 20]$ and $[0, 1000]$,

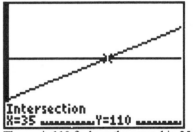

The car is 110 ft above the ground in 35 s.

19. For $s(t) = 150 - 16t^2$,

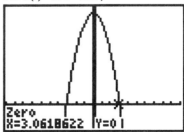

The rock reaches the ocean in approximately 3.1 s.

20. For $B(t) = 750t + 25{,}000$ and
$C(t) = 31{,}250 - 500t$ on [0, 8] and [0, 32 000],

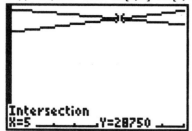

Intersection
X=5   Y=28750

The populations of the two cities will be equal in
2002 + 5 = 2007.

Cumulative Review Exercises

1. $\{x \mid -2 \le x \le 3\}$

2. True

3. $2 \cdot 3^2 - 4^3 \div (2 - 6) = 2 \cdot 9 - 64 \div (2 - 6)$
$= 18 - 64 \div (-4)$
$= 18 + 16$
$= 34$

4. For $-a^3b - 4ab^2$,
$-(-2)^3(4) - 4(-2)(4)^2 = -(-8)(4) - 4(-2)(16)$
$= 32 + 128$
$= 160$

5. For $3a + 2b - c^2$,
$3\left(\dfrac{5}{6}\right) + 2\left(-\dfrac{2}{3}\right) - \left(-\dfrac{3}{2}\right)^2 = \dfrac{5}{2} - \dfrac{4}{3} - \dfrac{9}{4}$
$= \dfrac{30}{12} - \dfrac{16}{12} - \dfrac{27}{12}$
$= -\dfrac{13}{12}$

6. $3 - 5(2a - 7) = 3 - 10a + 35 = -10a + 38$

7. Commutative Property of Multiplication

8.

Input, x	$\dfrac{3}{2}x - 3$	Output
−4	$\dfrac{3}{2}(-4) - 3$	−9
−2	$\dfrac{3}{2}(-2) - 3$	−6
0	$\dfrac{3}{2}(0) - 3$	−3
2	$\dfrac{3}{2}(2) - 3$	0
4	$\dfrac{3}{2}(4) - 3$	3
6	$\dfrac{3}{2}(6) - 3$	6

Using a [−10, 10] window,

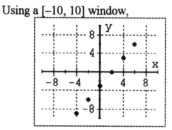

9. a.

Input, x	$0.4m$	Output
0	0.4(0)	0
100	0.4(100)	40
150	0.4(150)	60
200	0.4(200)	80
250	0.4(250)	100
300	0.4(300)	120
350	0.4(350)	140

b. When this car is driven 150 mi, it emits 60 g
of NO_x.

10. $y = 2 - \dfrac{x}{2}$

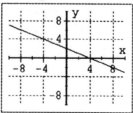

11. $f(x) = -\dfrac{2}{3}x$

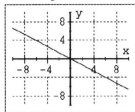

12.

Input, x	$x^2 - 6x + 1$	Output
-1	$(-1)^2 - 6(-1) + 1$	8
0	$(0)^2 - 6(0) + 1$	1
1	$(1)^2 - 6(1) + 1$	-4
2	$(2)^2 - 6(2) + 1$	-7
3	$(3)^2 - 6(3) + 1$	-8
4	$(4)^2 - 6(4) + 1$	-7
5	$(5)^2 - 6(5) + 1$	-4

Using a $[-10, 10]$ window,

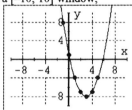

13.

Input, x	$-x^2 - 2x + 1$	Output
-4	$-(-4)^2 - 2(-4) + 1$	-7
-3	$-(-3)^2 - 2(-3) + 1$	-2
-2	$-(-2)^2 - 2(-2) + 1$	1
-1	$-(-1)^2 - 2(-1) + 1$	2
0	$-(0)^2 - 2(0) + 1$	1
1	$-(1)^2 - 2(1) + 1$	-2
2	$-(2)^2 - 2(2) + 1$	-7

Using a $[-10, 10]$ window,

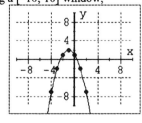

14. For $y = \dfrac{4}{3}x - 2$,

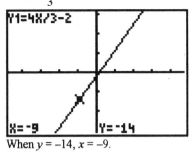

When $y = -14$, $x = -9$.

15. For $f(x) = -\dfrac{3}{2}x + 3$ and $y = -3$,

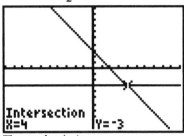

The number is 4.

16. a. $g(x) = \dfrac{x+3}{x-2}$

$g(-3) = \dfrac{-3+3}{-3-2} = \dfrac{0}{-5} = 0$

b. $g(x) = \dfrac{x+3}{x-2}$

$g(2) = \dfrac{2+3}{2-2} = \dfrac{5}{0}$ undefined

c. $g(x) = \dfrac{x+3}{x-2}$

$g(-4) = \dfrac{-4+3}{-4-2} = \dfrac{-1}{-6} = \dfrac{1}{6}$

17. $f(x) = x^2 + 2x - 3$
    $f(0) = (0)^2 + 2(0) - 3 = -3$

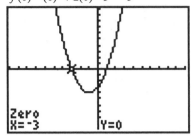

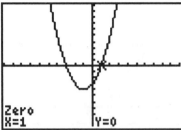

The x-intercepts are $(-3, 0)$ and $(1, 0)$.
The y-intercept is $(0, -3)$.

18. For $f(x) = 3x - 4$ and $g(x) = -x + 4$,

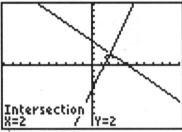

The number is 2.

19. For $P(t) = \dfrac{20}{t + 2}$ on $[0, 10]$ and $[0, 20]$

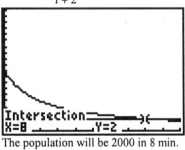

The population will be 2000 in 8 min.

20. For $G(n) = 0.75n + 8$ and $W(n) = -0.5n + 13$

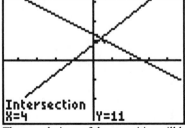

The populations of the two cities will be equal in
$2000 + 4 = 2004$.

Chapter 3: First-Degree Equations and Inequalities

Prep Test

1. $8 - 12 = -4$

2. $-9 + 3 = -6$

3. $\dfrac{-18}{-6} = 3$

4. $-\dfrac{3}{4}\left(-\dfrac{4}{3}\right) = \dfrac{12}{12} = 1$

5. $3x - 5 + 7x = 10x - 5$

6. $8x - 9 - 8x = -9$

7. $6x - 3(6 - x) = 6x - 18 + 3x$
   $ = 9x - 18$

8. $|-8| = 8$

9. $20 - n$

Go Figure

Since the other three smaller rectangles are of different sizes, the possible values for x cannot be the same as any of the three other rectangles. The first possible value of x is 1. The lengths of the sides of the rectangles are shown below.

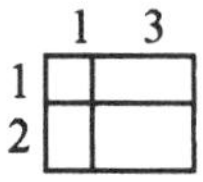

The second possible value of x is 4.
The first possible value of x is 4. The lengths of the sides of the rectangles are shown below.

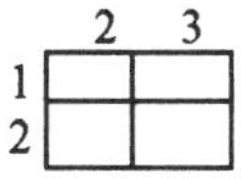

The third possible value of x is 9. The lengths of the sides of the rectangles are shown below.

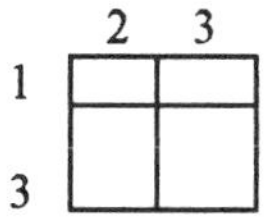

Section 3.1

1. An equation has an equals sign; an expression does not have an equals sign.

3. The goal of solving an equation is to find its solutions. The goal of simplifying an expression is to combine like terms and write the expression in simplest form.

5. The same number can be added to each side of an equation without changing the solution of the equation. This property is used to remove a term from one side of an equation.

7. $\begin{aligned} x - 2 &= 7 \\ x - 2 + 2 &= 7 + 2 \\ x &= 9 \end{aligned}$
   The solution is 9.

9. $\begin{aligned} 3x &= 12 \\ \dfrac{3x}{3} &= \dfrac{12}{3} \\ x &= 4 \end{aligned}$
   The solution is 4.

11. $\begin{aligned} \dfrac{2}{3}y &= 5 \\ \dfrac{3}{2}\left(\dfrac{2}{3}y\right) &= \dfrac{3}{2}(5) \\ y &= \dfrac{15}{2} \end{aligned}$
    The solution is $\dfrac{15}{2}$.

13. $\begin{aligned} -\dfrac{3}{5} &= \dfrac{3b}{10} \\ \dfrac{10}{3}\left(-\dfrac{3}{5}\right) &= \dfrac{10}{3}\left(\dfrac{3b}{10}\right) \\ -2 &= b \end{aligned}$
    The solution is -2.

15. $\begin{aligned} 0.25x &= 1.2 \\ \dfrac{0.25x}{0.25} &= \dfrac{1.2}{0.25} \\ x &= 4.8 \end{aligned}$
    The solution is 4.8.

17. $\begin{aligned} 3x + 5x &= 12 \\ 8x &= 12 \\ \dfrac{8x}{8} &= \dfrac{12}{8} \\ x &= \dfrac{3}{2} \end{aligned}$
    The solution is $\dfrac{3}{2}$.

19. $\begin{aligned} 3x + 8 &= 17 \\ 3x &= 9 \\ \dfrac{3x}{3} &= \dfrac{9}{3} \\ x &= 3 \end{aligned}$
    The solution is 3.

21.
$$5 = 3x - 10$$
$$15 = 3x$$
$$\frac{15}{3} = \frac{3x}{3}$$
$$5 = x$$
The solution is 5.

23.
$$\frac{2}{3}x + 5 = 3$$
$$\frac{2}{3}x = -2$$
$$\frac{3}{2}\left(\frac{2}{3}x\right) = \frac{3}{2}(-2)$$
$$x = -3$$
The solution is −3.

25.
$$2x + 2 = 3x + 5$$
$$2x - 2x + 2 = 3x - 2x + 5$$
$$2 = x + 5$$
$$2 - 5 = x + 5 - 5$$
$$-3 = x$$
The solution is −3.

27.
$$3b - 2b = 4 - 2b$$
$$3b - 2b + 2b = 4 - 2b + 2b$$
$$3b = 4$$
$$\frac{3b}{3} = \frac{4}{3}$$
$$b = \frac{4}{3}$$
The solution is $\frac{4}{3}$.

29.
$$d + \frac{1}{5}d = 2$$
$$\frac{6}{5}d = 2$$
$$\frac{5}{6}\left(\frac{6}{5}d\right) = \frac{5}{6}(2)$$
$$d = \frac{5}{3}$$
The solution is $\frac{5}{3}$.

31.
$$4(x - 5) = 8$$
$$4x - 20 = 8$$
$$4x - 20 + 20 = 8 + 20$$
$$4x = 28$$
$$\frac{4x}{4} = \frac{28}{4}$$
$$x = 7$$
The solution is 7.

33.
$$5 - 2(2x + 3) = 11$$
$$5 - 4x - 6 = 11$$
$$-4x - 1 = 11$$
$$-4x - 1 + 1 = 11 + 1$$
$$-4x = 12$$
$$\frac{-4x}{-4} = \frac{12}{-4}$$
$$x = -3$$
The solution is −3.

35.
$$5(2 - b) = -3(b - 3)$$
$$10 - 5b = -3b + 9$$
$$10 - 10 - 5b + 3b = -3b + 3b + 9 - 10$$
$$-2b = -1$$
$$\frac{-2b}{-2} = \frac{-1}{-2}$$
$$b = \frac{1}{2}$$
The solution is $\frac{1}{2}$.

37.
$$4 - 3x = 7x - 2(3 - x)$$
$$4 - 3x = 7x - 6 + 2x$$
$$4 - 3x = 9x - 6$$
$$4 - 3x + 3x = 9x + 3x - 6$$
$$4 = 12x - 6$$
$$4 + 6 = 12x - 6 + 6$$
$$10 = 12x$$
$$\frac{10}{12} = \frac{12x}{12}$$
$$\frac{5}{6} = x$$
The solution is $\frac{5}{6}$.

39.
$$3y = 2[5 - 3(2 - y)]$$
$$3y = 2(5 - 6 + 3y)$$
$$3y = 2(-1 + 3y)$$
$$3y = -2 + 6y$$
$$3y - 6y = -2 + 6y - 6y$$
$$-3y = -2$$
$$\frac{-3y}{-3} = \frac{-2}{-3}$$
$$y = \frac{2}{3}$$
The solution is $\frac{2}{3}$.

41.
$$3[x - (2 - x) - 2x] = 3(4 - x)$$
$$3(x - 2 + x - 2x) = 12 - 3x$$
$$3(-2) = 12 - 3x$$
$$-6 = 12 - 3x$$
$$-6 - 12 = 12 - 12 - 3x$$
$$-18 = -3x$$
$$\frac{-18}{-3} = \frac{-3x}{-3}$$
$$6 = x$$
The solution is 6.

Applying Concepts 3.1

43.
$$3x - 5 = 9x + 4$$
$$3x - 3x - 5 = 9x - 3x + 4$$
$$-5 = 6x + 4$$
$$-5 - 4 = 6x + 4 - 4$$
$$-9 = 6x$$
$$\frac{-9}{6} = \frac{6x}{6}$$
$$-\frac{3}{2} = x$$

Evaluate the expression $6x - 3$ at $x = -\frac{3}{2}$.

$$6x - 3$$
$$6\left(-\frac{3}{2}\right) - 3 = -9 - 3 = -12$$

45.
$$2[3(x + 4) - 2(x + 1)] = 5x + 3(1 - x)$$
$$2[3x + 12 - 2x - 2] = 5x + 3 - 3x$$
$$2[x + 10] = 2x + 3$$
$$2x + 20 = 2x + 3$$
$$2x - 2x + 20 - 20 = 2x - 2x + 3 - 20$$
$$0 \neq -17$$

There is no solution.

47.
$$\frac{1}{\frac{1}{x}} = 9$$
$$1 \div \frac{1}{x} = 9$$
$$1 \cdot \frac{x}{1} = 9$$
$$x = 9$$

The solution is 9.

49.
$$\frac{10}{\frac{3}{x}} - 5 = 4x$$
$$10 \div \frac{3}{x} - 5 = 4x$$
$$10 \cdot \frac{x}{3} - 5 = 4x$$
$$3\left(\frac{10}{3}x - 5\right) = 3(4x)$$
$$10x - 15 = 12x$$
$$10x - 10x - 15 = 12x - 10x$$
$$-15 = 2x$$
$$\frac{-15}{2} = \frac{2x}{2}$$
$$-\frac{15}{2} = x$$

The solution is $-\frac{15}{2}$.

51. a. For the first option,
$$4500 = 0.05x + 2500$$
$$4500 - 2500 = 0.05x$$
$$2000 = 0.05x$$
$$\frac{2000}{0.05} = \frac{0.05x}{0.05}$$
$$40,000 = x$$

For the second option,
$$4500 = 0.02x + 4000$$
$$4500 - 4000 = 0.02x + 4000 - 4000$$
$$500 = 0.02x$$
$$\frac{500}{0.02} = \frac{0.02x}{0.02}$$
$$25,000 = x$$

For the first option, the executive must sell $40,000. For the second option, the executive must sell $25,000.

b. For the first option,
$$5500 = 0.05x + 2500$$
$$5500 - 2500 = 0.05x$$
$$3000 = 0.05x$$
$$\frac{3000}{0.05} = \frac{0.05x}{0.05}$$
$$60,000 = x$$

For the second option,
$$5500 = 0.02x + 4000$$
$$5500 - 4000 = 0.02x + 4000 - 4000$$
$$1500 = 0.02x$$
$$\frac{1500}{0.02} = \frac{0.02x}{0.02}$$
$$75,000 = x$$

For the first option, the executive must sell $60,000. For the second option, the executive must sell $75,000.

c.
$$0.05x + 2500 = 0.02x + 4000$$
$$0.05x - 0.02x + 2500 = 0.02x - 0.02x + 4000$$
$$0.03x + 2500 - 2500 = 4000 - 2500$$
$$0.03x = 1500$$
$$\frac{0.03x}{0.03} = \frac{1500}{0.03}$$
$$x = 50,000$$

The executive must sell $50,000 for the plans are equal.

Section 3.2

1. $V = x(0.85) = 0.85x$

3. Yes, since the cost of the apple and cranberry juices per quart is less than the selling price of the mixture.
Sometimes; it depends on the ratio of the juices used.
No. The selling price is less than both of the ingredients.

5. The second jogger is the faster runner.

7. The total distance between the two objects = the distance traveled by the first object + the distance traveled by the second object.

9. The planes are headed toward each other, add their rates. $350 + 450 = 800$. The rate at which the distance between the planes is changing at 800 mph.

11. Strategy
Let x represent the cost of the resulting mixture. There are 64 ounces of olive oil costing $0.13 per ounce and 20 ounces of vinegar costing $0.09 per ounce. The resulting mixture will be $64 + 20 = 84$ pounds. Use the equation $V = AC$ to find the value of each:
Value of olive oil: $64(0.13)$
Value of vinegar: $20(0.09)$
Value of mixture: $84x$
Write an equation using the fact that the sum of the values before mixing equals the value after mixing.

Solution
$$64(0.13) + 20(0.09) = 84x$$
$$8.32 + 18 = 84x$$
$$10.12 = 84x$$
$$0.12 = x$$
The cost of the mixture is $0.12 per ounce.

13. Strategy
Let x represent the pounds of the $6-per-pound coffee. There will be 25 pounds of resulting coffee mixture costing $5.25 per pound. Thus, the weight of the $3.50-per-pound coffee is $25 - x$. Use the equation $V = AC$ to find the value of each:
Value of $6 coffee: $6x$
Value of $3.50 coffee: $3.50(25 - x)$
Value of mixture: $5.25(25)$
Write an equation using the fact that the sum of the values before mixing equals the value after mixing.

Solution
$$6x + 3.50(25 - x) = 5.25(25)$$
$$6x + 87.5 - 3.50x = 131.25$$
$$2.50x + 87.5 = 131.25$$
$$2.50x = 43.75$$
$$x = 17.5$$
$$25 - x = 25 - 17.5 = 7.5$$
The blend must contain 7.5 lb of the $3.50 grade of coffee and 17.5 lb of the $6 grade.

15. Strategy
Let x represent the number of adult tickets sold at $2.50 each. There were 113 tickets sold (for a total of $221). Thus, the number of children's tickets sold is $113 - x$, at $1 each. Use the equation $V = AC$ to find the value of each:
Value of adult tickets: $2.5x$
Value of children's tickets: $1(113 - x)$
Write an equation using the fact that the sum of the values of the adult tickets sold and the children's tickets sold is equal to $221.

Solution
$$2.5x + 1(113 - x) = 221$$
$$2.5x + 113 - x = 221$$
$$1.5x + 113 = 221$$
$$1.5x = 108$$
$$x = 72$$
72 adult tickets were sold.

17. Strategy
Let x represent the bushels of soybeans, costing $8.50 per bushel. There are 1000 bushels of the resulting mixture costing $5.50 per bushel. Thus, the number of bushels of the wheat used is $1000 - x$, costing $4.50 per bushel. Use the equation $V = AC$ to find the value of each:
Value of soybeans: $8.50x$
Value of wheat: $4.50(1000 - x)$
Value of mixture: $5.50(1000)$
Write an equation using the fact that the sum of the values before mixing equals the value after mixing

Solution
$$8.50x + 4.50(1000 - x) = 5.50(1000)$$
$$8.50x + 4500 - 4.50x = 5500$$
$$4x + 4500 = 5500$$
$$4x = 1000$$
$$x = 250$$
$$1000 - x = 1000 - 250 = 750$$
The mixture must contain 250 bushels of soybeans and 750 bushels of wheat.

19. Strategy
Let x represent the ounces of pure silver, costing $5.20 per ounce. There are 50 ounces of another alloy, costing $2.80 per ounce. Thus, there are $50 + x$ ounces of the resulting alloy, costing $4.40 per ounce. Use the equation $V = AC$ to find the value of each
Value of pure silver: $5.20x$
Value of silver alloy: $2.80(50)$
Value of mixture: $4.40(50 + x)$
Write an equation using the fact that the sum of the values before mixing equals the value after mixing.

Solution
$$5.20x + 2.80(50) = 4.40(50 + x)$$
$$5.20x + 140 = 220 + 4.40x$$
$$0.80x = 80$$
$$x = 100$$
100 oz of pure silver must be used.

21. Strategy
Let x represent the selling price per ounce of the mixture. There are 100 ounces of face cream costing $3.46 per ounce and 60 ounces of face cream costing $12.50 per ounce. Thus, there are $100 + 60 = 160$ ounces of the resulting mixture. Use the equation $V = AC$ to find the value of each
Value of $3.46 cream: $3.46(100)$
Value of $12.50 cream: $12.50(60)$
Value of mixture: $160(x)$
Write an equation using the fact that the sum of the values before mixing equals the value after mixing.

Solution
$$3.46(100) + 12.50(60) = 160x$$
$$346 + 750 = 160x$$
$$1096 = 160x$$
$$6.85 = x$$
The selling price of the mixture is $6.85 per ounce.

23. Strategy
Let x represent the kilograms of walnuts, costing $4.05 per kilogram. There are 50 kilograms of the resulting mixture, costing $6.25 per kilogram. Thus, the number of kilograms of cashews used is $50 - x$, costing $7.25 per kilogram. Use the equation $V = AC$ to find the value of each:
Value of walnuts: $4.05x$
Value of cashews: $7.25(50 - x)$
Value of mixture: $6.25(50)$
Write an equation using the fact that the sum of the values before mixing equals the value after mixing.

Solution
$$4.05x + 7.25(50 - x) = 6.25(50)$$
$$4.05x + 362.50 - 7.25x = 312.50$$
$$-3.20x + 362.50 = 312.50$$
$$-3.20x = -50$$
$$x = 15.625$$
$$50 - x = 50 - 15.625 = 34.375$$
The mixture must contain 15.6 kg of walnuts and 34.4 kg of cashews.

25. If a cyclist travels at a rate of 12 miles per hour, then in the equation $d = rt$, $r = 12$ miles per hour. An equation for the distance d that the car travels in t hours is $d = 12t$.

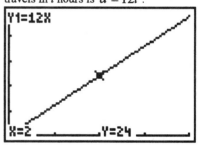

27. a. After four hours, Imogene has traveled farther. To verify this, find the 4-hour mark along the time axis. Looking at the graphs directly above this point, the graph representing the distance traveled by Imogene is higher than the graph representing Alice's distance. Therefore, Imogene has traveled farther in four hours than Alice.

b. No, Alice does not ever pass Imogene on this ride. We can tell because her graph does not intersect Imogene's graph.

29. Strategy

Let

r = the rate of the first car

$r + 10$ = the rate of the second car.

Both the first car and the second car travel for 2.5 hours. Use the uniform motion equation $d = rt$ (where d is the distance, r is the rate of speed, and t is the time) to write the distances traveled by each car:

Distance traveled by first car: $2.5r$

Distance traveled by second car: $2.5(r + 10)$

The total distance traveled by the two cars is 295 miles. Translate this fact into an equation:

$2.5r + 2.5(r + 10) = 295$

Solution

$$2.5r + 2.5(r + 10) = 295$$
$$2.5r + 2.5r + 25 = 295$$
$$5r + 25 = 295$$
$$5r = 270$$
$$r = 54$$
$$r + 10 = 54 + 10 = 64$$

The speed of the first car is 54 mph. The speed of the second car is 64 mph.

31. Strategy

Let

t = the time flying to a city

$4 - t$ = the time returning

Going to the city, the plane travels at 210 mph. Returning from the city, the plane travels at 140 mph. Use the uniform motion equation $d = rt$ (where d is the distance, r is the rate of speed, and t is the time) to write the distances traveled each way:

Distance to the city: $210t$

Distance returning from the city: $140(4 - t)$

The distance to the city is the same as the distance returning. Translate this fact into an equation:

$210t = 140(4 - t)$

Solution

$$210t = 140(4 - t)$$
$$210t = 560 - 140t$$
$$350t = 560$$
$$t = 1.6$$
$$d = rt = 210(1.6) = 336$$

The distance between the two airports is 336 mi.

33. Strategy

Let

r = the rate of the first hiker

$r + 0.5$ = the rate of the second hiker

Both hikers travel for 2 hours. Use the uniform motion equation $d = rt$ (where d is the distance, r is the rate of speed, and t is the time) to write the distances traveled by each hiker:

Distance traveled by the first hiker: $2r$

Distance traveled by the second hiker: $2(r + 0.5)$

The total distance traveled by the two hikers is 13 miles. Translate this fact into an equation:

$2r + 2(r + 0.5) = 13$

Solution

$$2r + 2(r + 0.5) = 13$$
$$2r + 2r + 1 = 13$$
$$4r + 1 = 13$$
$$4r = 12$$
$$r = 3$$
$$r + 0.5 = 3 + 0.5 = 3.5$$

The first hiker walks at 3 mph. The second hiker walks at 3.5 mph.

35. Strategy

Let

r = the rate of the freight train

$r + 18$ = the rate of the passenger train

The passenger train travels for 2.5 hours and the freight train travels for $1.5 + 2.5 = 4$ hours. Use the uniform motion equation $d = rt$ (where d is the distance, r is the rate of speed, and t is the time) to write the distances traveled by each train:

Distance traveled by freight train: $4r$

Distance traveled by passenger train: $2.5(r + 18)$

The distance the freight train travels is equal to the distance the passenger train travels. Translate this fact into an equation:

$4r = 2.5(r + 18)$

Solution

$$4r = 2.5(r + 18)$$
$$4r = 2.5r + 45$$
$$1.5r = 45$$
$$r = 30$$
$$r + 18 = 30 + 18 = 48$$

The rate of the freight train is 30 mph. The rate of the passenger train is 48 mph.

37. Strategy

Let

r = the rate of the jogger

$4r$ = the rate of the cyclist

Both the jogger and the cyclist traveled for 2 hours. Use the uniform motion equation $d = rt$ (where d is the distance, r is the rate of speed, and t is the time) to write the distances traveled by each:

Distance traveled by the jogger: $2r$

Distance traveled by the cyclist: $2(4r)$

In 2 hours, the cyclist is 33 miles ahead of the jogger. Translate this fact into an equation:

$2(4r) - 2r = 33$

Solution

$$2(4r) - 2r = 33$$
$$8r - 2r = 33$$
$$6r = 33$$
$$r = 5.5$$

The rate of the cyclist is 22 mph.

$d = rt = 22(2) = 44$

The cyclist traveled 44 miles.

Applying Concepts 3.2

39. Strategy

There are 20 lbs of peanuts costing $2.00 per lb. The mixture containing walnuts, cashews, and peanuts, is 50 pounds costing $2.72 per pound. The mixture of just cashews and walnuts is $50 - 20 = 30$ lbs.

Let x represent the number of pounds of walnuts. There are x pounds of walnuts costing $2.60 per pound. There are $30 - x$ pounds of cashews costing $3.50 per pound.

Use the equation $V = AC$ to find the value of each

Value of walnuts: $2.60x$

Value of cashews: $3.50(30 - x)$

Value of peanuts: $2.00(20)$

Value of mixture: $50(2.72)$

Write an equation using the fact that the sum of the values before mixing equals the value after mixing.

Solution

$$2.60x + 3.50(30 - x) + 2.00(20) = 50(2.72)$$
$$2.6x + 105 - 3.5x + 40 = 136$$
$$-0.9x = -9$$
$$x = 10$$

$30 - x = 30 - 10 = 20$

The mixture must contain 10 pounds of walnuts and 20 pounds of cashews.

41. Strategy

To find the distance solve the equation $d = rt$ for t using $d = 260$ trillion miles = 260,000,000 million miles, and $r = 18$ million mph.

Solution

$$d = rt$$
$$260,000,000 = 18t$$
$$t \approx 14,444,444 \text{ h}$$
$$= 14,444,444 \text{ h} \cdot \frac{1 \text{ day}}{24 \text{ h}} \cdot \frac{1 \text{ yr}}{365 \text{ day}}$$
$$\approx 1648 \text{ yr}$$
$$\approx 1600 \text{ yr}$$

It will take about 1600 years.

43. Strategy

The rate of the campers downstream was 12 mph and their rate upstream was 4 mph. Let t represent the time it took to go downstream. Because the total trip took 1 hour, the time it took to go upstream was $1 - t$. Then:

Distance traveled downstream: $12t$

Distance traveled upstream: $4(1 - t)$

Because the campers left their campsite and then returned to their campsite, the distance downstream equals the distance upstream. The equation is: $12t = 4(1 - t)$.

Solution

$$12t = 4(1 - t)$$
$$12t = 4 - 4t$$
$$12t + 4t = 4 - 4t + 4t$$
$$16t = 4$$
$$\frac{16t}{16} = \frac{4}{16}$$
$$t = \frac{1}{4}$$

The length of the trip downstream was $\frac{1}{4}$ hour or 15 minutes. The campers turned around downstream 15 minutes after they left at 10 A.M., or at 10:15 A.M.

Section 3.3

1. A right angle is an angle whose measure is 90°. An acute angle is an angle whose measure is between 0° and 90°. An obtuse angle is an angle whose measure is between 90° and 180°. A straight angle is an angle whose measure is 180°.

3. Vertical angles are nonadjacent angles formed by intersecting lines.

5. They are not parallel.

7. A central angle is formed by two radii of the circle. The measure of the central angle is equal to the measure of the intercepted arc.

9. **Strategy**
   The sum of the measures of complementary angles is 90°. Let x represent the measure of the complement of a 43° angle.

   Solution
   $$x + 43 = 90$$
   $$x + 43 - 43 = 90 - 43$$
   $$x = 47$$
   The complement of a 43° angle is a 47° angle.

11. **Strategy**
    The sum of the measures of supplementary angles is 180°. Let x represent the measure of the supplement of a 98° angle.

    Solution
    $$98 + x = 180$$
    $$98 - 98 + x = 180 - 98$$
    $$x = 82$$
    The supplement of a 98° angle is an 82° angle.

13. **Strategy**
    Let x represent the smaller angle. Because the angles are complements of one another, the measure of the other angle is $90 - x$. Thus:
    Measure of one angle: x
    Measure of other angle: $90 - x$
    The other angle is 6 degrees more than twice the one angle. Then, $90 - x = 2x + 6$.

    Solution
    $$90 - x = 2x + 6$$
    $$90 - x + x = 2x + x + 6$$
    $$90 = 3x + 6$$
    $$90 - 6 = 3x + 6 - 6$$
    $$84 = 3x$$
    $$\frac{84}{3} = \frac{3x}{3}$$
    $$28 = x$$
    The one angle has a measure of 28°. The other angle has a measure of 90 − 28 = 62°.

15. **Strategy**
    Let x represent the measure of the smaller angle. Because the two angles are supplementary, the measure of the other angle is $180 - x$.
    Measure of one angle: x
    Measure of the other angle: $180 - x$
    The other angle is 12 degrees less than three times the one angle. Thus, $180 - x = 3x - 12$.

    Solution
    $$180 - x = 3x - 12$$
    $$180 - x + x = 3x + x - 12$$
    $$180 = 4x - 12$$
    $$180 + 12 = 4x - 12 + 12$$
    $$192 = 4x$$
    $$\frac{192}{4} = \frac{4x}{4}$$
    $$48 = x$$
    The one angle has a measure of 48°. The other angle has a measure of $180 - 48 = 132\,°$.

17. The measure of a right angle is 90°.
    $$(2x - 9) + x = 90$$
    $$3x - 9 = 90$$
    $$3x = 99$$
    $$x = 33$$
    The value of x is 33°.

19. The measure of a right angle is 90°.
    $$7x + 11x = 90$$
    $$18x = 90$$
    $$x = 5$$
    The value of x is 5°.

21. The measure of a straight angle is 180°.
    $$5x + 30 + x = 180$$
    $$6x + 30 = 180$$
    $$6x = 150$$
    $$x = 25$$
    The value of x is 25°.

23. The measure of a straight angle is 180°.
    $$4x - 30 + x = 180$$
    $$5x - 30 = 180$$
    $$5x = 210$$
    $$x = 42$$
    The value of x is 42°.

25. The measure of a straight angle is 180°. The measure of a right angle is 90°.
    $$12 + 90 + b = 180$$
    $$102 + b = 180$$
    $$b = 78$$
    The measure of $\angle b$ is 78°.

27. Because the angles shown are vertical angles, their measures are equal.

$$4x + 3 = x + 15$$
$$3x + 3 = 15$$
$$3x = 12$$
$$x = 4$$

The value of x is 4.

29. Alternate interior angles have the same measure. Therefore, $m\angle b = 136°$. The sum of the measures of supplementary angles is 180°. Therefore:

$$a + b = 180$$
$$a + 136 = 180$$
$$a = 44$$

The measure of $\angle a$ is 44°.

31. Alternate interior angles have the same measure. Therefore, $m\angle a = 122°$. The sum of the measures of supplementary angles is 180°. Therefore:

$$a + b = 180$$
$$122 + b = 180$$
$$b = 58$$

The measure of $\angle b$ is 58°.

33. Corresponding angles have the same measure and the sum of the measures of supplementary angles is 180°. Therefore:

$$(x + 20) + 3x = 180$$
$$4x + 20 = 180$$
$$4x = 160$$
$$x = 40$$

35. Alternate interior angles have the same measure and the sum of the measures of supplementary angles is 180°. Therefore:

$$(3x) + (6x) = 18$$
$$9x = 180$$
$$x = 20$$

37. **Strategy**
Note from the figure that $\angle a$ and $\angle y$ are supplementary.

$$m\angle a + m\angle y = 180°$$
$$45° + m\angle y = 180°$$
$$m\angle y = 135°$$

Let $\angle c$ be the interior angle of the triangle that is adjacent to $\angle b$. Note from the figure that these angles are supplementary.

$$m\angle b + m\angle c = 180°$$
$$100° + m\angle c = 180°$$
$$m\angle c = 80°$$

Let $\angle d$ be the interior angle of the triangle that is opposite $\angle a$. Note from the figure that these are vertical angles. Therefore $m\angle d = 45°$.
The measure of the interior angle of the triangle that is adjacent to $\angle x$ is $180° - m\angle x$. Use the sum of the interior angles of the triangle to find the measure of $\angle x$.

Solution

$$m\angle c + m\angle d + 180° - m\angle x = 180°$$
$$80° + 45° + 180° - m\angle x = 180°$$
$$305° - m\angle x = 180°$$
$$-m\angle x = -125°$$
$$m\angle x = 125°$$

The measure of $\angle x$ is 125° and the measure of $\angle y$ is 135°.

39. **Strategy**
Note from the figure that $\angle a$ and $\angle y$ are supplementary angles. Thus,

$$m\angle a + m\angle y = 180°$$
$$25° + m\angle y = 180°$$
$$m\angle y = 155°$$

Let $\angle b$ be the interior angle of the triangle that is opposite $\angle a$. Note from the figure that these are vertical angles. Therefore $m\angle b = 25°$. Use the sum of the interior angles of the triangle to find the measure of $\angle x$.

Solution

$$90° + m\angle b + m\angle x = 180°$$
$$90° + 25° + m\angle x = 180°$$
$$115° + m\angle x = 180°$$
$$m\angle x = 65°$$

The measure of $\angle x$ is 65° and the measure of $\angle y$ is 155°.

41. Strategy

Let the measure of one acute angle of the right triangle be x. Then the measure of the other acute angle is $3x + 2$. Use the fact that the sum of the interior angles of a triangle is 180°.

Solution

$$x + (3x + 2) + 90 = 180$$
$$4x + 92 = 180$$
$$4x = 88$$
$$x = 22$$

The measure of one acute angle is 22° and the measure of the other acute angle is $3x + 2 =$ $3(22) + 2 = 66 + 2 = 68°$.

43. Because the angle shown is a central angle, the measure of the arc shown is equal to the measure of the central angle.

$$2x + 5 = 75$$
$$2x = 70$$
$$x = 35$$

45. Because the angle shown is an inscribed angle of the circle, the measure of the angle is equal to half the measure of the arc.

$$(3x - 37) = \frac{1}{2}(4x - 8)$$
$$3x - 37 = 2x - 4$$
$$3x - 37 = 2x - 4$$
$$x = 33$$

47. Because the inscribed angles intersect the same arc, their measures are equal.

$$5x + 10 = 9x - 30$$
$$10 = 4x - 30$$
$$40 = 4x$$
$$10 = x$$

49. The measure of $\angle x$ is half the measure of the arc it intercepts. So the measure of the arc intercepted by $\angle x$ is $(2x)°$. The arc measure of half a circle is 180°. Therefore,

$$30° + (2x)° + 94° = 180°$$
$$2x + 124° = 180°$$
$$2x = 56$$
$$x = 28$$

51. Because the angle shown is a central angle, the measure of the arc shown is equal to the measure of the central angle. The arc measure of half a circle is 180°. Therefore,

$$(2x + 4) + 48 = 180$$
$$2x + 52 = 180$$
$$2x = 128$$
$$x = 64$$

53. The three angles form a straight angle. The sum of the measures of the interior angles of a triangle is 180°.

55. Let $\angle x$ be the complement of 50°. Thus,

$$m\angle x + 50° = 90°$$
$$m\angle x + 50° - 50° = 90° - 50°$$
$$m\angle x = 40°$$

The measure of the complement of 50° is 40°. We are told that 50° is the complement of the supplement of $\angle a$. Thus, 40° is the supplement of $\angle a$.
$$40° + m\angle a = 180°$$
$$40° - 40° + m\angle a = 180° - 40°$$
$$m\angle a = 140°$$

Therefore, the measure of angle a is 140°.

Section 3.4

1.) and (indicate that the endpoint of an interval is not included in the solution set;] and [indicate that the endpoint of an of an interval is included in the solution set.

3. The Multiplication Property of Inequalities states that when each side of an inequality is multiplied by a positive number, the inequality symbol remains the same; when each side of an inequality is multiplied by a negative number, the inequality symbol must be reversed.

5. A number cannot be less than –3 *and* greater than 4.

7.
$$x - 5 > -2$$
$$x - 5 + 5 > -2 + 5$$
$$x > 3$$

The solution set is $\{x \mid x > 3\}$. The graph is shown below.

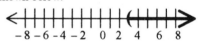

9.
$$-2 + n \geq 0$$
$$-2 + 2 + n \geq 0 + 2$$
$$n \geq 2$$

The solution set is $\{n \mid n \geq 2\}$. The graph is shown below.

11.
$$-4x < 8$$
$$\frac{-4x}{-4} > \frac{8}{-4}$$
$$x > -2$$

The solution set is $\{x \mid x > -2\}$. The graph is shown below.

13. $-2n \le -8$

$\dfrac{-2n}{-2} \ge \dfrac{-8}{-2}$

$n \ge 4$

The solution set is $\{n \mid n \ge 4\}$. The graph is shown below.

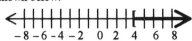

15. $4x \le 8$

$\dfrac{4x}{4} \le \dfrac{8}{4}$

$x \le 2$

In set-builder notation, the solution set is $\{x \mid x \le 2\}$.

17. $3x - 1 > 2x + 2$

$3x - 2x - 1 > 2x - 2x + 2$

$x - 1 > 2$

$x - 1 + 1 > 2 + 1$

$x > 3$

In set-builder notation, the solution set is $\{x \mid x > 3\}$.

19. $5x - 2 \le 8$

$5x - 2 + 2 \le 8 + 2$

$5x \le 10$

$\dfrac{5x}{5} \le \dfrac{10}{5}$

$x \le 2$

In set-builder notation, the solution set is $\{x \mid x \le 2\}$.

21. $8x + 1 \ge 2x + 13$

$8x - 2x + 1 \ge 2x - 2x + 13$

$6x + 1 \ge 13$

$6x + 1 - 1 \ge 13 - 1$

$6x \ge 12$

$\dfrac{6x}{6} \ge \dfrac{12}{6}$

$x \ge 2$

In set-builder notation, the solution set is $\{x \mid x \ge 2\}$.

23. $7 - 2x \ge 1$

$7 - 7 - 2x \ge 1 - 7$

$-2x \ge -6$

$\dfrac{-2x}{-2} \le \dfrac{-6}{-2}$

$x \le 3$

In set-builder notation, the solution set is $\{x \mid x \le 3\}$.

25. $4x - 2 < x - 11$

$4x - x - 2 < x - x - 11$

$3x - 2 < -11$

$3x - 2 + 2 < -11 + 2$

$3x < -9$

$\dfrac{3x}{3} < \dfrac{-9}{3}$

$x < -3$

In set-builder notation, the solution set is $\{x \mid x < -3\}$.

27. $3x + 2 \le 7x + 4$

$3x - 7x + 2 \le 7x - 7x + 4$

$-4x + 2 \le 4$

$-4x + 2 - 2 \le 4 - 2$

$-4x \le 2$

$\dfrac{-4x}{-4} \ge \dfrac{2}{-4}$

$x \ge -\dfrac{1}{2}$

In interval notation, the solution set is

$\left[-\dfrac{1}{2}, \infty \right)$.

29. $\dfrac{2}{3}x - \dfrac{3}{2} < \dfrac{7}{6} - \dfrac{1}{3}x$

$\dfrac{2}{3}x + \dfrac{1}{3}x - \dfrac{3}{2} < \dfrac{7}{6} - \dfrac{1}{3}x + \dfrac{1}{3}x$

$x - \dfrac{3}{2} < \dfrac{7}{6}$

$x - \dfrac{3}{2} + \dfrac{3}{2} < \dfrac{7}{6} + \dfrac{3}{2}$

$x < \dfrac{16}{6}$

$x < \dfrac{8}{3}$

In interval notation, the solution set is

$\left(-\infty, \dfrac{8}{3} \right)$.

31. $0.5x + 4 > 1.3x - 2.5$

$0.5x - 1.3x + 4 > 1.3x - 1.3x - 2.5$

$-0.8x + 4 > -2.5$

$-0.8x + 4 - 4 > -2.5 - 4$

$-0.8x > -6.5$

$\dfrac{-0.8x}{-0.8} < \dfrac{-6.5}{-0.8}$

$x < 8.125$

In interval notation, the solution set is $(-\infty, 8.125)$.

33.
$$2 - 5(x+1) \geq 3(x-1) - 8$$
$$2 - 5x - 5 \geq 3x - 3 - 8$$
$$-5x - 3 \geq 3x - 11$$
$$-5x - 3x - 3 \geq 3x - 3x - 11$$
$$-8x - 3 \geq -11$$
$$-8x - 3 + 3 \geq -11 + 3$$
$$-8x \geq -8$$
$$\frac{-8x}{-8} \leq \frac{-8}{-8}$$
$$x \leq 1$$

In interval notation, the solution set is $(-\infty, 1]$.

35.
$$3 + 2(x+5) \geq x + 5(x+1) + 1$$
$$3 + 2x + 10 \geq x + 5x + 5 + 1$$
$$2x + 13 \geq 6x + 6$$
$$2x - 6x + 13 \geq 6x - 6x + 6$$
$$-4x + 13 \geq 6$$
$$-4x + 13 - 13 \geq 6 - 13$$
$$-4x \geq -7$$
$$\frac{-4x}{-4} \leq \frac{-7}{-4}$$
$$x \leq \frac{7}{4}$$

In interval notation, the solution set is

$$\left(-\infty, \frac{7}{4}\right].$$

37.
$$12 - 2(3x - 2) \geq 5x - 2(5 - x)$$
$$12 - 6x + 4 \geq 5x - 10 + 2x$$
$$-6x + 16 \geq 7x - 10$$
$$-6x - 7x + 16 \geq 7x - 7x - 10$$
$$-13x + 16 \geq -10$$
$$-13x + 16 - 16 \geq -10 - 16$$
$$-13x \geq -26$$
$$\frac{-13x}{-13} \leq \frac{-26}{-13}$$
$$x \leq 2$$

In interval notation, the solution set is $(-\infty, 2]$.

39. Strategy
Let x be the amount of income tax that must be paid by April 15. Because at least 90% must be paid to avoid a penalty, write an inequality.

Solution
$$x \geq 0.90(3500)$$
$$x \geq 3150$$
To avoid a penalty, the self-employed person must pay $3150 or more by April 15.

41. Strategy
Let x represent the total monthly dollar amounts of sales. Because we are interested in when the commissions will be more than the monthly salary, write an inequality.

Solution
$$0.35x > 2000$$
$$\frac{0.35x}{0.35} > \frac{2000}{0.35}$$
$$x > 5714$$
The commissions are more attractive if the sales person makes more than $5714 worth of sales each month.

43. Strategy
Let x represent the number of minutes the service is used. Because we are interested in when the per-minute charge exceeds the flat fee of $10, write an inequality.

Solution
$$4 + 0.10x > 10$$
$$4 - 4 + 0.10x > 10 - 4$$
$$0.10x > 6$$
$$\frac{0.10x}{0.10} > \frac{6}{0.10}$$
$$x > 60$$
The cost for this service exceeds $10 when more than 60 minutes are used.

45. Strategy
Let x represent how far away is the ski area. If the skiers take the shuttle service, they will pay $4(8) = \$32$ each way or a total of $2(32) = \$64$. If the skiers take the shuttle service, the cost must be less than the cost to rent a car. Write an inequality. (Note: first find the cost of renting the car for a round trip to make a proper comparison to the cost of taking the shuttle each way.).

Solution
$$64 < 45 + 0.25(2x)$$
$$64 < 45 + 0.5x$$
$$64 - 0.5x < 45 + 0.5x - 0.5x$$
$$64 - 0.5x < 45$$
$$64 - 64 - 0.5x < 45 - 64$$
$$-0.5x < -19$$
$$\frac{-0.5x}{-0.5} > \frac{-19}{-0.5}$$
$$x > 38$$
The ski area must be more than 38 miles away for the skiers to choose to take the shuttle service.

47. Strategy
To find the number of pages, write and solve an inequality using P to represent the number of pages. Then $P - 400$ is the number of pages for which you are charged an extra fee per page.
Cost of Top Page: $6.95 + 0.10(P - 400)$
Cost of competitor: $3.95 + 0.15(P - 400)$

Solution
Cost of Top Page < Cost of competitor
$6.95 + 0.10(P - 400) < 3.95 + 0.15(P - 400)$
$6.95 + 0.10P - 40 < 3.95 + 0.15P - 60$
$0.10P - 33.05 < 0.15P - 56.05$
$-0.05P < -23$
$\dfrac{-0.05P}{-0.05} > \dfrac{-23}{-0.05}$
$P > 460$
The Top Page plan is less expensive when service is for more than 460 pages per month.

49. Strategy
To find the temperature range in Fahrenheit degrees, write and solve a compound inequality using F to represent Fahrenheit degrees.

Solution
$$0 \le \frac{5(F - 32)}{9} \le 30$$
$$9(0) \le 9\left(\frac{5(F - 32)}{9}\right) \le 9(30)$$
$$0 \le 5(F - 32) \le 270$$
$$\frac{0}{5} \le \frac{5(F - 32)}{5} \le \frac{270}{5}$$
$$0 \le F - 32 \le 54$$
$$0 + 32 \le F - 32 + 32 \le 54 + 32$$
$$32 \le F \le 86$$
The temperature range is 32°F to 86°F.

51. Strategy
To find the number of checks, write and solve an inequality using N to represent the number of checks.
Cost of Glendale checking: $8 + 0.12(N - 100)$
Cost of competitor checking: $5 + 0.15(N - 100)$

Solution
Cost of Glendale < Cost of competitor
$8 + 0.12(N - 100) < 5 + 0.15(N - 100)$
$8 + 0.12N - 12 < 5 + 0.15N - 15$
$0.12N - 4 < 0.15N - 10$
$-0.03N < -6$
$\dfrac{-0.03N}{-0.03} > \dfrac{-6}{-0.03}$
$N > 200$
The Glendale checking account is less expensive if more than 200 checks are written.

53. Strategy
To find the range of scores, write and solve an inequality using N to represent the score on the last test.

Solution
$$70 \le \frac{56 + 91 + 83 + 62 + N}{5} \le 79$$
$$70 \le \frac{292 + N}{5} \le 79$$
$$5(70) \le 5\left(\frac{292 + N}{5}\right) \le 5(79)$$
$$350 \le 292 + N \le 395$$
$$350 - 292 \le 292 - 292 + N \le 395 - 292$$
$$58 \le N \le 103$$
Since 100 is the maximum score, the range of scores to receive a C grade is $58 \le N \le 100$.

55. $2x < 6$ or $x - 4 > 1$
$\dfrac{2x}{2} < \dfrac{6}{2}$ $x - 4 + 4 > 1 + 4$
$x < 3$ $x > 5$
$\{x \mid x < 3\}$ $\{x \mid x > 5\}$
The solution of the compound inequality is the union of the solution sets for each inequality.
$\{x \mid x < 3\} \cup \{x \mid x > 5\} = \{x \mid x < 3 \text{ or } x > 5\}$

57. $3x < -9$ and $x - 2 < 2$
$\dfrac{3x}{3} < \dfrac{-9}{3}$ $x - 2 + 2 < 2 + 2$
$x < -3$ $x < 4$
$\{x \mid x < -3\}$ $\{x \mid x < 4\}$
The solution of the compound inequality is the intersection of the solution sets for each inequality.
$\{x \mid x < -3\} \cap \{x \mid x < 4\} = \{x \mid x < -3\}$

59. $6x - 2 < -14$ or $5x + 1 > 11$
$6x - 2 + 2 < -14 + 2$ $5x + 1 - 1 > 11 - 1$
$6x < -12$ $5x > 10$
$\dfrac{6x}{6} < \dfrac{-12}{6}$ $\dfrac{5x}{5} > \dfrac{10}{5}$
$x < -2$ $x > 2$
$\{x \mid x < -2\}$ $\{x \mid x > 2\}$
The solution of the compound inequality is the union of the solution sets for each inequality.
$\{x \mid x < -2\} \cup \{x \mid x > 2\} = \{x \mid x < -2 \text{ or } x > 2\}$

61.

$$3x - 5 > 10 \quad \text{or} \quad 3x - 5 < -10$$
$$3x - 5 + 5 > 10 + 5 \qquad 3x - 5 + 5 < -10 + 5$$
$$3x > 15 \qquad\qquad 3x < -5$$
$$\frac{3x}{3} > \frac{15}{3} \qquad\qquad \frac{3x}{3} < \frac{-5}{3}$$
$$x > 5 \qquad\qquad x < -\frac{5}{3}$$

$$\{x \mid x > 5\} \qquad \left\{x \mid x < -\frac{5}{3}\right\}$$

The solution of the compound inequality is the union of the solution sets for each inequality.

$$\{x \mid x > 5\} \cup \left\{x \mid x < -\frac{5}{3}\right\} = \left\{x \mid x > 5 \text{ or } x < -\frac{5}{3}\right\}$$

63.

$$5x + 12 \geq 2 \quad \text{or} \quad 7x - 1 \leq 13$$
$$5x + 12 - 12 \geq 2 - 12 \qquad 7x - 1 + 1 \leq 13 + 1$$
$$5x \geq -10 \qquad\qquad 7x \leq 14$$
$$\frac{5x}{5} \geq \frac{-10}{5} \qquad\qquad \frac{7x}{7} \leq \frac{14}{7}$$
$$x \geq -2 \qquad\qquad x \leq 2$$

$$\{x \mid x \geq -2\} \qquad \{x \mid x \leq 2\}$$

The solution of the compound inequality is the union of the solution sets for each inequality.

$$\{x \mid x \geq -2\} \cup \{x \mid x \leq 2\}$$
$$= \{x \mid x \in \text{real numbers}\}$$

65.

$$6x + 5 < -1 \quad \text{or} \quad 1 - 2x < 7$$
$$6x + 5 - 5 < -1 - 5 \qquad 1 - 1 - 2x < 7 - 1$$
$$6x < -6 \qquad\qquad -2x < 6$$
$$\frac{6x}{6} < \frac{-6}{6} \qquad\qquad \frac{-2x}{-2} > \frac{6}{-2}$$
$$x < -1 \qquad\qquad x > -3$$

$$\{x \mid x < -1\} \qquad \{x \mid x > -3\}$$

The solution of the compound inequality is the union of the solution sets for each inequality.

$$\{x \mid x < -1\} \cup \{x \mid x > -3\}$$
$$= \{x \mid x \in \text{real numbers}\}$$

67.

$$7 - 2b \leq 15 - 5b$$
$$7 - 2b + 5b \leq 15 - 5b + 5b$$
$$7 + 3b \leq 15$$
$$7 - 7 + 3b \leq 15 - 7$$
$$3b \leq 8$$
$$\frac{3b}{3} \leq \frac{8}{3}$$
$$b \leq 2\frac{2}{3}$$

The positive integers that are less than or equal to $2\frac{2}{3}$ make up the solution set for this inequality: $\{1, 2\}$.

69.

$$2(2c - 3) < 5(6 - c)$$
$$4c - 6 < 30 - 5c$$
$$4c + 5c - 6 < 30 - 5c + 5c$$
$$9c - 6 < 30$$
$$9c - 6 + 6 < 30 + 6$$
$$9c < 36$$
$$\frac{9c}{9} < \frac{36}{9}$$
$$c < 4$$

The positive integers that are less than 4 make up the solution set to this inequality: $\{1, 2, 3\}$.

71.

$$5x - 12 \leq x + 8$$
$$5x - x - 12 \leq x - x + 8$$
$$4x - 12 \leq 8$$
$$4x - 12 + 12 \leq 8 + 12$$
$$4x \leq 20$$
$$\frac{4x}{4} \leq \frac{20}{4}$$
$$x \leq 5$$

$$3x - 4 \geq 2 + x$$
$$3x - x - 4 \geq 2 + x - x$$
$$2x - 4 \geq 2$$
$$2x - 4 + 4 \geq 2 + 4$$
$$2x \geq 6$$
$$\frac{2x}{2} \geq \frac{6}{2}$$
$$x \geq 3$$

The intersection of the solution sets of the two inequalities is $\{3, 4, 5\}$.

73.

$$4(x - 2) \leq 3x + 5$$
$$4x - 8 \leq 3x + 5$$
$$x - 8 \leq 5$$
$$x \leq 13$$

$$7(x - 3) \geq 5x - 1$$
$$7x - 21 \geq 5x - 1$$
$$2x - 21 \geq -1$$
$$2x \geq 20$$
$$x \geq 10$$

The intersection of the solution sets of the two inequalities is $\{10, 11, 12, 13\}$.

75. **a.** Always true

b. Sometimes true

c. Sometimes true (true when the integer is negative)

d. Sometimes true (true when $0 < a < 1$)

e. Always true

Section 3.5

1. **a.** Always true

   b. Never true $|x| < a$ is equivalent to $-a < x < a$.

   c. Never true If $|x + 3| = 12$, then $x + 3 = 12$ and $x + 3 = -12$.

   d. Sometimes true

   e. Never true If $|x + b| < c$, then $-c < x + b < c$.

3. Parts **b**, **d**, and **f** have no solution. For parts **a**, **c**, and **e**, the solution set is all real numbers.

5. The solution set of $|ax + b| \le c$ contains the endpoints of the interval. The solution set of $|ax + b| < c$ does not contain the endpoints.

7. $|x| = 2$
   $x = 2 \quad x = -2$

   The solutions are -2 and 2.

9. $|-a| = 9$
   $$-a = 9 \qquad -a = -9$$
   $$a = -9 \qquad a = 9$$
   The solutions are -9 and 9.

11. $|-y| = -2$
   Because the absolute value of a number is never negative, this equation has no solution.

13. $|x + 5| = 2$
   $$x + 5 = 2 \qquad x + 5 = -2$$
   $$x = -3 \qquad x = -7$$
   The solutions are -7 and -3.

15. $|y - 8| = 4$
   $$y - 8 = 4 \qquad y - 8 = -4$$
   $$y = 12 \qquad y = 4$$
   The solutions are 4 and 12.

17. $|a + 7| = 0$
   $$a + 7 = 0 \qquad a + 7 = -0$$
   $$a = -7 \qquad a = -7$$
   The solution is -7.

19. $|x + 8| = -2$
   Because the absolute value of a number is never negative, this equation has no solution.

21. $|4 - 3x| = 4$
   $$4 - 3x = 4 \qquad 4 - 3x = -4$$
   $$-3x = 0 \qquad -3x = -8$$
   $$x = 0 \qquad x = \frac{8}{3}$$
   The solutions are 0 and $\frac{8}{3}$.

23. $|2x - 3| = 0$
   $$2x - 3 = 0$$
   $$2x = 3$$
   $$x = \frac{3}{2}$$
   The solution is $\frac{3}{2}$.

25. $|3x - 2| = -4$
   Because the absolute value of a number is never negative, this equation has no solution.

27. $|x - 2| - 2 = 3$
   $$|x - 2| = 5$$
   $$x - 2 = 5 \qquad x - 2 = -5$$
   $$x = 7 \qquad x = -3$$
   The solutions are -3 and 7.

29. $|3a + 2| - 4 = 4$
   $$|3a + 2| = 8$$
   $$3a + 2 = 8 \qquad 3a + 2 = -8$$
   $$3a = 6 \qquad 3a = -10$$
   $$a = 2 \qquad a = -\frac{10}{3}$$
   The solutions are $-\frac{10}{3}$ and 2.

31. $|2x - 3| + 3 = 3$
   $$|2x - 3| = 0$$
   $$2x - 3 = 0$$
   $$2x = 3$$
   $$x = \frac{3}{2}$$
   The solution is $\frac{3}{2}$.

33. $|2x - 3| + 4 = -4$
   $$|2x - 3| = -8$$
   Because the absolute value of a number is never negative, this equation has no solution.

35. $|6x - 5| - 2 = 4$
   $$|6x - 5| = 6$$
   $$6x - 5 = 6 \qquad 6x - 5 = -6$$
   $$6x = 11 \qquad 6x = -1$$
   $$x = \frac{11}{6} \qquad x = -\frac{1}{6}$$
   The solutions are $-\frac{1}{6}$ and $\frac{11}{6}$.

37.
$$| \ 3t+2 \ |+3=4$$
$$| \ 3t+2 \ |=1$$

$3t+2=1$	$3t+2=-1$
$3t=-1$	$3t=-3$
$t=-\dfrac{1}{3}$	$t=-1$

The solutions are -1 and $-\dfrac{1}{3}$.

39.
$$3-| \ x-4 \ |=5$$
$$-| \ x-4 \ |=2$$
$$| \ x-4 \ |=-2$$

Because the absolute value of a number is never negative, this equation has no solution.

41.
$$| \ 2x-8 \ |+12=2$$
$$| \ 2x-8 \ |=-10$$

Because the absolute value of a number is never negative, this equation has no solution.

43.
$$2+| \ 3x-4 \ |=5$$
$$| \ 3x-4 \ |=3$$

$3x-4=3$	$3x-4=-3$
$3x=7$	$3x=1$
$x=\dfrac{7}{3}$	$x=\dfrac{1}{3}$

The solutions are $\dfrac{1}{3}$ and $\dfrac{7}{3}$.

45.
$$5-| \ 2x+1 \ |=5$$
$$-| \ 2x+1 \ |=0$$
$$| \ 2x+1 \ |=0$$
$$2x+1=0$$
$$2x=-1$$
$$x=-\dfrac{1}{2}$$

The solution is $-\dfrac{1}{2}$.

47.
$$8-| \ 1-3x \ |=-1$$
$$8=| \ 1-3x \ |-1$$
$$9=| \ 1-3x \ |$$

$1-3x=9$	$1-3x=-9$
$-3x=8$	$-3x=-10$
$x=-\dfrac{8}{3}$	$x=\dfrac{10}{3}$

The solutions are $-\dfrac{8}{3}$ and $\dfrac{10}{3}$.

49.
$$| \ x \ |<5$$
$$-5<x<5$$

The solution set is $\{x \mid -5<x<5\}$.

51.
$$| \ x-2 \ |>1$$

$x-2<-1$	or	$x-2>1$
$x<1$		$x>3$

The solution set is $\{x \mid x<1 \text{ or } x>3\}$.

53.
$$| \ x-4 \ |\le 3$$
$$-3\le x-4\le 3$$
$$-3+4\le x-4+4\le 3+4$$
$$1\le x\le 7$$

The solution set is $\{x \mid 1\le x\le 7\}$.

55.
$$| \ 3-x \ |\ge 2$$

$3-x\le -2$		$3-x\ge 2$
$-x\le -5$	or	$-x\ge -1$
$x\ge 5$		$x\le 1$

The solution set is $\{x \mid x\le 1 \text{ or } x\ge 5\}$.

57.
$$| \ 3x-2 \ |<4$$
$$-4<3x-2<4$$
$$-4+2<3x-2+2<4+2$$
$$-2<3x<6$$
$$\dfrac{-2}{3}<\dfrac{3x}{3}<\dfrac{6}{3}$$
$$-\dfrac{2}{3}<x<2$$

The solution set is $\left\{x \mid -\dfrac{2}{3}<x<2\right\}$.

59.
$$| \ 7x-1 \ |>13$$

$7x-1<-13$		$7x-1>13$
$7x<-12$	or	$7x>14$
$x<-\dfrac{12}{7}$		$x>2$

The solution set is $\left\{x \mid x<-\dfrac{12}{7} \text{ or } x>2\right\}$.

61.
$$| \ 5x+1 \ |\le -4$$

Because the absolute value of a number is never negative, this inequality has no solution. The solution set is $\varnothing$.

63.
$$| \ 3x-1 \ |>-4$$

Because the absolute value of a number is always nonnegative, this inequality is always true. The solution set is $\{x \mid x \in \text{real numbers}\}$.

65.
$$| \ 7-2x \ |>9$$

$7-2x<-9$		$7-2x>9$
$-2x<-16$	or	$-2x>2$
$x>8$		$x<-1$

The solution set is $\{x \mid x<-1 \text{ or } x>8\}$.

67. $\quad |\,3-7x\,|<17$

$$-17<3-7x<17$$
$$-17-3<3-3-7x<17-3$$
$$-20<-7x<14$$
$$\frac{-20}{-7}>\frac{-7x}{-7}>\frac{14}{-7}$$
$$\frac{20}{7}>x>-2$$

The solution set is $\left\{x\,|-2<x<\dfrac{20}{7}\right\}$.

69. $\quad |\,10-5x\,|\ge 0$

Because the absolute value of a number is always nonnegative, this inequality is always true. The solution set is $\{x\,|\,x\in\text{real numbers}\}$.

71. $\quad |\,5x-1\,|<16$

$$-16<5x-1<16$$
$$-16+1<5x-1+1<16+1$$
$$-15<5x<17$$
$$\frac{-15}{5}<\frac{5x}{5}<\frac{17}{5}$$
$$-3<x<\frac{17}{5}$$

The solution set is $\left\{x\,|-3<x<\dfrac{17}{5}\right\}$.

73. Strategy

Let d represent the diameter of the bushing, T the tolerance, and x the lower and upper limits of the diameter. Solve the absolute value inequality $|\,x-d\,|\le T$ for x.

Solution
$$|x-d|\le T$$
$$|x-3.48|\le 0.004$$
$$-0.004\le x-3.48\le 0.004$$
$$-0.004+3.48\le x-3.48+3.48\le 0.004+3.48$$
$$3.476\le x\le 3.484$$

The lower and upper limits of the diameter of the bushing are 3.476 inches and 3.484 inches.

75. Strategy

Let v represent the prescribed number of volts, T the tolerance, and m the lower and upper limits of the amount of voltage. Solve the absolute value inequality $|\,m-v\,|\le T$ for m.

Solution
$$|\,m-v\,|\le T$$
$$|\,m-110\,|\le 16.5$$
$$-16.5\le m-110\le 16.5$$
$$-16.5+110\le m-110+110\le 16.5+110$$
$$93.5\le m\le 126.5$$

The lower and upper limits of the amount of voltage to the computer are 93.5 volts and 126.5 volts.

77. Strategy

Let r represent the length of the piston rod, T the tolerance, and L the lower and upper limits of the length. Solve the absolute value inequality $|\,L-r\,|\le T$ for L.

Solution
$$|\,L-r\,|\le T$$
$$\left|\,L-10\frac{3}{8}\,\right|\le\frac{1}{32}$$
$$-\frac{1}{32}\le L-10\frac{3}{8}\le\frac{1}{32}$$
$$-\frac{1}{32}+10\frac{3}{8}\le L-10\frac{3}{8}+10\frac{3}{8}\le\frac{1}{32}+10\frac{3}{8}$$
$$10\frac{11}{32}\le L\le 10\frac{13}{32}$$

The lower and upper limits of the length of the piston rod are $10\frac{11}{32}$ inches and $10\frac{13}{32}$ inches.

79. Strategy

Let M represent the amount of ohms, T the tolerance, and r the given amount of the resistor. Find the tolerance. Then solve the absolute value inequality $|\,M-r\,|\le T$ for M.

Solution
$$T=(0.02)(29,000)=580\text{ ohms}$$
$$|\,M-r\,|\le T$$
$$|\,M-29,000\,|\le 580$$
$$-580\le M-29,000\le 580$$
$$28,420\le M\le 29,580$$

The lower and upper limits of the resistor are 28,420 ohms and 29,580 ohms.

81. Strategy

Let M represent the amount of ohms, T the tolerance, and r the given amount of the resistor. Find the tolerance. Then solve the absolute value inequality $|\,M-r\,|\le T$ for M.

Solution
$$T=(0.05)(25,000)=1250\text{ ohms}$$
$$|\,M-r\,|\le T$$
$$|\,M-25,000\,|\le 1250$$
$$-1250\le M-25,000\le 1250$$
$$23,750\le M\le 26,250$$

The lower and upper limits of the resistor are 23,750 ohms and 26,250 ohms.

83. $\quad \dfrac{|\,x-250\,|}{11.18}<1.96$

$$|\,x-250\,|<21.9128$$
$$-21.9128<x-250<21.9128$$
$$228.0872<x<271.9128$$
$$228<x<271$$

One would be reasonably sure that the coin is fair if the number of heads falls between 228 and 272.

85. $\dfrac{\mid x-12.4 \mid}{2.6} > 1.96$

$\mid x-12.4 \mid > 5.096$

$x-12.4 < -5.096 \qquad x-12.4 > 5.096$

$\qquad x < 7.304 \quad$ or $\quad x > 17.496$

$\qquad x < 7.3 \qquad\qquad x > 17.5$

The diameters of pumpkins that satisfy this condition are less than 7.3 inches or greater than 17.5 inches.

Applying Concepts 3.5

87. $\mid 1-3x \mid = \mid x+2 \mid$

$1-3x = x+2 \qquad\qquad 1-3x = -(x+2)$

$1-4x = 2 \qquad\qquad\quad 1-3x = -x-2$

$-4x = 1 \qquad\qquad\qquad 1-2x = -2$

$x = -0.25 \qquad\qquad\quad -2x = -3$

$\qquad\qquad\qquad\qquad\qquad x = 1.5$

The solutions are −0.25 and 1.5.

89. $\mid 2x-4 \mid + \mid x \mid = 5$

$2x-4+x = 5 \qquad\qquad 2x-4+x = -5$

$3x-4 = 5 \qquad\qquad\quad 3x-4 = -5$

$3x = 9 \qquad\qquad\qquad 3x = -1$

$x = 3 \qquad\qquad\qquad x = -\dfrac{1}{3}$

The solutions are $-\dfrac{1}{3}$ and 3.

91. $\mid x+4 \mid = 4x$

$x+4 = 4x \qquad\qquad x+4 = -4x$

$4 = 3x \qquad\qquad\quad 4 = -5x$

$\dfrac{4}{3} = x \qquad\qquad\quad -\dfrac{4}{5} = x$

Because the absolute value of a number is never negative, the solution $-\dfrac{4}{5}$ is not valid.

The solution is $\dfrac{4}{3}$.

93. $\mid 3x-2 \mid < \mid x-3 \mid$

Use a graphing calculator to graph the left side of the of the inequality as Y1 and the right side of the inequality as Y2. Then look to see where the graph of Y1 is below the graph of Y2.

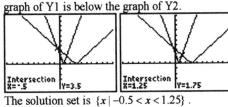

The solution set is $\{x \mid -0.5 < x < 1.25\}$.

95. a. $\mid x+a \mid \le b$

$-b \le x+a \le b$

$-b-a \le x \le b-a$

b. $\mid x-a \mid > b$

$x-a > b \qquad\qquad x-a < -b$

$x > a+b \qquad\qquad x < a-b$

The solution is $x < a-b$ or $x > a+b$.

c. $\mid x+a \mid > a$

$x+a > a \qquad\qquad x+a < -a$

$x > 0 \qquad\qquad\quad x < -2a$

The solution is $x < -2a$ or $x > 0$.

d. $\mid x-a \mid \le a$

$-a \le x-a \le a$

$0 \le x \le 2a$

97. $x = -7 \qquad\qquad x = 3$

$x+2 = -7+2 \qquad x+2 = 3+2$

$x+2 = -5 \qquad\quad x+2 = 5$

$\qquad\qquad \mid x+2 \mid = 5$

99. For $c > 0$, the solution set $-c \le x-4 \le c$. For $c = 0$, the solution is 4. For $c < 0$, the solution set is the empty set.

Chapter Review Exercises

1. $m-\dfrac{3}{5} = -\dfrac{1}{4}$

$m-\dfrac{3}{5}+\dfrac{3}{5} = -\dfrac{1}{4}+\dfrac{3}{5}$

$m = -\dfrac{5}{20}+\dfrac{12}{20}$

$m = \dfrac{7}{20}$

2. $\dfrac{3}{2}y = 4$

$\dfrac{2}{3}\left(\dfrac{3}{2}y\right) = \dfrac{2}{3}(4)$

$y = \dfrac{8}{3}$

3. $9-4b = 5b+8$

$9-4b+4b = 5b+4b+8$

$9 = 9b+8$

$9-8 = 9b+8-8$

$1 = 9b$

$\dfrac{1}{9} = \dfrac{9b}{9}$

$\dfrac{1}{9} = b$

4. $2[x + 3(4 - x) - 5x] = 6(x + 4)$
$2(x + 12 - 3x - 5x) = 6x + 24$
$2(12 - 7x) = 6x + 24$
$24 - 14x = 6x + 24$
$24 - 24 - 14x = 6x + 24 - 24$
$-14x = 6x$
$-14x - 6x = 6x - 6x$
$-20x = 0$
$\dfrac{-20x}{-20} = \dfrac{0}{-20}$
$x = 0$

5. $5x - 3 < x + 9$
$5x - x - 3 < x - x + 9$
$4x - 3 < 9$
$4x - 3 + 3 < 9 + 3$
$4x < 12$
$\dfrac{4x}{4} < \dfrac{12}{4}$
$x < 3$
The solution set is $\{x \mid x < 3\}$.

6. $-1 \le 3x + 5 \le 8$
$-1 - 5 \le 3x + 5 - 5 \le 8 - 5$
$-6 \le 3x \le 3$
$-\dfrac{6}{3} \le \dfrac{3x}{3} \le \dfrac{3}{3}$
$-2 \le x \le 1$
The solution is $[-2, 1]$.

7. $5x - 2 > 8$ and $3x + 2 < -4$
$\quad 5x > 10 \qquad\qquad 3x < -6$
$\quad\ x > 2 \qquad\qquad\ x < -2$
The solution set is $(-\infty, -2) \cup (2, \infty)$.

8. $\mid 6x + 4 \mid - 3 = 7$
$\mid 6x + 4 \mid = 10$
$6x + 4 = 10 \qquad 6x + 4 = -10$
$6x = 6 \qquad\qquad 6x = -14$
$x = 1 \qquad\qquad\ x = -\dfrac{7}{3}$

The solutions are $-\dfrac{7}{3}$ and 1.

9. $\mid 5 - 4x \mid > 3$
$5 - 4x < -3 \qquad\quad 5 - 4x > 3$
$-4x < -8 \quad$ or $\quad -4x > -2$
$x > 2 \qquad\qquad\quad x < \dfrac{1}{2}$

The solution set is $\left\{ x \mid x < \dfrac{1}{2} \text{ or } x > 2 \right\}$.

10. $\left| \dfrac{3x - 1}{5} \right| < 4$
$-4 < \dfrac{3x - 1}{5} < 4$
$5(-4) < 5\left(\dfrac{3x - 1}{5} \right) < 5(4)$
$-20 < 3x - 1 < 20$
$-20 + 1 < 3x - 1 + 1 < 20 + 1$
$-19 < 3x < 21$
$\dfrac{-19}{3} < \dfrac{3x}{3} < \dfrac{21}{3}$
$-\dfrac{19}{3} < x < 7$
The solution set is $\left\{ x \mid -\dfrac{19}{3} < x < 7 \right\}$.

11. The sum of angles forming a straight angle is
180°.
$34 + 90 + 2x = 180$
$124 + 2x = 180$
$124 - 124 + 2x = 180 - 124$
$2x = 56$
$\dfrac{2x}{2} = \dfrac{56}{2}$
$x = 28$
The value of x is 28.

12. Strategy
Note from the figure that $\angle a$ and $\angle y$ are
supplementary.
$m\angle a + m\angle y = 180°$
$103° + m\angle y = 180°$
$m\angle y = 77°$

Let $\angle c$ be the interior angle of the triangle that is
adjacent to $\angle b$. Note from the figure that these
angles are supplementary.
$m\angle b + m\angle c = 180°$
$143° + m\angle c = 180°$
$m\angle c = 37°$

Let $\angle d$ be the interior angle of the triangle that is
opposite $\angle a$. Note from the figure that these are
vertical angles. Therefore $m\angle d = 103°$.
The measure of the interior angle of the triangle
that is adjacent to $\angle x$ is $180° - m\angle x$. Use the
sum of the interior angles of the triangle to find
the measure of $\angle x$.

Solution
$m\angle c + m\angle d + 180° - m\angle x = 180°$
$37° + 103° + 180° - m\angle x = 180°$
$320° - m\angle x = 180°$
$320° - 320° - m\angle x = 180° - 320°$
$-m\angle x = -140°$
$m\angle x = 140°$
The measure of $\angle x$ is 140° and the measure of
$\angle y$ is 77°.

13. Alternate interior angles have the same measure.
Therefore, $m\angle a = 138°$. The sum of the measures
of supplementary angles is 180°. Therefore:
$$a + b = 180$$
$$138 + b = 180$$
$$b = 42$$
The measure of $\angle b$ is 42°.

14. Because the angles shown are central angles, the
measure of each arc is equal to the measure of
the central angle. The arc measure of half a circle
is 180°. Therefore,
$$2x + 3 + 61 = 180$$
$$2x + 64 = 180$$
$$2x = 116$$
$$x = 58$$

15. Strategy
The sum of the measures of supplementary
angles is 180°. Let x represent the measure of the
supplement of a 32° angle.

Solution
$$x + 32 = 180$$
$$x + 32 - 32 = 180 - 32$$
$$x = 148$$
The supplement of a 32° angle is a 148° angle.

16. $\left| \dfrac{x - 70}{10} \right| < 1.96$

$$-1.96 < \frac{x - 70}{10} < 1.96$$
$$10(-1.96) < 10\left(\frac{x - 70}{10}\right) < 10(1.96)$$
$$-19.6 < x - 70 < 19.6$$
$$-19.6 + 70 < x - 70 + 70 < 19.6 + 70$$
$$50.4 < x < 89.6$$
The range of scores that 95% of the students
taking the pretest will have is $50.4 < x < 89.6$.

17. Strategy
Let t = the time that each plane flies before they
pass. We know that the first plane's rate is 320
mph and the second plane's rate is 280 mph. Use
the uniform motion equation $d = rt$ (where d is
the distance, r is the rate of speed, and t is the
time) to write the distances traveled by each
plane:
Distance traveled by first plane: 320t
Distance traveled by second plane: 280t
The total distance traveled by the two planes is
800 miles. Translate this fact into an equation:
$320t + 280t = 800$

Solution
$$320t + 280t = 800$$
$$600t = 800$$
$$\frac{600t}{600} = \frac{800}{600}$$
$$t = 1\frac{1}{3}$$
The planes pass after 1 1/3 hours, that is, one
hour and 20 minutes. The time when the planes
pass is 2:20 P.M.

18. Strategy
Let d represent the diameter of the bushing, T the
tolerance, and x the lower and upper limits of the
diameter. Solve the absolute value inequality
$|x - d| \leq T$ for x.

Solution
$$|x - d| \leq T$$
$$|x - 2.75| \leq 0.003$$
$$-0.003 \leq x - 2.75 \leq 0.003$$
$$-0.003 + 2.75 \leq x - 2.75 + 2.75 \leq 0.003 + 2.75$$
$$2.747 \leq x \leq 2.753$$
The lower and upper limits of the diameter of the
bushing are 2.747 in. and 2.753 in., respectively.

19. Strategy
To find the range of scores, write and solve an
inequality using N to represent the score on the
last test.

Solution
$$80 \leq \frac{92 + 66 + 72 + 88 + N}{5} \leq 89$$
$$80 \leq \frac{318 + N}{5} \leq 89$$
$$5(80) \leq 5\left(\frac{318 + N}{5}\right) \leq 5(89)$$
$$400 \leq 318 + N \leq 445$$
$$400 - 318 \leq 318 - 318 + N \leq 445 - 318$$
$$82 \leq N \leq 127$$
Since 100 is the maximum score, the range of
scores to receive a B grade is $82 \leq N \leq 100$.

20. Strategy
Let x represent the gallons of apple juice, costing $3.20 per gallon. There are 40 gallons of cranberry juice, costing $5.50 per gallon. The resulting mixture, costing $4.20 per gallon, consists of $40 + x$ gallons. Use the equation $V = AC$ to find the value of each:
Value of cranberry juice: $5.50(40)$
Value of apple juice: $3.20(x)$
Value of mixture: $4.20(40 + x)$
Write an equation using the fact that the sum of the values before mixing equals the value after mixing.

Solution
$$5.50(40) + 3.2x = 4.2(40 + x)$$
$$220 + 3.2x = 168 + 4.2x$$
$$220 = 168 + x$$
$$52 = x$$
The mixture must contain 52 gal of apple juice.

Chapter Test

1.
$$\frac{2}{3} = b + \frac{3}{4}$$
$$\frac{2}{3} - \frac{3}{4} = b + \frac{3}{4} - \frac{3}{4}$$
$$-\frac{1}{12} = b$$

2.
$$\frac{2}{3}d = \frac{4}{9}$$
$$\frac{3}{2} \cdot \frac{2}{3}d = \frac{3}{2} \cdot \frac{4}{9}$$
$$d = \frac{2}{3}$$

3.
$$4x + 1 = 7x - 7$$
$$4x - 4x + 1 = 7x - 4x - 7$$
$$1 = 3x - 7$$
$$1 + 7 = 3x - 7 + 7$$
$$8 = 3x$$
$$\frac{8}{3} = \frac{3x}{3}$$
$$\frac{8}{3} = x$$

4.
$$5x - 4(x + 2) = 7 - 2(3 - 2x)$$
$$5x - 4x - 8 = 7 - 6 + 4x$$
$$x - 8 = 1 + 4x$$
$$x - 4x - 8 = 1 + 4x - 4x$$
$$-3x - 8 = 1$$
$$-3x - 8 + 8 = 1 + 8$$
$$-3x = 9$$
$$\frac{-3x}{-3} = \frac{9}{-3}$$
$$x = -3$$

5.
$$2 - 2(7 - 2x) \le 4(5 - 3x)$$
$$2 - 14 + 4x \le 20 - 12x$$
$$-12 + 4x \le 20 - 12x$$
$$-12 + 4x + 12x \le 20 - 12x + 12x$$
$$16x - 12 \le 20$$
$$16x - 12 + 12 \le 20 + 12$$
$$16x \le 32$$
$$\frac{16x}{16} \le \frac{32}{16}$$
$$x \le 2$$
The solution set is $\{x \mid x \le 2\}$.

6.
$$2 - 5(x + 1) \ge 3(x - 1) - 8$$
$$2 - 5x - 5 \ge 3x - 3 - 8$$
$$-5x - 3 \ge 3x - 11$$
$$-5x - 3x - 3 \ge 3x - 3x - 11$$
$$-8x - 3 \ge -11$$
$$-8x - 3 + 3 \ge -11 + 3$$
$$-8x \ge -8$$
$$\frac{-8x}{-8} \le \frac{-8}{-8}$$
$$x \le 1$$
The solution set is $\{x \mid x \le 1\}$.

7.
$$-5 < 4x - 1 < 7$$
$$-5 + 1 < 4x - 1 + 1 < 7 + 1$$
$$-4 < 4x < 8$$
$$-\frac{4}{4} < \frac{4x}{4} < \frac{8}{4}$$
$$-1 < x < 2$$
The solution is $(-1, 2)$.

8.
$$3x - 2 > -4 \quad \text{and} \quad 7x - 5 < 3x + 3$$
$$3x > -2 \qquad\qquad 7x < 3x + 8$$
$$x > -\frac{2}{3} \qquad\qquad 4x < 8$$
$$\qquad\qquad\qquad x < 2$$
The solution set is $(-\infty, \infty)$.

9.
$$9x - 2 > 7 \quad \text{and} \quad 3x - 5 < 10$$
$$9x > 9 \qquad\qquad 3x < 15$$
$$x > 1 \qquad\qquad x < 5$$
The solution set is $\{x \mid 1 < x < 5\}$.

10.
$$|2x - 3| = 8$$
$$2x - 3 = 8 \qquad\qquad 2x - 3 = -8$$
$$2x = 11 \qquad\qquad 2x = -5$$
$$x = \frac{11}{2} \qquad\qquad x = -\frac{5}{2}$$
The solutions are $-\frac{5}{2}$ and $\frac{11}{2}$.

11.
$$|2x - 5| \le 3$$
$$-3 \le 2x - 5 \le 3$$
$$-3 + 5 \le 2x - 5 + 5 \le 3 + 5$$
$$-2 \le 2x \le 8$$
$$1 \le x \le 4$$
The solution set is $\{x \mid 1 \le x \le 4\}$.

12. $|4x-7|\geq 5$

$$4x-7\leq -5 \qquad\quad 4x-7\geq 5$$
$$4x\leq 2 \quad \text{or} \quad 4x\geq 12$$
$$x\leq\frac{1}{2} \qquad\qquad x\geq 3$$

The solution set is $\left\{x \middle| x\leq\frac{1}{2} \text{ or } x\geq 3\right\}$.

13. $|5x-4|<-2$

Because the absolute value of a number is never negative, this inequality has no solution. The solution set is $\varnothing$.

14. The measures of vertical angles are equal.

$$3x+5=x+17$$
$$3x-x+5=x-x+17$$
$$2x+5=17$$
$$2x+5-5=17-5$$
$$2x=12$$
$$\frac{2x}{2}=\frac{12}{2}$$
$$x=6$$

The value of x is 6.

15. Alternate exterior angles have the same measure. Therefore, $m\angle b=39°$. The sum of the measures of supplementary angles is $180°$. Therefore:

$$a+b=180$$
$$a+39=180$$
$$a=141$$

The measure of $\angle a$ is $141°$.

16. The measure of the arc intercepted by the $48°$ angle is twice the angle measure, or $2(48°)=96°$. The measure of the arc intercepted by the $32°$ angle is twice the angle measure, or $2(32°)=64°$. There are a total of $360°$ in a circle. Therefore,

$$118+96+64+x=360$$
$$278+x=360$$
$$x=82$$

17. Strategy
Let the measure of one acute angle of the right triangle be x. Then the measure of the other acute angle is $2x$. Use the fact that the sum of the interior angles of a triangle is $180°$.

Solution
$$x+2x+90=180$$
$$3x+90=180$$
$$3x=90$$
$$x=30$$

The measure of the right angle is $90°$. The measure of one acute angle is $30°$ and the measure of the other acute angle is $2x=2(30)=60°$.

18. Strategy
Let
$r=$ the rate of the first plane
$r+80=$ the rate of the second plane.
Both the first plane and the second plane travel for 1.75 hours. Use the uniform motion equation $d=rt$ (where d is the distance, r is the rate of speed, and t is the time) to write the distances traveled by each plane:
Distance traveled by first plane: $1.75r$
Distance traveled by second plane: $1.75(r+80)$
The total distance traveled by the two planes is 1680 miles. Translate this fact into an equation:
$1.75r+1.75(r+80)=1680$

Solution
$$1.75r+1.75(r+80)=1680$$
$$1.75r+1.75r+140=1680$$
$$3.5r+140=1680$$
$$3.5r=1540$$
$$r=440$$
$$r+80=440+80=520$$
The speed of the first plane is 440 mph. The speed of the second plane is 520 mph.

19. Strategy
Let x represent the selling price per pound of the mixture. There are 40 pounds of tea costing \$6.40 per pound and 65 pounds of tea costing \$3.80 per pound. Thus, there are $40+65=105$ pounds of the resulting mixture. Use the equation $V=AC$ to find the value of each:
Value of \$6.40 tea: $6.40(40)$
Value of \$3.80 tea: $3.80(65)$
Value of mixture: $105(x)$
Now write an equation using the fact that the sum of the values before mixing equals the value after mixing.

Solution
$$6.40(40)+3.80(65)=105x$$
$$256+247=105x$$
$$503=105x$$
$$4.79\approx x$$
The cost of the mixture is \$4.79 per pound.

20. Strategy
Let p represent the prescribed amount of medication, T the tolerance, and m the lower and upper limits of the amount of medication. Solve the absolute value inequality $|m-p|\leq T$ for m.

Solution
$$|m-p|\leq T$$
$$|m-5|\leq 0.2$$
$$-0.2\leq m-5\leq 0.2$$
$$-0.2+5\leq m-5+5\leq 0.2+5$$
$$4.8\leq m\leq 5.2$$
The lower and upper limits of the amount of medicine to be given to the patient are 4.8 mg and 5.2 mg.

Cumulative Review Exercises

1. Use trial and error:
If K = 0,
  103104 is a multiple of 12 and a multiple of 9.
If K = 1,
  113114 is not a multiple of 12.
If K = 2,
  123124 is not a multiple of 12.
If K = 3,
  133134 is not a multiple of 12.
If K = 4,
  143144 is not a multiple of 12.
If K = 5,
  153154 is not a multiple of 12.
If K = 6,
  163164 is a multiple of 12 and not a multiple of 9.

2. The statements are arranged in the order:
(B) All birds have feathers.
(C) An eagle is a bird.
(A) An eagle has feathers.

3. The odd natural numbers less than 9: $\{1, 3, 5, 7\}$.

4. If $E = \{0, 3, 6, 9, 12\}$ and
$F = \{-6, -4, -2, 0, 2, 4, 6\}$, then
$E \cup F = \{-6, -4, -2, 0, 2, 3, 4, 6, 9, 12\}$
and $E \cap F = \{0, 6\}$.

5. $2(b+c) - 2a^2$
$2(3 + -2) - 2(-1)^2 = 2(1) - 2(1) = 2 - 2 = 0$

6. $-8°C + 12°C = 4°C$

7. $y - z$
$-3.597 - (-4.826) = -3.597 + 4.826 = 1.229$

8. Let $a = 6.5$ m, $b = 9.5$ m, and $h = 5$ m.
$A = \dfrac{1}{2}h(a+b)$
$A = \dfrac{1}{2}(5)(6.5 + 9.5)$
$= \dfrac{5}{2}(16)$
$= 40$
The area is 40 m^2.

9. $5(3y - 8) - 4(1 - 2y) = 15y - 40 - 4 + 8y$
$= 23y - 44$

10. a number and twenty: $x + 20$
a number minus the sum of the number and
twenty: $x - (x + 20)$
$x - (x + 20) = x - x - 20 = -20$

11. a. The graphing calculator screen is given below. Y1 represents the distance d, and X represents the gallons of gasoline.

X	Y1	
0	0	
2	56	
4	112	
6	168	
8	224	
10	280	
12	336	

Y1 ⬛28X

b. The car can travel 280 mi on 10 gal of gasoline.

12. $f(t) = t^2 + t - 4$
$f(-2) = (-2)^2 + (-2) - 4$
$= 4 - 2 - 4$
$= -2$

13. $s(t) = 2t^3 - t^2 - 3t + 4$
$s(-4) = 2(-4)^3 - (-4)^2 - 3(-4) + 4$
$= 2(-64) - 16 + 12 + 4$
$= -128 - 16 + 16$
$= -128$
$s(-2) = 2(-2)^3 - (-2)^2 - 3(-2) + 4$
$= 2(-8) - 4 + 6 + 4$
$= -16 - 4 + 10$
$= -10$
$s(0) = 2(0)^3 - (0)^2 - 3(0) + 4$
$= 4$
$s(2) = 2(2)^3 - (2)^2 - 3(2) + 4$
$= 2(8) - 4 - 6 + 4$
$= 16 - 4 - 6 + 4$
$= 10$
$s(4) = 2(4)^3 - (4)^2 - 3(4) + 4$
$= 2(64) - 16 - 12 + 4$
$= 128 - 16 - 12 + 4$
$= 104$
The range is $\{-128, -10, 4, 10, 104\}$

14. $F(x) = x^2 + x - 6$
$F(0) = (0)^2 + 0 - 6 = -6$

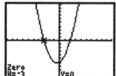 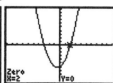

The x-intercepts are $(-3, 0)$ and $(2, 0)$. The y-intercept is $(0, -6)$.

15. For the functions $f(x) = 4x - 2$ and $g(x) = -3x + 5$, use the graphing calculator to find the point of intersection.

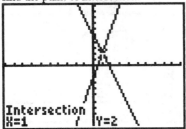

The input value is 1.

16.
$$3(2x - 3) + 1 = 2(1 - 2x)$$
$$6x - 9 + 1 = 2 - 4x$$
$$6x - 8 = 2 - 4x$$
$$6x + 4x - 8 = 2 - 4x + 4x$$
$$10x - 8 + 8 = 2 + 8$$
$$10x = 10$$
$$x = 1$$

17.
$$3x - 2 \geq 6x + 7$$
$$3x - 3x - 2 \geq 6x - 3x + 7$$
$$-2 - 7 \geq 3x$$
$$-9 \geq 3x$$
$$-3 \geq x$$

The solution in set-builder notation: $(-\infty, -3]$.

18.
$$3 - |2x - 3| = -8$$
$$-|2x - 3| = -11$$
$$|2x - 3| = 11$$

$$2x - 3 = -11 \quad \text{or} \quad 2x - 3 = 11$$
$$2x = -8 \qquad\qquad 2x = 14$$
$$x = -4 \qquad\qquad x = 7$$

The solution is –4, 7.

19.
$$|3x - 5| \leq 4$$
$$-4 \leq 3x - 5 \leq 4$$
$$-4 + 5 \leq 3x - 5 + 5 \leq 4 + 5$$
$$1 \leq 3x \leq 9$$
$$\frac{1}{3} \leq \frac{3x}{3} \leq \frac{9}{3}$$
$$\frac{1}{3} \leq x \leq 3$$
$$\left\{ x \middle| \frac{1}{3} \leq x \leq 3 \right\}$$

20. Strategy

Let
r = the rate of the first plane
$r + 1200$ = the rate of the second plane.
Both the first plane and the second plane travel for 2.5 hours. Use the uniform motion equation $d = rt$ (where d is the distance, r is the rate of speed, and t is the time) to write the distances traveled by each plane:
Distance traveled by first plane: $2.5r$
Distance traveled by second plane: $2.5(r + 120)$
The total distance traveled by the two planes is 1400 miles. Translate this fact into an equation:
$2.5r + 2.5(r + 120) = 1400$

Solution
$$2.5r + 2.5(r + 120) = 1400$$
$$2.5r + 2.5r + 300 = 1400$$
$$5r + 300 = 1400$$
$$5r = 1100$$
$$r = 220$$
$$r + 120 = 220 + 120 = 340$$

The speed of the first plane is 220 mph. The speed of the second plane is 340 mph.

Chapter 4: Linear Functions

Prep Test

1. $-4(x-3) = -4x + 12$

2. $y - (-5) = y + 5$

3. $\frac{1}{4}(3x - 16) = \frac{3}{4}x - \frac{16}{4} = \frac{3}{4}x - 4$

4. $\frac{3 - (-5)}{2 - 6} = \frac{8}{-4} = -2$

5. $8r + 240$
   $8(0) + 240 = 240$

6. $\frac{3 - (-2)}{-3 - 2} = \frac{3 + 2}{-5} = \frac{5}{-5} = -1$

7. $3x - 4(0) = 12$
   $3x = 12$
   $x = 4$

8. $3x + 6 = 0$
   $3x = -6$
   $x = -2$

9. $y + 8 = 0$
   $y = -8$

10.
$$-4 < x + 3$$
$$-4 - 3 < x$$
$$-7 < x$$
$$x > -7$$
   The solutions are a, b, and c.

Go Figure

If two fractions are inserted between $\frac{1}{4}$ and $\frac{1}{2}$, then there are three steps from $\frac{1}{4}$ to $\frac{1}{2}$. First, to find the two fractions, we find the difference:
$$\frac{1}{2} - \frac{1}{4} = \frac{1}{4}$$
Second, since there are 3 steps between the fractions, divide the difference by 3.
$$\frac{1}{4} \cdot \frac{1}{3} = \frac{1}{12}$$ This is the difference between each step.
Next, find the value of each fraction
$$\frac{1}{4} + \frac{1}{12} = \frac{3}{12} + \frac{1}{12} = \frac{4}{12}$$
$$\frac{4}{12} + \frac{1}{12} = \frac{5}{12}$$
The four fractions are $\frac{1}{4}, \frac{4}{12}, \frac{5}{12}, \frac{1}{2}$. Each consecutive fraction has the same difference. Finally find the sum of these four fractions.
$$\frac{1}{4} + \frac{4}{12} + \frac{5}{12} + \frac{1}{2} = \frac{3 + 4 + 5 + 6}{12} = \frac{18}{12} = \frac{3}{2}$$

Section 4.1

1. Answers will vary. For example,
   a. $y = 3x - 4$
   b. $2x - 5y = 10$

3. The graph of a line with zero slope is horizontal. The graph of a line with no slope is vertical.

5. No. For instance, the graph of $x = 3$ is a line but is not the graph of a function.

7. The graph of $x = a$ is a vertical line passing through $(a, 0)$. The graph of $y = b$ is a horizontal line passing through $(0, b)$.

9. Yes. $-\frac{3x}{4} = -\frac{3}{4}x$. It is a function of the form $f(x) = mx + b$.

11. No. The exponent on the variable is 2, not 1.

13. $P_1(1, 3)$, $P_2(3, 1)$
$$m = \frac{y_2 - y_1}{x_2 - x_1} = \frac{1 - 3}{3 - 1} = \frac{-2}{2} = -1$$
The slope is -1.

15. $P_1(-1, 4)$, $P_2(2, 5)$
$$m = \frac{y_2 - y_1}{x_2 - x_1} = \frac{5 - 4}{2 - (-1)} = \frac{1}{3}$$
The slope is $\frac{1}{3}$.

17. $P_1(-1, 3)$, $P_2(-4, 5)$
$$m = \frac{y_2 - y_1}{x_2 - x_1} = \frac{5 - 3}{-4 - (-1)} = \frac{2}{-3} = -\frac{2}{3}$$
The slope is $-\frac{2}{3}$.

19. $P_1(0, 3)$, $P_2(4, 0)$
$$m = \frac{y_2 - y_1}{x_2 - x_1} = \frac{0 - 3}{4 - 0} = \frac{-3}{4} = -\frac{3}{4}$$
The slope is $-\frac{3}{4}$.

21. $P_1(2, 4)$, $P_2(2, -2)$
$$m = \frac{y_2 - y_1}{x_2 - x_1} = \frac{-2 - 4}{2 - 2} = \frac{-6}{0}$$
The slope is undefined.

23. $P_1(2, 5)$, $P_2(-3, -2)$
$$m = \frac{y_2 - y_1}{x_2 - x_1} = \frac{-2 - 5}{-3 - 2} = \frac{-7}{-5} = \frac{7}{5}$$
The slope is $\frac{7}{5}$.

25. $P_1(2, 3),\ P_2(-1, 3)$

$m = \dfrac{y_2 - y_1}{x_2 - x_1} = \dfrac{3-3}{-1-2} = \dfrac{0}{-3} = 0$

The line has zero slope.

27. $P_1(0, 4),\ P_2(-2, 5)$

$m = \dfrac{y_2 - y_1}{x_2 - x_1} = \dfrac{5-4}{-2-0} = \dfrac{1}{-2} = -\dfrac{1}{2}$

The slope is $-\dfrac{1}{2}$.

29. $P_1(-3, -1),\ P_2(-3, 4)$

$m = \dfrac{y_2 - y_1}{x_2 - x_1} = \dfrac{4-(-1)}{-3-(-3)} = \dfrac{5}{0}$

The slope is undefined.

31.

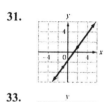

33.

35.

37.

39.

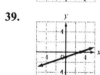

41. $m = \dfrac{4.8-2}{12-5} = \dfrac{2.8}{7} = 0.40$

The slope of 0.40 means that the cellular call costs $0.40 per minute.

43. $m = \dfrac{4-1}{100-25} = \dfrac{3}{75} = 0.04$

Each second, 0.04 megabyte is downloaded.

45. $m = \dfrac{275-125}{20-50} = \dfrac{150}{-30} = -5$

The temperature of the oven decreases 5° per minute.

47. $m = \dfrac{240-80}{6-2} = \dfrac{160}{4} = 40$

The average speed of the motorist is 40 mph.

49. $m = \dfrac{15,260-6188.28}{54,500-22,101} = \dfrac{9071.72}{32,399} = 0.28$

The tax rate is 28%.

51. $m = \dfrac{13-6}{40-180} = \dfrac{7}{-140} = -0.05$

For each mile the car is driven, approximately 0.05 gallons of fuel is used.

53. a. To find the x-intercept, replace $f(x)$ by 0 and solve for x.

$f(x) = 7x - 30$
$0 = 7x - 30$
$30 = 7x$
$\dfrac{30}{7} = x$

The x-intercept is $\left(\dfrac{30}{7},\ 0\right)$. This means that

when the temperature is $\dfrac{30}{7}$ °C, the number of

chirps per minute is 0. In other words, the cricket no longer chirps at this temperature.

b. The slope of 7 means that the number of chirps per minute increases by 7 chirps for every 1°C increase in temperature.

55. a. To find the intercept on the vertical axis, evaluate the function when x is 0.

$T(x) = 20x - 100$
$T(0) = 20(0) - 100$
$\quad\ \ = 0 - 100 = -100$

The vertical axis intercept is $(0, -100)$. This means that when the object was taken from the freezer, its temperature was -100°F.

To find the intercept on the horizontal axis, replace $T(x)$ by 0 and solve for x.

$T(x) = 20x - 100$
$0 = 20x - 100$
$100 = 20x$
$5 = x$

The horizontal axis intercept is $(5, 0)$. This means that 5 hours after the object was removed from the freezer, its temperature was 0°F.

b. The slope of 20 means that the temperature of the object increases 20°F per hour.

57. $m = -6.5$. The slope of -6.5 means that the temperature is decreasing 6.5°C for each 1-kilometer increase in height above sea level.

59. $m = 50$. The slope of 50 means that the pigeon flies 50 mph.

61. Strategy

Find a length x for which $\dfrac{14}{x} \le \dfrac{1}{12}$.

Solution

Solve $\dfrac{14}{x} \le \dfrac{1}{12}$

$$14 \le \dfrac{1}{12}x$$
$$x \ge 14(12)$$
$$x \ge 168$$

The ramp must be at least 168 inches long.

63. Let the points on the line be represented by $(-1, 2)$ and $(1, y)$. If the slope is -3, then we have the relationship:

$$\dfrac{y-2}{1-(-1)} = -3$$
$$\dfrac{y-2}{2} = -3$$
$$y - 2 = -6$$
$$y = -4$$

The y-coordinate of the point is -4 when $x = 1$.

65. Let the points on the line be represented by $(-2, -1)$ and $(-6, y)$. If the slope is $\dfrac{3}{2}$, then we have the relationship:

$$\dfrac{y-(-1)}{-6-(-2)} = \dfrac{3}{2}$$
$$\dfrac{y+1}{-4} = \dfrac{3}{2}$$
$$y + 1 = -6$$
$$y = -7$$

The y-coordinate of the point is -7 when $x = -6$.

67. Strategy

Look at the slopes of the lines to see which line represents the depth of water in each can.

Solution

Since Can 2 has a wider diameter and the water is filling both cans at the same rate, the depth of Can 1 will increase faster. Since line A has a steeper slope, it represents Can 1. Line B represents Can 2.

69.
$$2x + y = 5$$
$$2x - 2x + y = -2x + 5$$
$$y = -2x + 5$$

71.
$$5x - y = 7$$
$$5x - 5x - y = -5x + 7$$
$$-y = -5x + 7$$
$$\dfrac{-y}{-1} = \dfrac{-5x}{-1} + \dfrac{7}{-1}$$
$$y = 5x - 7$$

73.
$$3x + 2y = 6$$
$$3x - 3x + 2y = -3x + 6$$
$$2y = -3x + 6$$
$$\dfrac{2y}{2} = \dfrac{-3x}{2} + \dfrac{6}{2}$$
$$y = -\dfrac{3}{2}x + 3$$

75.
$$2x - 5y = 10$$
$$2x - 2x - 5y = -2x + 10$$
$$-5y = -2x + 10$$
$$\dfrac{-5y}{-5} = \dfrac{-2x}{-5} + \dfrac{10}{-5}$$
$$y = \dfrac{2}{5}x - 2$$

77.
$$x + 3y = 6$$
$$x - x + 3y = -x + 6$$
$$3y = -x + 6$$
$$\dfrac{3y}{3} = \dfrac{-x}{3} + \dfrac{6}{3}$$
$$y = -\dfrac{1}{3}x + 2$$

79.
$$6x - 5y = 10$$
$$6x - 6x - 5y = -6x + 10$$
$$-5y = -6x + 10$$
$$\dfrac{-5y}{-5} = \dfrac{-6x}{-5} + \dfrac{10}{-5}$$
$$y = \dfrac{6}{5}x - 2$$

81.

x-intercept:	y-intercept:
$3x + y = 3$	$3x + y = 3$
$3x + 0 = 3$	$3(0) + y = 3$
$3x = 3$	$y = 3$
$x = 1$	
$(1, 0)$	$(0, 3)$

83.

x-intercept:	y-intercept:
$4x - y = 8$	$4x - y = 8$
$4x - (0) = 8$	$4(0) - y = 8$
$4x = 8$	$-y = 8$
$x = 2$	$y = -8$
$(2, 0)$	$(0, -8)$

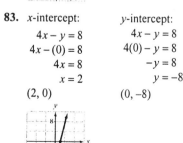

85. *x*-intercept:
$$2x + y = 6$$
$$2x + 0 = 6$$
$$2x = 6$$
$$x = 3$$
$$(3, 0)$$

y-intercept:
$$2x + y = 6$$
$$2(0) + y = 6$$
$$y = 6$$
$$(0, 6)$$

87. *x*-intercept:
$$4x - 3y = 12$$
$$4x - 3(0) = 12$$
$$4x = 12$$
$$x = 3$$
$$(3, 0)$$

y-intercept:
$$4x - 3y = 12$$
$$4(0) - 3y = 12$$
$$-3y = 12$$
$$y = -4$$
$$(0, -4)$$

89. *x*-intercept:
$$2x - 3y = 18$$
$$2x - 3(0) = 18$$
$$2x = 18$$
$$x = 9$$
$$(9, 0)$$

y-intercept:
$$2x - 3y = 18$$
$$2(0) - 3y = 18$$
$$-3y = 18$$
$$y = -6$$
$$(0, -6)$$

91. *x*-intercept:
$$4x - 3y = 24$$
$$4x - 3(0) = 24$$
$$4x = 24$$
$$x = 6$$
$$(6, 0)$$

y-intercept:
$$4x - 3y = 24$$
$$4(0) - 3y = 24$$
$$-3y = 24$$
$$y = -8$$
$$(0, -8)$$

93. $y = -3$

95. If $f(1) = -6$ and $f(-1) = -6$, then f represents a horizontal line at –6. So, $f(4) = -6$.

Applying Concepts 4.1

97. From the three points, *A*, *B*, and *C*, create three pairs of points, *A* and *B*, *A* and *C*, and *B* and *C*. Determine whether the lines containing each pair of points have the same slope.

   a. $A = (2, 5)$, $B = (-1, -1)$, and $C = (3, 7)$

      A to *B*: $m = \dfrac{5 - (-1)}{2 - (-1)} = \dfrac{6}{3} = 2$

      B to *C*: $m = \dfrac{7 - (-1)}{3 - (-1)} = \dfrac{8}{4} = 2$

      A to *C*: $m = \dfrac{7 - 5}{3 - 2} = \dfrac{2}{1} = 2$

      The points lie on the same line.

   b. $A = (-1, 5)$, $B = (0, 3)$, and $C = (-3, 4)$

      A to *B*: $m = \dfrac{5 - 3}{-1 - 0} = \dfrac{2}{-1} = -2$

      B to *C*: $m = \dfrac{4 - 3}{-3 - 0} = \dfrac{1}{-3} = -\dfrac{1}{3}$

      A to *C*: $m = \dfrac{5 - 4}{-1 - (-3)} = \dfrac{1}{2}$

      The points do not lie on the same line.

99. No; for example, $x = 2$.

101. Rewrite the slope as $m = 3 = \dfrac{3}{1} = \dfrac{-3}{-1}$. Starting from the given point on the line (8, 12), move down 3 and to the left 1 until the desired point is found:
$$(8 - 1, 12 - 3) = (7, 9)$$
$$(7 - 1, 9 - 3) = (6, 6)$$
$$(6 - 1, 6 - 3) = (5, 3)$$
$$(5 - 1, 3 - 3) = (4, 0)$$
$$(4 - 1, 0 - 3) = (3, -3) = (C, -3)$$
The value of *C* is 3.

103. Answers will vary.

Section 4.2

1. The slope, *m*, and the *y*-intercept, (0, *b*), can be read directly from the equation.

3. *m* would be positive because as the age of the tree increases, the height of the tree increases.

5. **a.** Parallel lines have equal slopes.

   b. The product of the slopes of perpendicular lines is –1; that is, their slopes are negative reciprocals.

7. $y = -2x + b$
$$-1 = -2(0) + b$$
$$-1 = b$$
$$y = -2x - 1$$

9. $y = -\dfrac{1}{4}x + b$

$2 = -\dfrac{1}{4}(0) + b$

$2 = b$

$y = -\dfrac{1}{4}x + 2$

11. $y = \dfrac{1}{6}x + b$

$0 = \dfrac{1}{6}(0) + b$

$0 = b$

$y = \dfrac{1}{6}x$

13. $y = 2x + b$

$5 = 2(0) + b$

$5 = b$

$y = 2x + 5$

15. $y = -\dfrac{5}{4}x + b$

$0 = -\dfrac{5}{4}(4) + b$

$0 = -5 + b$

$5 = b$

$y = -\dfrac{5}{4}x + 5$

17. $y = 3x + b$

$-3 = 3(2) + b$

$-3 = 6 + b$

$-9 = b$

$y = 3x - 9$

19. $y = (0)x + b$

$-3 = (0)(-2) + b$

$-3 = b$

$y = -3$

21. $x = 3$

23. $m = \dfrac{y_2 - y_1}{x_2 - x_1} = \dfrac{5 - 2}{3 - 0} = \dfrac{3}{3} = 1$

$y - y_1 = m(x - x_1)$

$y - 2 = 1(x - 0)$

$y - 2 = 1x$

$y = x + 2$

25. $m = \dfrac{y_2 - y_1}{x_2 - x_1} = \dfrac{3 - 0}{4 - 0} = \dfrac{3}{4}$

$y - y_1 = m(x - x_1)$

$y - 0 = \dfrac{3}{4}(x - 0)$

$y = \dfrac{3}{4}x$

27. $m = \dfrac{y_2 - y_1}{x_2 - x_1} = \dfrac{-2 - (-}{-1 - (}$

$y - y_1 = m(x - x_1)$

$y - (-3) = 1(x - (-2))$

$y + 3 = 1x + 2$

$y = x - 1$

29. $m = \dfrac{y_2 - y_1}{x_2 - x_1} = \dfrac{0 - (-3)}{2 - 4} = \dfrac{3}{-2} = -\dfrac{3}{2}$

$y - y_1 = m(x - x_1)$

$y - (0) = -\dfrac{3}{2}(x - 2)$

$y = -\dfrac{3}{2}x + 3$

31. $m = \dfrac{y_2 - y_1}{x_2 - x_1} = \dfrac{4 - 3}{2 - (-1)} = \dfrac{1}{3}$

$y - y_1 = m(x - x_1)$

$y - 3 = \dfrac{1}{3}[x - (-1)]$

$y - 3 = \dfrac{1}{3}(x + 1)$

$y - 3 = \dfrac{1}{3}x + \dfrac{1}{3}$

$y = \dfrac{1}{3}x + \dfrac{10}{3}$

33. $m = \dfrac{y_2 - y_1}{x_2 - x_1} = \dfrac{-4 - (-4)}{-2 - 3} = \dfrac{0}{-5} = 0$

$y - y_1 = m(x - x_1)$

$y - (-4) = 0(x - 3)$

$y + 4 = 0$

$y = -4$

35. $m = \dfrac{y_2 - y_1}{x_2 - x_1} = \dfrac{-5 - 5}{-2 - (-2)} = \dfrac{-10}{0}$

The slope is undefined. The line is a vertical line. All points on the line have an abscissa of –2. The equation of the line is $x = -2$.

37. Strategy
Use the slope-intercept form to determine the equation of the line.

Solution
y-intercept = 0
$m = 1200$
$y = mx + b$
$y = 1200x + 0$
The equation that represents the ascent of the plane is $y = 1200x$ where x stands for the number of minutes after take-off. To find the height of the plane when $x = 11$
$y = 1200(11)$
$y = 13{,}200$
After 11 min, the plane will be 13,200 ft in the air.

Strategy
Use the slope-intercept form of the equation.

Solution
The y-intercept is 5200 and the slope is 1000.
$$y = mx + b$$
$$y = 1000x + 5200$$
The equation representing the height in terms of time after take-off is $y = 1000x + 5200$. To find the height of the plane 8 minutes after take-off
$$y = 1000 \cdot 8 + 5200$$
$$y = 13,200$$
After 8 min, the height of the plane will be 13,200 ft.

41. Strategy
Use the point-slope formula.

Solution
$(x_1, y_1) = (0, 100), \ (x_2, y_2) = (2, 93)$
$$m = \frac{y_2 - y_1}{x_2 - x_1} = \frac{93 - 100}{2 - 0} = -\frac{7}{2}$$
$$y - y_1 = m(x - x_1)$$
$$y - 100 = -\frac{7}{2}(x - 0)$$
$$y - 100 = -\frac{7}{2}x$$
$$y = -\frac{7}{2}x + 100$$
The equation to predict the boiling point is $y = -\frac{7}{2}x + 100$ or $y = -3.5x + 100$, where x is the altitude above sea level. To predict the boiling point for an altitude of 8.85 kilometers,
$$y = -\frac{7}{2}(8.85) + 100$$
$$y = -31.0 + 100 = 69$$
The boiling point on the top of Mount Everest is approximately 69°C.

43. Strategy
Use the point-slope form where all y-values are in millions.

Solution
$(x_1, y_1) = (91, 24)$
$m = 2.4$
$$y - y_1 = m(x - x_1)$$
$$y - 24 = 2.4(x - 91)$$
$$y - 24 = 2.4x - 218.4$$
$$y = 2.4x - 194.4$$
The equation to find the number of computers in homes is $y = 2.4x - 194.4$ where x is the years after 1900. To predict the number of computers in homes in 2004,
$$y = 2.4(104) - 194.4$$
$$y = 55.2$$
48 million computers are predicted to be in homes in the year 2001.

45. Strategy
Use the point-slope formula.

Solution
$(x_1, y_1) = (1000, 1480)$
$m = 0.017$
$$y - y_1 = m(x - x_1)$$
$$y - 1480 = 0.017(x - 1000)$$
$$y - 1480 = 0.017x - 17$$
$$y = 0.017x + 1463$$
The equation that can be used to approximate the speed of sound below sea level is $y = 0.017x + 1463$. To find the speed of sound 2500 meters below sea level,
$$y = 0.017(2500) + 1463$$
$$y = 1505.5$$
The approximate speed of sound 2500 meters below sea level is 1506 m/s.

47. Strategy
Use the point-slope formula.

Solution
Let y represent the number of trucks sold at a price of x dollars. Then $y = 50,000$ when $x = 9000$. And $y = 55,000$ when $x = 8750$. The slope is
$$m = \frac{55,000 - 50,000}{8750 - 9000} = \frac{5000}{-250} = -20$$
$$y - y_1 = m(x - x_1)$$
$$y - 50,000 = -20(x - 9000)$$
$$y - 50,000 = -20x + 180,000$$
$$y = -20x + 230,000$$
To predict the number of trucks that would be sold at a price of \$8500, evaluate the model when $x = 8500$:
$$y = -20x + 230,000$$
$$y = -20(8500) + 230,000$$
$$= -170,000 + 230,000$$
$$= 60,000$$
60,000 trucks will be sold when the price is \$8500.

49. Strategy
Use the point-slope formula.

Solution
Let y represent the number of rooms rented at a rate of x dollars per night.
Then $y = 500$ when $x = 75$. Because a \$10 increase in price results in 6 fewer rooms being rented, we have $y = 500 - 6 = 494$ when $x = 75 + 10 = 85$. The slope is

$$m = \frac{500 - 494}{75 - 85} = \frac{6}{-10} = -\frac{3}{5}$$

$$y - y_1 = m(x - x_1)$$
$$y - 500 = -\frac{3}{5}(x - 75)$$
$$y - 500 = -\frac{3}{5}x + 45$$
$$y = -\frac{3}{5}x + 545$$

To predict the number of rooms that would be rented at a price of \$100 per night, evaluate the model when $x = 100$:

$$y = -\frac{3}{5}x + 545$$
$$y = -\frac{3}{5}(100) + 545$$
$$= -60 + 545 = 485$$

485 rooms will be rented when the price is \$100 per night.

51. a. $m = \dfrac{-0.558 - (-0.372)}{30 - 20} = \dfrac{-0.186}{10} = -0.0186$

$$y - y_1 = m(x - x_1)$$
$$y - (-0.372) = -0.0186(x - 20)$$
$$y + 0.372 = -0.0186x + 0.372$$
$$y = -0.0186x$$

b. For every 1 g of sugar added, the freezing point decreases 0.0186°C.

c. $y = -0.0186x$
$y = -0.0186(50) = -0.93$
When 50 g of sugar has been added, the freezing point of water is −0.93°C.

53. Yes, the line $x = -2$ is perpendicular to the line $y = 3$ because $x = -2$ is a vertical line and $y = 3$ is a horizontal line.

55. No, the line $x = -3$ is not parallel to the line $y = -3$ because $x = -3$ is a vertical line and $y = -3$ is a horizontal line. Vertical and horizontal lines are perpendicular, not parallel.

57. Yes, both lines have the same slope of $-\dfrac{3}{2}$.

59. To determine whether the lines are parallel, find the slope of each line.
Slope between $(3, 2)$ and $(1, 6)$:
$$m = \frac{6 - 2}{1 - 3} = \frac{4}{-2} = -2$$
Slope between $(-1, 3)$ and $(-1, -1)$:
$$m = \frac{-1 - 3}{-1 - (-1)} = \frac{-4}{0} \text{ undefined slope}$$
The slopes are not equal. No, the lines are not parallel.

61. Because the lines are parallel, the slope of the unknown line is the same as the slope of the given line. The given line is $y = -3x - 1$, whose slope is −3. Therefore, the slope of the unknown line is −3. Use the point-slope formula to find the equation of the line.
$$y - y_1 = m(x - x_1)$$
$$y - 4 = -3(x - 1)$$
$$y - 4 = -3x + 3$$
$$y = -3x + 7$$

63. Because the lines are parallel, the slope of the unknown line is the same as the slope of the given line. Write the equation of the given line in slope-intercept form by solving for y.
$$2x - 3y = 2$$
$$-3y = -2x + 2$$
$$y = \frac{2}{3}x - \frac{2}{3}$$

The slope of the given line is $\dfrac{2}{3}$. Because the lines are parallel, the slope of the unknown line is also $\dfrac{2}{3}$. Use the point-slope formula to find the equation of the line.
$$y - y_1 = m(x - x_1)$$
$$y - (-4) = \frac{2}{3}[x - (-2)]$$
$$y + 4 = \frac{2}{3}(x + 2)$$
$$y + 4 = \frac{2}{3}x + \frac{4}{3}$$
$$y = \frac{2}{3}x - \frac{8}{3}$$

65. No, the slopes are reciprocals, not negative reciprocals.
$$\left(-\frac{5}{2}\right)\left(-\frac{2}{5}\right) = 1$$

67. To determine whether the lines are perpendicular, find the slope of each line.

Slope between $(-3, 2)$ and $(4, -1)$:

$$m = \frac{-1-2}{4-(-3)} = \frac{-3}{7} = -\frac{3}{7}$$

Slope between $(1, 3)$ and $(-2, -4)$:

$$m = \frac{-4-3}{-2-1} = \frac{-7}{-3} = \frac{7}{3}$$

Find the product of the slopes:

$$\left(-\frac{3}{7}\right)\left(\frac{7}{3}\right) = -1$$

Yes, because the product of the slopes is -1, these two lines are perpendicular.

69. Because the lines are perpendicular, the value of the slope of the unknown line is the negative reciprocal of the slope of the given line. The slope of the given line is -3. Therefore, the slope of the unknown perpendicular line is $\frac{1}{3}$.

Now use the point-slope formula to find the equation of the line.

$$y - y_1 = m(x - x_1)$$
$$y - 1 = \frac{1}{3}(x - 4)$$
$$y - 1 = \frac{1}{3}x - \frac{4}{3}$$
$$y = \frac{1}{3}x - \frac{1}{3}$$

71. Because the lines are perpendicular, the value of the slope of the unknown line is the negative reciprocal of the slope of the given line. The equation of the given line is $3x - 5y = 2$. Rewrite this equation in slope-intercept form:

$$3x - 5y = 2$$
$$-5y = -3x + 2$$
$$y = \frac{3}{5}x - \frac{2}{5}$$

The slope is $\frac{3}{5}$. Therefore, the slope of the unknown perpendicular line is $-\frac{5}{3}$. Now use the point-slope formula to find the equation of the line.

$$y - y_1 = m(x - x_1)$$
$$y - (-3) = -\frac{5}{3}[x - (-1)]$$
$$y + 3 = -\frac{5}{3}(x + 1)$$
$$y + 3 = -\frac{5}{3}x - \frac{5}{3}$$
$$y = -\frac{5}{3}x - \frac{14}{3}$$

73. Strategy
To find the equation of the line on the initial path
• Find the slope of the line of the string
• Find the slope of the line on the initial path which is perpendicular to the line of the string.
• Use the point slope form to find the equation of the line of the initial path.

Solution
Slope of the string,

$$m_1 = \frac{9-0}{1-0} = 9$$

Slope of the line on the initial path,

$$m_1 \cdot m_2 = -1$$
$$9 \cdot m_2 = -1$$
$$m_2 = -\frac{1}{9}$$

Equation of the line,

$$y - y_1 = m(x - x_1)$$
$$y - 9 = -\frac{1}{9}[x - 1]$$
$$y - 9 = -\frac{1}{9}x + \frac{1}{9}$$
$$y = -\frac{1}{9}x + \frac{82}{9}$$

The equation of the line is $y = -\frac{1}{9}x + \frac{82}{9}$.

Applying Concepts 4.2

75. Find the equation of the line that contains $(5, 1)$ and $(4, 2)$.

$$m = \frac{2-1}{4-5} = \frac{1}{-1} = -1$$
$$y - y_1 = m(x - x_1)$$
$$y - 1 = -1(x - 5)$$
$$y - 1 = -x + 5$$
$$y = -x + 6$$

Does $(0, 6)$ satisfy this equation?

$$y = -x + 6$$
$$6 = -0 + 6$$
$$6 = 6$$

$(0, 6)$ satisfies $y = -x + 6$.
$y = -x + 6$ contains all three ordered pairs.

77. Find the equation of the line that contains
$(-1, -5)$ and $(2, 4)$.
$$m = \frac{4-(-5)}{2-(-1)} = \frac{4+5}{2+1} = \frac{9}{3} = 3$$
$$y - y_1 = m(x - x_1)$$
$$y - (-5) = 3[x - (-1)]$$
$$y + 5 = 3(x + 1)$$
$$y + 5 = 3x + 3$$
$$y = 3x - 2$$
Does $(0, 2)$ satisfy this equation?
$$y = 3x - 2$$
$$2 \neq 3(0) - 2$$
$$2 \neq -2$$
$(0, 2)$ does not satisfy $y = 3x - 2$.
There is no linear equation that contains all of the given ordered pairs.

79. Find the equation of the line that contains $(0, 1)$ and $(4, 9)$.
$$m = \frac{9-1}{4-0} = \frac{8}{4} = 2$$
$$y - y_1 = m(x - x_1)$$
$$y - 1 = 2(x - 0)$$
$$y - 1 = 2x$$
$$y = 2x + 1$$
Substitute $x = 3$, $y = n$ into this equation, and solve for n.
$$n = 2(3) + 1$$
$$n = 6 + 1$$
$$n = 7$$

81. Find the equation of the line that contains $(2, -2)$ and $(-2, -4)$.
$$m = \frac{-4-(-2)}{-2-2} = \frac{-4+2}{-4} = \frac{-2}{-4} = \frac{1}{2}$$
$$y - y_1 = m(x - x_1)$$
$$y - (-2) = \frac{1}{2}(x - 2)$$
$$y + 2 = \frac{1}{2}x - 1$$
$$y = \frac{1}{2}x - 3$$
Substitute $x = 4$, $y = n$ into this equation and solve for n.
$$n = \frac{1}{2}(4) - 3$$
$$n = 2 - 3$$
$$n = -1$$

83. Write the equations of the lines in slope-intercept form.
(1) $A_1 x + B_1 y = C_1$
$$B_1 y = C_1 - A_1 x$$
$$y = \frac{C_1}{B_1} - \frac{A_1}{B_1}x$$
(2) $A_2 x + B_2 y = C_2$
$$B_2 y = C_2 - A_2 x$$
$$y = \frac{C_2}{B_2} - \frac{A_2}{B_2}x$$
The slopes of the two lines must be the same for the lines to be parallel, so $\dfrac{A_1}{B_1} = \dfrac{A_2}{B_2}$.

85. Find the slope of the line containing the points $(4, -1)$ and $(2, 1)$:
$$m = \frac{1-(-1)}{2-4} = \frac{2}{-2} = -1$$
Because the slope is -1, move down 1 unit and to the right 1 unit from one of the given points or move up 1 unit and to the left 1 unit from one of the given points to find another point on the line. Possible points are:
$$(2 - 1, 1 + 1) = (1, 2)$$
$$(4 - 1, -1 + 1) = (3, 0)$$
$$(1 - 1, 2 + 1) = (0, 3)$$

87. Notice from the slopes of the two given lines that these two lines are not perpendicular. To form a right triangle, the third line must be perpendicular to one of the first two lines but should not contain the point $(6, -1)$. A line perpendicular to the first equation has a slope of 2 and will be of the form $y = 2x + b$, where $b \neq 13$ because if $b = 13$, this line would contain the point $(6, -1)$. A line perpendicular to the second equation has a slope of $-\dfrac{3}{2}$ and will be of the form $y = -\dfrac{3}{2}x + c$, where $c \neq 8$ because if $c = 8$, this line would contain the point $(6, -1)$.

89. Let x represent the steepness of the hill in degrees and let y represent the speed of your car in kilometers per hour. Then we have two ordered pairs: $(5, 77)$ and $(-2, 154)$. First find the slope of the line:

$$m = \frac{154 - 77}{-2 - 5} = \frac{77}{-7} = -11$$

Now use the point-slope formula to find a linear equation:

$$y - y_1 = m(x - x_1)$$
$$y - 77 = -11(x - 5)$$
$$y - 77 = -11x + 55$$
$$y = -11x + 132$$

Let $y = 99$ and solve for x:

$$y = -11x + 132$$
$$99 = -11x + 132$$
$$-33 = -11x$$
$$3 = x$$

When the top speed is 99 kilometers per hour, the hill is 3° up.

Section 4.3

1. Answers will vary.

3. Answers will vary. For example, we can use the equation to project possible future outcomes.

5. r would be positive because as the number of months increases, the weight increases.

7. r would be close to 0 because there is no correlation between height and history exam scores.

9. a. Answers will vary. Find the equation of the line through the points $(95, 14)$ and $(99, 141)$: First find the slope of the line:

$$m = \frac{141 - 14}{99 - 95} = \frac{127}{4} = 31.75$$

Now use the point-slope formula to find a linear equation:

$$y - y_1 = m(x - x_1)$$
$$y - 14 = 31.75(x - 95)$$
$$y - 14 = 31.75x - 3016.25$$
$$y = 31.75x - 3002.25$$

b. The slope of 31.75 means that the wolf population increased by approximately 32 wolves from 1995 to 2000.

11. a. Answers will vary.
The linear regression equation is

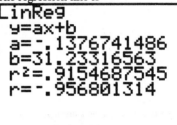

$$y = 66.4857x - 129,626.\overline{6}$$

b. The slope of 66.4857 means that electricity sales increased 66.4857 billion kilowatt hours per year from 1990 to 2000.

13. a. The regression line is

```
LinReg
y=ax+b
a=-.1376741486
b=31.23316563
r²=.9154687545
r=-.956801314
```

$$y = -0.1376741486x + 31.23316563 .$$

b. $y = -0.1376741486x + 31.23316563$
$y = -0.1376741486(65) + 31.23316563 \approx 22$
Traveling at 65 mph, the car will get 22 mpg.

c. The slope is negative; as x increases, y decreases.

15. a. The regression line is

```
LinReg
y=ax+b
a=.3213184476
b=.4003189793
r²=.9673122878
r=.9835203546
```

$$y = 0.3213184476x + 0.4003189793$$

b. $y = 0.3213184476x + 0.4003189793$
$y = 0.3213184476(10) + 0.4003189793 \approx 3.6$
A mouse 10 cm long is expected to run at 3.6 m/s.

c. With an increase of 1 cm in body length, an animal's running speed increases approximately 0.32 m/s.

d. The y-intercept of approximately 0.4 represents the running speed of an animal of length 0 cm.

17. a. The regression line is

```
LinReg
y=ax+b
a=.3325053996
b=37.29859611
r²=.9999844943
r=.9999922471
```

$y = 0.3325054x + 37.2985961$.

b. $r = 0.99999$; The fit of the data to the regression line is very good.

c. $y = 0.3325054x + 37.2985961$
$y = 0.3325054(110) + 37.2985961 \approx 73.9$
In 2010, there are expected to be 73.9 million children under age 18.

d. The slope of approximately 0.333 means that the number of children in the United States is increasing at a rate of about 0.333 million per year.

e. The y-intercept of approximately 37.299 means that in 1900 there were 37.299 million children in the United States.

19. a. The regression line is

```
LinReg
y=ax+b
a=1.551862378
b=1.986390721
r²=.9991430632
r=.9995714398
```

$y = 1.551862378x + 1.986390721$.

b. The slope of approximately 1.55 means that a state receives 1.55 electoral college votes per 1 million residents.

c. The y-intercept of approximately 1.986 means that a state with a population of 0 people would have 1.986 electoral college votes. (Note: each state receives 2 electoral college votes for its 2 senators.)

d. The r value is not exactly 1 because the data are not completely linear. States cannot have a fractional part of a vote. The number of votes a state receives is rounded to a whole number.

21. a. For $y = 0.9x + 1.\overline{7}$, the points are farther away from the regression line and the slope of the line is positive. **ii** $r = 0.787$.

b. For $y = -0.8\overline{6}x + 1.\overline{5}$, the points are close to the regression line and the slope of the line is negative. **iii** $r = -0.995$.

c. For $y = 0.8\overline{6}x + 1.\overline{5}$, the points are close to the regression line and the slope of the line is positive. **iv** $r = 0.995$.

d. For $y = -0.9x + 1.\overline{7}$, the points are farther away from the regression line and the slope of the line is negative. **i** $r = -0.787$.

23. The regression line is

```
LinReg
y=ax+b
a=-2.5
b=9
r²=1
r=-1
```

$y = -2.5x + 9$.

b. The r^2 value would decrease because the data values would not as closely fit a straight line.

25. a. The regression line is

```
LinReg
y=ax+b
a=34.14285714
b=-3234.428571
r²=.9940967835
r=.9970440229
```

$y = 34.142857x - 3234.4286$.

b. The r^2 value would decrease because the data values would not as closely fit a straight line.

Applying Concepts 4.3

27. The value of r is between -1 and 1; it cannot be greater than 1.

29. a. The linear regression line is

```
LinReg
y=ax+b
a=.3672004201
b=315.6241382
r²=.4213347926
r=.6491030678
```

$y = 0.36720042x + 315.62414$.
The correlation coefficient is $r = 0.6491$.

b. The linear regression line is

```
LinReg
y=ax+b
a=1.147424593
b=⁻66.26976216
r²=.4213347926
r=.6491030678
```

$y = 1.1474245x - 66.269762$.
The correlation coefficient is $r = 0.6491$.

c. No. The r values indicate that there is not a strong relationship between the two variables.

Section 4.4

1. No

3. No. There are ordered pairs with the same first component and different second components.

5. $y \le \dfrac{3}{2}x - 3$

$y \le \dfrac{3}{2}x - 3$

$-3 \le \dfrac{3}{2}(4) - 3$

$-3 \le 6 - 3$

$-3 \le 3$

Yes

7. $y < -\dfrac{1}{3}x + 2$

$y < -\dfrac{1}{3}x + 2$

$6 < -\dfrac{1}{3}(-3) + 2$

$6 < 1 + 2$

$6 \not< 3$

No

9. $y < \dfrac{4}{5}x - 2$

$y < \dfrac{4}{5}x - 2$

$-1 < \dfrac{4}{5}(5) - 2$

$-1 < 4 - 2$

$-1 < 2$

Yes

11. $x + 3y < 6$

$3y < -x + 6$

$y < -\dfrac{1}{3}x + 2$

$x + 3y < 6$

$1 + 3(2) < 6$

$1 + 6 < 6$

$7 < 6$

No

13. $2x + 3y \ge 6$

$3y \ge -2x + 6$

$y \ge -\dfrac{2}{3}x + 2$

$2x + 3y \ge 6$

$2(6) + 3(-1) \ge 6$

$12 - 3 \ge 6$

$9 \ge 6$

Yes

15. $-x + 2y > -8$
$$2y > x - 8$$
$$y > \frac{1}{2}x - 4$$

$$-x + 2y > -8$$
$$-5 + 2(-3) > -8$$
$$-5 - 6 > -8$$
$$-11 \not> -8$$
No

17. $y < 4$

$$y < 4$$
$$2 < 4$$
Yes

19. $6x + 5y < 15$
$$5y < -6x + 15$$
$$y < -\frac{6}{5}x + 3$$

$$6x + 5y < 15$$
$$6(-6) + 5(0) < 15$$
$$-12 < 15$$
Yes

21. $-5x + 3y \geq -12$
$$3y \geq 5x - 12$$
$$y \geq \frac{5}{3}x - 4$$

$$-5x + 3y \geq -12$$
$$-5(2) + 3(-2) \geq -12$$
$$-10 - 6 \geq -12$$
$$-16 \not\geq -12$$
No

23. $x \geq -2$

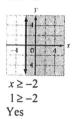

$$x \geq -2$$
$$1 \geq -2$$
Yes

25. $y \leq -2$

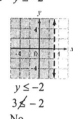

$$y \leq -2$$
$$3 \not\leq -2$$
No

Applying Concepts 4.4

27. $y + 3 < 6(x + 1)$
$$y + 3 < 6x + 6$$
$$y < 6x + 3$$

29. $2x - 3(y + 1) \geq y - (4 - x)$
$$2x - 3y - 3 \geq y - 4 + x$$
$$2x - 3y \geq y - 1 + x$$
$$-3y \geq y - 1 - x$$
$$-4y \geq -x - 1$$
$$y \leq \frac{1}{4}x + \frac{1}{4}$$

31. First find the equation of the line with x-intercept $(3, 0)$ and y-intercept $(0, 2)$.
Find the slope of the line.
$P_1(3, 0)$, $P_2(0, 2)$
$$m = \frac{y_2 - y_1}{x_2 - x_1} = \frac{2 - 0}{0 - 3} = \frac{2}{-3} = -\frac{2}{3}$$
The line has slope $-\frac{2}{3}$.

The equation of the line is $y = -\frac{2}{3}x + 2$.

The line is dashed, and the lower half-plane is shaded.

The inequality is $y < -\frac{2}{3}x + 2$.

33. No. The solution sets do not intersect, which means that there are no ordered pairs that satisfy both inequalities.

Chapter Review Exercises

1. $P_1(-1, 3), P_2(-2, 4)$

$$m = \frac{y_2 - y_1}{x_2 - x_1} = \frac{4 - 3}{-2 - (-1)} = \frac{1}{-1} = -1$$

The slope is -1.

2. $P_1(-6, 5), P_2(-6, 4)$

$$m = \frac{y_2 - y_1}{x_2 - x_1} = \frac{4 - 5}{-6 - (-6)} = \frac{-1}{0} \text{ undefined}$$

The slope is undefined.

3.

4.

5.

6.

7. $y = -\frac{4}{3}x + b$

$$-5 = -\frac{4}{3}(0) + b$$

$$-5 = b$$

$$y = -\frac{4}{3}x - 5$$

8. $y = 4x + b$

$$2 = 4(1) + b$$

$$-2 = b$$

$$y = 4x - 2$$

9. $m = \dfrac{y_2 - y_1}{x_2 - x_1} = \dfrac{9 - 6}{-4 - 2} = \dfrac{3}{-6} = -\dfrac{1}{2}$

$$y - y_1 = m(x - x_1)$$

$$y - 6 = -\frac{1}{2}(x - 2)$$

$$y - 6 = -\frac{1}{2}x + 1$$

$$y = -\frac{1}{2}x + 7$$

10. $m = \dfrac{y_2 - y_1}{x_2 - x_1} = \dfrac{-4 - (-4)}{-2 - 3} = \dfrac{0}{-5} = 0$

$$y - y_1 = m(x - x_1)$$

$$y - (-4) = 0(x - 3)$$

$$y + 4 = 0$$

$$y = -4$$

11. To determine whether the lines are parallel, find the slope of each line.

Slope between $(4, 3)$ and $(6, 2)$:

$$m = \frac{2 - 3}{6 - 4} = \frac{-1}{2} = -\frac{1}{2}$$

Slope between $(3, 2)$ and $(1, 4)$:

$$m = \frac{4 - 2}{1 - 3} = \frac{2}{-2} = -1$$

The slopes are not equal. No, the lines are not parallel.

12. $3x + y = 4$

$$y = -3x + 4$$

$$m = -3$$

$$y - y_1 = m(x - x_1)$$

$$y - (-2) = -3(x - 3)$$

$$y + 2 = -3x + 9$$

$$y = -3x + 7$$

The equation of the line is $y = -3x + 7$.

13. To determine whether the lines are perpendicular, find the slope of each line.

Slope between $(3, 5)$ and $(-3, 3)$:

$$m = \frac{3 - 5}{-3 - 3} = \frac{-2}{-6} = -\frac{1}{3}$$

Slope between $(2, -5)$ and $(-4, 4)$:

$$m = \frac{4 - (-5)}{-4 - 2} = \frac{9}{-6} = -\frac{3}{2}$$

Find the product of the slopes:

$$\left(-\frac{1}{3}\right)\left(-\frac{3}{2}\right) = \frac{1}{2}$$

No, because the product of the slopes is not -1, these two lines are not perpendicular.

14. $y = -\dfrac{2}{3}x + 6$

$$m_1 = -\dfrac{2}{3}$$

$$m_1 \cdot m_2 = -1$$

$$-\dfrac{2}{3}m_2 = -1$$

$$m_2 = \dfrac{3}{2}$$

$$y - y_1 = m(x - x_1)$$

$$y - 5 = \dfrac{3}{2}(x - 2)$$

$$y - 5 = \dfrac{3}{2}x - 3$$

$$y = \dfrac{3}{2}x + 2$$

The equation of the line is $y = \dfrac{3}{2}x + 2$.

15.

16. The y-intercept is $(0, 60,000)$.
The slope is 90.
$$y = mx + b$$
$$y = 90x + 60,000$$
The linear function is $y = 90x + 60,000$.
Predict the cost of building a house with 2500 ft^2.
$$y = 90(2500) + 60,000$$
$$y = 285,000$$
The house will cost $285,000 to build.

17. $m = \dfrac{148 - 130}{30 - 55} = \dfrac{18}{-25} = -0.72$

The maximum recommended exercise heart rate decreases -0.72 beat per minute for every year older.

18. a. $m = \dfrac{2500 - 1750}{60 - 30} = \dfrac{750}{30} = 25$

$$y - y_1 = m(x - x_1)$$
$$y - 1750 = 25(x - 30)$$
$$y - 1750 = 25x - 750$$
$$y = 25x + 1000$$

b. Water is being added to the pond at a rate of 25 gal/min.

c. There are 360 minutes in 6 hours.
$$y = 25x + 1000$$
$$y = 25(360) + 1000$$
$$= 9000 + 1000$$
$$= 10,000$$
After 6 hours, there is 10,000 gallons of water in the pond.

19. a. It costs $0.25 per minute to use the phone.

b. The y-intercept is 19.95. When the phone is used for 0 minutes during the month, the phone bill is $19.95.

20. a. The regression line is

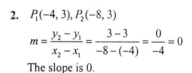

$y = 0.28928571x + 74.07142857$.

b. $y = 0.28928571x + 74.07142857$
$y = 0.28928571(75) + 74.07142857 \approx 95.8$
When the relative humidity is 75, the apparent temperature is 95.8°F.

Chapter Test

1. $P_1(-2, 6), P_2(-1, 4)$

$$m = \dfrac{y_2 - y_1}{x_2 - x_1} = \dfrac{4 - 6}{-1 - (-2)} = \dfrac{-2}{1} = -2$$

The slope is -2.

2. $P_1(-4, 3), P_2(-8, 3)$

$$m = \dfrac{y_2 - y_1}{x_2 - x_1} = \dfrac{3 - 3}{-8 - (-4)} = \dfrac{0}{-4} = 0$$

The slope is 0.

3.

4.

5.

6.

7. $3x - 4y = 8$
$$-4y = -3x + 8$$
$$y = \frac{3}{4}x - 2$$

8. $6x - y > 6$
$$-y > -6x + 6$$
$$y < 6x - 6$$

9. $y = -\frac{5}{3}x + b$
$$-4 = -\frac{5}{3}(0) + b$$
$$-4 = b$$
$$y = -\frac{5}{3}x - 4$$

10. $y = \frac{1}{2}x + b$
$$-2 = \frac{1}{2}(3) + b$$
$$-\frac{7}{2} = b$$
$$y = \frac{1}{2}x - \frac{7}{2}$$

11. $m = \dfrac{y_2 - y_1}{x_2 - x_1} = \dfrac{0 - 1}{-1 - 0} = \dfrac{-1}{-1} = 1$
$$y - y_1 = m(x - x_1)$$
$$y - 1 = 1(x - 0)$$
$$y - 1 = x$$
$$y = x + 1$$

12. $m = \dfrac{y_2 - y_1}{x_2 - x_1} = \dfrac{8 - (-2)}{-4 - 4} = \dfrac{10}{-8} = -\dfrac{5}{4}$
$$y - y_1 = m(x - x_1)$$
$$y - (-2) = -\frac{5}{4}(x - 4)$$
$$y + 2 = -\frac{5}{4}x + 5$$
$$y = -\frac{5}{4}x + 3$$

13. To determine whether the lines are parallel, find the slope of each line.
Slope between $(3, 3)$ and $(-3, 7)$:
$$m = \frac{7 - 3}{-3 - 3} = \frac{4}{-6} = -\frac{2}{3}$$
Slope between $(6, -5)$ and $(-6, 3)$:
$$m = \frac{3 - (-5)}{-6 - 6} = \frac{8}{-12} = -\frac{2}{3}$$
The slopes are equal. Yes, the lines are parallel.

14. $4x - y = 2$
$$-y = -4x + 2$$
$$y = 4x - 2$$
$$m = 4$$
$$y - y_1 = m(x - x_1)$$
$$y - 1 = 4(x - (-3))$$
$$y - 1 = 4x + 12$$
$$y = 4x + 13$$
The equation of the line is $y = 4x + 13$.

15. To determine whether the lines are perpendicular, find the slope of each line.
Slope between $(4, 1)$ and $(-2, 4)$:
$$m = \frac{4 - 1}{-2 - 4} = \frac{3}{-6} = -\frac{1}{2}$$
Slope between $(-1, -6)$ and $(3, 2)$:
$$m = \frac{2 - (-6)}{3 - (-1)} = \frac{8}{4} = 2$$
Find the product of the slopes:
$$\left(-\frac{1}{2}\right)(2) = -1$$

Yes, because the product of the slopes is -1, these two lines are perpendicular.

16. $y = 3x + 2$
$$m_1 = 3$$
$$m_1 \cdot m_2 = -1$$
$$3m_2 = -1$$
$$m_2 = -\frac{1}{3}$$
$$y - y_1 = m(x - x_1)$$
$$y - 4 = -\frac{1}{3}(x - 3)$$
$$y - 4 = -\frac{1}{3}x + 1$$
$$y = -\frac{1}{3}x + 5$$

The equation of the line is $y = -\frac{1}{4}x + 5$.

17. a. $m = \dfrac{23{,}000 - 20{,}000}{3 - 1} = \dfrac{3000}{2} = 1500$
$$y - y_1 = m(x - x_1)$$
$$y - 20{,}000 = 1500(x - 1)$$
$$y - 20{,}000 = 1500x - 1500$$
$$y = 1500x + 18{,}500$$

b. The slope of 1500 means that the profit is increasing by $1500 per month.

c. $y = 1500x + 18{,}500$
$$y = 1500(12) + 18{,}500$$
$$= 18{,}000 + 18{,}500$$
$$= 36{,}500$$
The profit in December will be $36,500.

18. $m = \dfrac{161 - 133}{5 - 1} = \dfrac{28}{4} = 7$

The prices are increasing 7 cents per month.

19. a. $m = \dfrac{2400 - 2500}{20 - 15} = \dfrac{-100}{5} = -20$

$$y - y_1 = m(x - x_1)$$
$$y - 2500 = -20(x - 15)$$
$$y - 2500 = -20x + 300$$
$$y = -20x + 2800$$

b. The slope of -20 means the metal is cooling $20°F$ per minute.

c. There are 120 minutes in 2 hours.
$$y = -20x + 2800$$
$$y = -20(120) + 2800$$
$$= -2400 + 2800$$
$$= 400$$
After 2 hours, the temperature will be $400°F$.

20. a. The regression line is

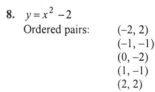

$y = 0.098x - 80.079$.

b. $y = 0.098x - 80.079$
$y = 0.098(2700) - 80.079 \approx 186$

The equation predicts that a car that weighs 2700 lb has an engine that delivers approximately 186 hp.

Cumulative Review Exercises

1. List all of the possibilities.

On	On	On	On
On	On	On	Off
On	On	Off	On
On	Off	On	On
On	Off	On	Off
Off	On	On	On
Off	On	On	Off
Off	On	Off	On

There are eight different ways the switches can be set.

2. $a @ b = a + ab$
$$\begin{aligned}(x @ y) @ z &= (x + xy) @ z \\ &= (2 + 2 \cdot 3) @ z \\ &= (2 + 6) @ z \\ &= 8 @ z \\ &= 8 + 8(z) \\ &= 8 + 8(4) \\ &= 8 + 32 \\ &= 40\end{aligned}$$

3. $E \cup F = \{-10, -5, 0, 5, 10, 15\}$
$E \cap F = \{0, 5, 10\}$

4. $2(a - d)^2 + (bc)^2$
$$\begin{aligned}2[-2 - (-4)]^2 + [(-1)(3)]^2 &= 2(-2 + 4)^2 + (-3)^2 \\ &= 2(2)^2 + 9 \\ &= 8 + 9 \\ &= 17\end{aligned}$$

5. Let $s = 3$ and $h = 5$.
$$V = \frac{1}{3}s^2 h$$
$$V = \frac{1}{3}(3)^2(5)$$
$$= 15$$
The volume is $15\ \text{ft}^3$.

6. $-3[4x - (2x - 1)] = -3[4x - 2x + 1]$
$$= -3[2x + 1]$$
$$= -6x - 3$$

7. one-fifth of a number: $\dfrac{1}{5}x$

product of twenty and one-fifth of a number: $20\left(\dfrac{1}{5}x\right)$

$$20\left(\dfrac{1}{5}x\right) = 4x$$

8. $y = x^2 - 2$
Ordered pairs: $(-2, 2)$
$(-1, -1)$
$(0, -2)$
$(1, -1)$
$(2, 2)$

9. Domain: $\{-1, 0, 1\}$
Range: $\{-1, 0, 1, 2\}$
No, the relation is not a function.

10. $p(s) = -2s^2 + 5s - 4$
$$p(-1) = -2(-1)^2 + 5(-1) - 4$$
$$= -2 - 5 - 4$$
$$= -11$$

11. *y*-intercept:

$$h(x) = x^2 - 2x - 3$$
$$h(0) = (0)^2 - 2(0) - 3 = -3$$

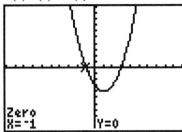

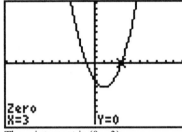

The *y*-intercept is $(0, -3)$.
The *x*-intercepts are $(-1, 0)$ and $(3, 0)$.

12. For $f(x) = 3x - 4$ and $g(x) = 6x + 5$

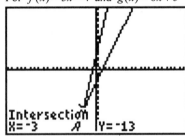

$$f(x) = 3x - 4$$
$$f(-3) = 3(-3) - 4 = -9 - 4 = -13$$

$$g(x) = 6x + 5$$
$$g(-3) = 6(-3) + 5 = -18 + 5 = -13$$

The input value is -3.

13.
$$3t - 8t = 0$$
$$-5t = 0$$
$$t = 0$$

14.
$$8 - z = 6z - 3(4 - z)$$
$$8 - z = 6z - 12 + 3z$$
$$8 - z = 9z - 12$$
$$8 = 10z - 12$$
$$20 = 10z$$
$$2 = z$$

15. Strategy
Pounds of coffee costing \$3.00: x
Pounds of coffee costing \$8.00: $80 - x$
Value of the \$3.00 coffee: $3x$
Value of the \$8.00 coffee: $8(80 - x)$
Value of the \$5.00 mixture: $5(80)$
The sum of the values of each part of the mixture equals the value of the mixture.
$$3x + 8(80 - x) = 5(80)$$

Solution
$$3x + 640 - 8x = 400$$
$$-5x + 640 = 400$$
$$-5x = -240$$
$$x = 48$$
$$80 - x = 32$$
The mixture consists of 48 lb of \$3 coffee and 32 lb of \$8 coffee.

16. Corresponding angles have the same measure. Therefore $m\angle b = 134°$. The sum of the measures of supplementary angles is 180°. Therefore:
$$a + b = 180$$
$$a + 134 = 180$$
$$a = 46$$
The measure of $\angle a$ is 46°.

17.
$$2 - 4(x + 1) \geq 11 + 3(2x - 6)$$
$$2 - 4x - 4 \geq 11 + 6x - 18$$
$$-4x - 2 \geq 6x - 7$$
$$-10x - 2 \geq -7$$
$$-10x \geq -5$$
$$x \leq \frac{1}{2}$$
$$\left(-\infty, \frac{1}{2}\right]$$

18.
$$2 + |3x + 1| = 7$$
$$|3x + 1| = 5$$

$$3x + 1 = 5 \qquad 3x + 1 = -5$$
$$3x = 4 \qquad 3x = -6$$
$$x = \frac{4}{3} \qquad x = -2$$

The solutions are -2 and $\frac{4}{3}$.

19. *x*-intercept: *y*-intercept:

$$4x - 6y = 12 \qquad 4x - 6y = 12$$
$$4x - 6(0) = 12 \qquad 4(0) - 6y = 12$$
$$4x = 12 \qquad -6y = 12$$
$$x = 3 \qquad y = -2$$
$$(3, 0) \qquad (0, -2)$$

20. $y = -\frac{2}{3}x + 6$

$m_1 = -\frac{2}{3}$

$m_1 \cdot m_2 = -1$

$-\frac{2}{3}m_2 = -1$

$m_2 = \frac{3}{2}$

$y - y_1 = m(x - x_1)$

$y - 5 = \frac{3}{2}(x - 2)$

$y - 5 = \frac{3}{2}x - 3$

$y = \frac{3}{2}x + 2$

The equation of the line is $y = \frac{3}{2}x + 2$.

Chapter 5: Systems of Linear Equations and Inequalities

Prep Test

1. $10\left(\dfrac{3}{5}x+\dfrac{1}{2}y\right)=\dfrac{30}{5}x+\dfrac{10}{2}y$
$\qquad = 6x+5y$

2. $3x+2y-z$
$3(-1)+2(4)-(-2)$
$=-3+8+2$
$=7$

3. $3x-2(-2)=4$
$\quad 3x+4=4$
$\qquad 3x=0$
$\qquad\; x=0$

4. $3x+4(-2x-5)=-5$
$\;\;3x-8x-20=-5$
$\qquad\quad -5x=15$
$\qquad\qquad x=-3$

5. $0.45x+0.06(-x+4000)=630$
$\;0.45x-0.06x+240=630$
$\qquad\qquad\;\; 0.39x=390$
$\qquad\qquad\qquad\;\; x=1000$

6. $y=\dfrac{1}{2}x-4$

7. $3x-2y=6$
$\quad -2y=-3x+6$
$\qquad\; y=\dfrac{3}{2}x-3$

8. $y>-\dfrac{3}{5}x+1$

Go Figure

If I have two more sisters than brothers and each of my sisters have two more sisters than brothers, then I must be a sister. If I have one brother, then I must have three sisters. So then my brother has zero brothers and four sisters.

Similarly, if I have two brothers, then I must have four sisters. Then my youngest brother has one brother and five sisters. He has four more sisters than brothers.

Section 5.1

1. Explanations will vary. For example, the solution is represented by an ordered pair (x, y).

3. Explanations will vary. For example, for a dependent system, the resulting equation is true; for an inconsistent system, the resulting equation is false.

5. $y=2x-1$
$y=-x+5$

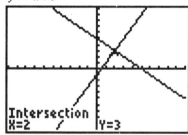

The solution is $(2, 3)$.

7. Solve each equation for y.
$\quad x+y=1 \qquad\quad 3x-y=-5$
$\qquad y=-x+1 \qquad -y=-3x-5$
$\qquad\qquad\qquad\qquad\quad\; y=3x+5$

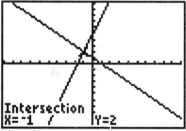

The solution is $(-1, 2)$.

9. Solve each equation for y.

$$-3x + 2y = 11 \qquad 2x + 5y = 18$$
$$2y = 3x + 11 \qquad 5y = -2x + 18$$
$$y = \frac{3}{2}x + \frac{11}{2} \qquad y = -\frac{2}{5}x + \frac{18}{5}$$

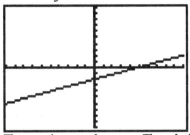

The solution is $(-1, 4)$.

11. Solve each equation for y.

$$2x - 5y = 10$$
$$-5y = -2x + 10 \qquad y = \frac{2}{5}x - 2$$
$$y = \frac{2}{5}x - 2$$

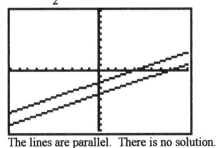

The equations are the same. The solution is

$$\left(x, \frac{2}{5}x - 2\right).$$

13. Solve each equation for y.

$$x - 2y = 8$$
$$-2y = -x + 8 \qquad y = \frac{1}{2}x - 2$$
$$y = \frac{1}{2}x - 4$$

The lines are parallel. There is no solution.

15. Solve each equation for y.

$$4x + 3y = -1 \qquad 2x - 2y = -11$$
$$3y = -4x - 1 \qquad -2y = -2x - 11$$
$$y = -\frac{4}{3}x - \frac{1}{3} \qquad y = x + \frac{11}{2}$$

The solution is $(-2.5, 3)$.

17. (1) $3x - 2y = 4$

(2) $x = 2$

Substitute the value of x into equation (1).

$$3x - 2y = 4$$
$$3(2) - 2y = 4$$
$$6 - 2y = 4$$
$$-2y = -2$$
$$y = 1$$

The solution is $(2, 1)$.

19. (1) $4x - 3y = 5$

(2) $y = 2x - 3$

Substitute $2x - 3$ for y in equation (1).

$$4x - 3y = 5$$
$$4x - 3(2x - 3) = 5$$
$$4x - 6x + 9 = 5$$
$$-2x + 9 = 5$$
$$-2x = -4$$
$$x = 2$$

Substitute into equation (2).

$$y = 2x - 3$$
$$y = 2(2) - 3$$
$$y = 4 - 3$$
$$y = 1$$

The solution is $(2, 1)$.

21. (1) $5x + 4y = -1$

(2) $y = 2 - 2x$

Substitute $2 - 2x$ for y in equation (1).

$$5x + 4y = -1$$
$$5x + 4(2 - 2x) = -1$$
$$5x + 8 - 8x = -1$$
$$-3x + 8 = -1$$
$$-3x = -9$$
$$x = 3$$

Substitute into equation (2).

$$y = 2 - 2x$$
$$y = 2 - 2(3)$$
$$y = 2 - 6$$
$$y = -4$$

The solution is $(3, -4)$.

23. (1) $2x + 2y = 7$
(2) $\quad\quad y = 4x + 1$
Substitute $4x + 1$ for y in equation (1).
$2x + 2y = 7$
$2x + 2(4x + 1) = 7$
$2x + 8x + 2 = 7$
$10x + 2 = 7$
$10x = 5$
$x = \dfrac{1}{2}$
Substitute into equation (2).
$y = 4x + 1$
$y = 4\left(\dfrac{1}{2}\right) + 1$
$y = 2 + 1$
$y = 3$
The solution is $\left(\dfrac{1}{2}, 3\right)$.

25. (1) $x + 3y = 5$
(2) $2x + 3y = 4$
Solve equation (1) for x.
$x + 3y = 5$
$x = -3y + 5$
Substitute into equation (2).
$2x + 3y = 4$
$2(-3y + 5) + 3y = 4$
$-6y + 10 + 3y = 4$
$-3y + 10 = 4$
$-3y = -6$
$y = 2$
Substitute into equation (1).
$x + 3y = 5$
$x + 3(2) = 5$
$x + 6 = 5$
$x = -1$
The solution is $(-1, 2)$.

27. (1) $3x + 5y = 0$
(2) $x - 4y = 0$
Solve equation (2) for x.
$x - 4y = 0$
$x = 4y$
Substitute into equation (1).
$3x + 5y = 0$
$3(4y) + 5y = 0$
$12y + 5y = 0$
$17y = 0$
$y = 0$
Substitute into equation (2).
$x - 4y = 0$
$x - 4(0) = 0$
$x = 0$
The solution is $(0, 0)$.

29. (1) $y = 3x + 2$
(2) $y = 2x + 3$
Substitute $2x + 3$ for y in equation (1).
$y = 3x + 2$
$2x + 3 = 3x + 2$
$2x = 3x - 1$
$-x = -1$
$x = 1$
Substitute into equation (2).
$y = 2x + 3$
$y = 2(1) + 3$
$y = 2 + 3$
$y = 5$
The solution is $(1, 5)$.

31. (1) $\quad\quad y = -2x + 1$
(2) $6x + 3y = 3$
Substitute the value of y into equation (2).
$6x + 3(-2x + 1) = 3$
$6x - 6x + 3 = 3$
$3 = 3$
The system of equations is dependent.
The solution is the ordered pairs $(x, -2x + 1)$

33. Strategy
Let x represent the cost per unit of electricity and y represent the cost per unit of gas. Because the homeowner used 400 units of electricity and 120 units of gas for a total of $147.20 the first month, one equation is $400x + 120y = 147.20$. An equation for the second month (350 units of electricity and 200 units of gas for a total cost of $144) is $350x + 200y = 144$.

Solution
(1) $400x + 120y = 147.20$
(2) $350x + 200y = 144$
Solve equation (2) for y.
$350x + 200y = 144$
$200y = -350x + 144$
$y = -1.75x + 0.72$
Substitute into equation (1).
$400x + 120(-1.75x + 0.72) = 147.20$
$400x - 210x + 86.4 = 147.20$
$190x = 60.8$
$x = 0.32$
Substitute into equation (2).
$350(0.32) + 200y = 144$
$112 + 200y = 144$
$200y = 32$
$y = 0.16$
The gas costs $0.16 per unit.

35. Strategy
Let the measure of one angle be x and the second angle be y. We are told that the measure of one angle is twice the measure of the second angle. Thus, $x = 2y$. The sum of the measures of the angles in this right triangle are $x + y + 90 = 180$. The system of equations is
$$x = 2y$$
$$x + y + 90 = 180$$

Solution
$$x + y + 90 = 180$$
$$2y + y + 90 = 180$$
$$3y + 90 = 180$$
$$3y = 90$$
$$y = 30$$
To find the value of x, substitute for y in the first equation:
$$x = 2y$$
$$x = 2(30)$$
$$x = 60$$
The measures of the two acute angles are 30 degrees and 60 degrees.

37. Strategy
Let x represent the amount of the first powder to be used and y represent the amount of the second powder to be used. First write an equation for vitamin B_1. The first powder is 25% vitamin B_1 and the second powder is 15% vitamin B_1. The total amount of vitamin B_1 needed is 117.5. An equation is $0.25x + 0.15y = 117.5$. Now write an equation for vitamin B_2. The first powder is 15% vitamin B_2 and the second powder is 20% vitamin B_2. The total amount of vitamin B_2 needed is 20. An equation is $0.15x + 0.20y = 120$.

Solution
(1) $0.25x + 0.15y = 117.5$
(2) $0.15x + 0.20y = 120$
Solve equation (2) for y.
$$0.15x + 0.20y = 120$$
$$0.2y = -0.15x + 120$$
$$y = -0.75x + 600$$
Substitute into equation (1).
$$0.25x + 0.15(-0.75x + 600) = 117.5$$
$$0.25x - 0.1125x + 90 = 117.5$$
$$0.1375x = 27.5$$
$$x = 200$$
Substitute into equation (2).
$$0.15(200) + 0.20y = 120$$
$$30 + 0.2y = 120$$
$$0.2y = 90$$
$$y = 450$$
The pharmacist should use 200 mg of the first powder and 450 mg of the second powder.

39. Strategy
The total interest on both investments is $870. Let x represent the amount invested in the 9.5% account and y represent the amount invested in the 7.5% account. The total of the two investments is $10,000, thus $x + y = 10,000$. The interest earned on the 9.5% account is $0.095x$ and the interest earned on the 7.5% account is $0.075y$. The total interest earned is $4860. Thus, $0.095x + 0.075y = 870$. The system of equations is
$$x + y = 10,000$$
$$0.095x + 0.075y = 870$$

Solution
$$x + y = 10,000$$
$$y = 10,000 - x$$
$$0.095x + 0.075y = 870$$
$$0.095x + 0.075(10,000 - x) = 870$$
$$0.095x + 750 - 0.075x = 870$$
$$750 - 0.02x = 870$$
$$-0.02x = -120$$
$$x = 6000$$
To find y, replace x by 6000 in the first equation and solve for y:
$$x + y = 10,000$$
$$6000 + y = 54,000$$
$$y = 4000$$
There is $6000 at 9.5% and $4000 at 7.5%.

Applying Concepts 5.1

41. Inconsistent equations have the same slope but different y-intercepts. Solve the two equations for y, and then set the slopes equal to each other.
(1) $6x - 3y = 4$
$$y = 2x - \frac{4}{3}$$
(2) $3x - ky = 1$
$$-ky = -3x + 1$$
$$y = \frac{3}{k}x - \frac{1}{k}$$
$$\frac{3}{k} = 2$$
$$3 = 2k$$
$$\frac{3}{2} = k$$

43. Inconsistent equations have the same slope but different y-intercepts. Solve the two equations for y, and then set the slopes equal to each other.
(1) $x = 2y + 2$
$$\frac{1}{2}x - 1 = y$$
(2) $kx - 8y = 2$
$$-8y = -kx + 2$$
$$y = \frac{k}{8}x - \frac{1}{4}$$
$$\frac{k}{8} = \frac{1}{2}$$
$$k = 4$$

45. $\dfrac{2}{a}+\dfrac{1}{b}=1$

$2\left(\dfrac{1}{a}\right)+\dfrac{1}{b}=1$

(1) $2x+y=1$

$\dfrac{8}{a}-\dfrac{2}{b}=0$

$8\left(\dfrac{1}{a}\right)-2\left(\dfrac{1}{b}\right)=0$

(2) $8x-2y=0$

Solve equation (1) for y.

$2x+y=1$

$y=-2x+1$

Substitute $-2x+1$ for y in equation (2).

$8x-2y=0$

$8x-2(-2x+1)=0$

$8x+4x-2=0$

$12x-2=0$

$12x=2$

$x=\dfrac{1}{6}$

Substitute into equation (1).

$2x+y=1$

$2\left(\dfrac{1}{6}\right)+y=1$

$\dfrac{1}{3}+y=1$

$y=\dfrac{2}{3}$

Replace x by $\dfrac{1}{a}$.

$x=\dfrac{1}{6}$

$\dfrac{1}{a}=\dfrac{1}{6}$

$6a\left(\dfrac{1}{a}\right)=6a\left(\dfrac{1}{6}\right)$

$6=a$

Replace y by $\dfrac{1}{b}$.

$y=\dfrac{2}{3}$

$\dfrac{1}{b}=\dfrac{2}{3}$

$3b\left(\dfrac{1}{b}\right)=3b\left(\dfrac{2}{3}\right)$

$3=2b$

$\dfrac{3}{2}=b$

The solution is $\left(6,\dfrac{3}{2}\right)$.

47. $\dfrac{3}{a}+\dfrac{4}{b}=-1$

$3\left(\dfrac{1}{a}\right)+4\left(\dfrac{1}{b}\right)=-1$

(1) $3x+4y=-1$

$\dfrac{1}{a}+\dfrac{6}{b}=2$

$\dfrac{1}{a}+6\left(\dfrac{1}{b}\right)=2$

(2) $x+6y=2$

Solve equation (1) for y.

$3x+4y=-1$

$4y=-3x-1$

$y=-\dfrac{3}{4}x-\dfrac{1}{4}$

Substitute $-\dfrac{3}{4}x-\dfrac{1}{4}$ for y in equation (2).

$x+6y=2$

$x+6\left(-\dfrac{3}{4}x-\dfrac{1}{4}\right)=2$

$x-\dfrac{9}{2}x-\dfrac{3}{2}=2$

$-\dfrac{7}{2}x-\dfrac{3}{2}=2$

$-\dfrac{7}{2}x=\dfrac{7}{2}$

$x=-1$

Substitute into equation (1).

$3x+4y=-1$

$3(-1)+4y=-1$

$-3+4y=-1$

$4y=2$

$y=\dfrac{1}{2}$

Replace x by $\dfrac{1}{a}$.

$x=-1$

$\dfrac{1}{a}=-1$

$-a\left(\dfrac{1}{a}\right)=-a(-1)$

$-1=a$

Replace y by $\dfrac{1}{b}$.

$y=\dfrac{1}{2}$

$\dfrac{1}{b}=\dfrac{1}{2}$

$2b\left(\dfrac{1}{b}\right)=2b\left(\dfrac{1}{2}\right)$

$2=b$

The solution is $(-1,2)$.

49. Because an absolute value can never be negative, the only way $|x+y-17|+|x-y-5|$ can equal zero is if each addend is equal to zero. Therefore, we have the system

   (1) $x+y-17=0 \Rightarrow x+y=17$
   (2) $x-y-5=0 \Rightarrow x-y=5$

Add the equations.
$$2x=22$$
$$x=11$$
Replace x in equation (1).
$$x+y=17$$
$$11+y=17$$
$$y=6$$
The numerical value of y is 6.

Section 5.2

1. The result of one of the steps will be an equation that is never true.

3. A three-dimensional coordinate system is one formed by three mutually perpendicular axes.

5. The planes intersect at one point.

7. Between 10% and 20% apple juice.

9. Since the boat is traveling with the current, the rates are added, resulting in a speed of 12 mph.

11.   (1) $x-y=5$
      (2) $x+y=7$
Eliminate y. Add the equations.
$$2x=12$$
$$x=6$$
Replace x in equation (1).
$$x-y=5$$
$$6-y=5$$
$$-y=-1$$
$$y=1$$
The solution is (6, 1).

13.   (1) $3x+y=7$
      (2) $x+2y=4$
Eliminate y.
$$-2(3x+y)=-2(7)$$
$$x+2y=4$$

$$-6x-2y=-14$$
$$x+2y=4$$
Add the equations.
$$-5x=-10$$
$$x=2$$
Replace x in equation (2).
$$x+2y=4$$
$$2+2y=4$$
$$2y=2$$
$$y=1$$
The solution is (2, 1).

15.   (1) $2x+5y=9$
      (2) $4x-7y=-16$
Eliminate x.
$$-2(2x+5y)=-2(9)$$
$$4x-7y=-16$$

$$-4x-10y=-18$$
$$4x-7y=-16$$
Add the equations.
$$-17y=-34$$
$$y=2$$
Replace y in equation (1).
$$2x+5y=9$$
$$2x+5(2)=9$$
$$2x+10=9$$
$$2x=-1$$
$$x=-\frac{1}{2}$$
The solution is $\left(-\frac{1}{2},2\right)$.

17.   (1) $3x-5y=7$
      (2) $x-2y=3$
Eliminate x.
$$3x-5y=7$$
$$-3(x-2y)=-3(3)$$

$$3x-5y=7$$
$$-3x+6y=-9$$
Add the equations.
$$y=-2$$
Replace y in equation (2).
$$x-2y=3$$
$$x-2(-2)=3$$
$$x+4=3$$
$$x=-1$$
The solution is (−1, −2).

19. (1) $4x + 4y = 5$

(2) $2x - 8y = -5$

Eliminate y.

$2(4x + 4y) = 2(5)$

$2x - 8y = -5$

$8x + 8y = 10$

$2x - 8y = -5$

Add the equations.

$10x = 5$

$x = \dfrac{1}{2}$

Replace x in equation (1).

$4x + 4y = 5$

$4\left(\dfrac{1}{2}\right) + 4y = 5$

$2 + 4y = 5$

$4y = 3$

$y = \dfrac{3}{4}$

The solution is $\left(\dfrac{1}{2}, \dfrac{3}{4}\right)$.

21. (1) $3x - 6y = 6$

(2) $9x - 3y = 8$

Eliminate y.

$3x - 6y = 6$

$-2(9x - 3y) = -2(8)$

$3x - 6y = 6$

$-18x + 6y = -16$

Add the equations.

$-15x = -10$

$x = \dfrac{2}{3}$

Replace x in the equation (1).

$3x - 6y = 6$

$3\left(\dfrac{2}{3}\right) - 6y = 6$

$2 - 6y = 6$

$-6y = 4$

$y = -\dfrac{2}{3}$

The solution is $\left(\dfrac{2}{3}, -\dfrac{2}{3}\right)$.

23. (1) $\dfrac{2}{3}x - \dfrac{1}{2}y = 3$

(2) $\dfrac{1}{3}x - \dfrac{1}{4}y = \dfrac{3}{2}$

Clear the fractions.

$6\left(\dfrac{2}{3}x - \dfrac{1}{2}y\right) = 6(3)$

$12\left(\dfrac{1}{3}x - \dfrac{1}{4}y\right) = 12\left(\dfrac{3}{2}\right)$

$4x - 3y = 18$

$4x - 3y = 18$

Eliminate x.

$-1(4x - 3y) = -1(18)$

$4x - 3y = 18$

$-4x + 3y = -18$

$4x - 3y = 18$

Add the equations.

$0 = 0$

This is a true equation. The equations are dependent. The solutions are the ordered pairs $\left(x, \dfrac{4}{3}x - 6\right)$.

25. (1) $\dfrac{3}{4}x + \dfrac{2}{5}y = -\dfrac{3}{20}$

(2) $\dfrac{3}{2}x - \dfrac{1}{4}y = \dfrac{3}{4}$

Clear the fractions.

$20\left(\dfrac{3}{4}x + \dfrac{2}{5}y\right) = 20\left(-\dfrac{3}{20}\right)$

$4\left(\dfrac{3}{2}x - \dfrac{1}{4}y\right) = 4\left(\dfrac{3}{4}\right)$

$15x + 8y = -3$

$6x - y = 3$

Eliminate y.

$15x + 8y = -3$

$8(6x - y) = 8(3)$

$15x + 8y = -3$

$48x - 8y = 24$

Add the equations.

$63x = 21$

$x = \dfrac{1}{3}$

Replace x in equation (2).

$\dfrac{3}{2}x - \dfrac{1}{4}y = \dfrac{3}{4}$

$\dfrac{3}{2}\left(\dfrac{1}{3}\right) - \dfrac{1}{4}y = \dfrac{3}{4}$

$\dfrac{1}{2} - \dfrac{1}{4}y = \dfrac{3}{4}$

$-\dfrac{1}{4}y = \dfrac{1}{4}$

$y = -1$

The solution is $\left(\dfrac{1}{3}, -1\right)$.

27. (1) $2x + 5y = 5x + 1$

(2) $3x - 2y = 3y + 3$

Write the equations in the form $Ax + By = C$.

$2x + 5y = 5x + 1$
$-3x + 5y = 1$

$3x - 2y = 3y + 3$
$3x - 5y = 3$

Solve the system.

$-3x + 5y = 1$
$3x - 5y = 3$

Add the equations.

$0 = 4$

This is not a true equation. The system of equations is inconsistent and therefore has no solution.

29. (1) $x + 2y - z = 1$

(2) $2x - y + z = 6$

(3) $x + 3y - z = 2$

Eliminate z. Add equations (1) and (2).

$x + 2y - z = 1$
$2x - y + z = 6$

(4) $3x + y = 7$

Add equations (2) and (3).

$2x - y + z = 6$
$x + 3y - z = 2$

(5) $3x + 2y = 8$

Multiply equation (4) by -1 and add to equation (5).

$-1(3x + y) = -1(7)$
$3x + 2y = 8$

$-3x - y = -7$
$3x + 2y = 8$

$y = 1$

Replace y by 1 in equation (4).

$3x + y = 7$
$3x + 1 = 7$
$3x = 6$
$x = 2$

Replace x by 2 and y by 1 in equation (1).

$x + 2y - z = 1$
$2 + 2(1) - z = 1$
$2 + 2 - z = 1$
$4 - z = 1$
$-z = -3$
$z = 3$

The solution is $(2, 1, 3)$.

31. (1) $2x - y + 2z = 7$

(2) $x + y + z = 2$

(3) $3x - y + z = 6$

Eliminate y. Add equations (1) and (2).

$2x - y + 2z = 7$
$x + y + z = 2$

$3x + 3z = 9$

Multiply both sides of the equation by $\frac{1}{3}$.

(4) $x + z = 3$

Add equations (2) and (3).

$x + y + z = 2$
$3x - y + z = 6$

$4x + 2z = 8$

Multiply both sides of the equation by $\frac{1}{2}$.

(5) $2x + z = 4$

Multiply equation (4) by -1 and add to equation (5).

$-1(x + z) = -1(3)$
$2x + z = 4$

$-x - z = -3$
$2x + z = 4$
$x = 1$

Replace x by 1 in equation (4).

$x + z = 3$
$1 + z = 3$
$z = 2$

Replace x by 1 and z by 2 in equation (2).

$x + y + z = 2$
$1 + y + 2 = 2$
$3 + y = 2$
$y = -1$

The solution is $(1, -1, 2)$.

33. (1) $3x - 2y + 3z = -4$

(2) $2x + y - 3z = 2$

(3) $3x + 4y + 5z = 8$

Eliminate y. Multiply equation (2) by 2 and add to equation (1).

$3x - 2y + 3z = -4$

$2(2x + y - 3z) = 2(2)$

$3x - 2y + 3z = -4$

$4x + 2y - 6z = 4$

(4) $7x - 3z = 0$

Multiply equation (2) by -4 and add to equation (3).

$-4(2x + y - 3z) = -4(2)$

$3x + 4y + 5z = 8$

$-8x - 4y + 12z = -8$

$3x + 4y + 5z = 8$

(5) $-5x + 17z = 0$

Multiply equation (4) by 5 and equation (5) by 7. Then add the equations.

$5(7x - 3z) = 5(0)$

$7(-5x + 17z) = 7(0)$

$35x - 15z = 0$

$-35x + 119z = 0$

$104z = 0$

$z = 0$

Replace z by 0 in equation (4).

$7x - 3z = 0$

$7x - 3(0) = 0$

$7x = 0$

$x = 0$

Replace x by 0 and z by 0 in equation (2).

$2x + y - 3z = 2$

$2(0) + y - 3(0) = 2$

$y = 2$

The solution is $(0, 2, 0)$.

35. (1) $2x + 4y - 2z = 3$

(2) $x + 3y + 4z = 1$

(3) $x + 2y - z = 4$

Eliminate x. Multiply equation (2) by -2 and add to equation (1).

$2x + 4y - 2z = 3$

$-2(x + 3y + 4z) = -2(1)$

$2x + 4y - 2z = 3$

$-2x - 6y - 8z = -2$

(4) $-2y - 10z = 1$

Multiply equation (2) by -1 and add to equation (3).

$-1(x + 3y + 4z) = -1(1)$

$x + 2y - z = 4$

$-x - 3y - 4z = -1$

$x + 2y - z = 4$

(5) $-y - 5z = 3$

Multiply equation (5) by -2 and add to equation (4).

$-2y - 10z = 1$

$-2(-y - 5z) = -2(3)$

$-2y - 10z = 1$

$2y + 10z = -6$

$0 = -5$

This is not a true equation. The system of equations is inconsistent and therefore has no solution.

37.
(1) $3x + 2y - 3z = 8$
(2) $2x + 3y + 2z = 10$
(3) $4x + 3y + 5z = 28$

Eliminate z. Multiply equation (1) by 2 and equation (2) by 3.
Then add the equations.
$2(3x + 2y - 3z) = 2(8)$
$3(2x + 3y + 2z) = 3(10)$

$6x + 4y - 6z = 16$
$6x + 9y + 6z = 30$

(4) $12x + 13y = 46$
Multiply equation (2) by 5 and equation (3) by –2. Add to equations.
$5(2x + 3y + 2z) = 5(10)$
$-2(4x + 3y + 5z) = -2(28)$

$10x + 15y + 10z = 50$
$-8x - 6y - 10z = -56$

(5) $2x + 9y = -6$
Multiply equation (5) by –6 and add to equation (4).
$12x + 13y = 46$
$-6(2x + 9y) = -6(-6)$

$12x + 13y = 46$
$-12x - 54y = 36$

$-41y = 82$
$y = -2$
Replace y by –2 in equation (5).
$2x + 9y = -6$
$2x + 9(-2) = -6$
$2x - 18 = -6$
$2x = 12$
$x = 6$
Replace x by 6 and y by –2 in equation (3).
$4x + 3y + 5z = 28$
$4(6) + 3(-2) + 5z = 28$
$24 - 6 + 5z = 28$
$5z = 10$
$z = 2$
The solution is $(6, -2, 2)$.

39.
(1) $2x - 3y + 7z = 0$
(2) $4x - 5y + 2z = -11$
(3) $x - 2y + 3z = -1$

Eliminate x. Multiply equation (3) by –2 and add to equation (1).
$2x - 3y + 7z = 0$
$-2(x - 2y + 3z) = -2(-1)$

$2x - 3y + 7z = 0$
$-2x + 4y - 6z = 2$

(4) $y + z = 2$
Multiply equation (1) by –2 and add to equation (2).
$-2(2x - 3y + 7z) = 2(0)$
$4x - 5y + 2z = -11$

$-4x + 6y - 14z = 0$
$4x - 5y + 2z = -11$

(5) $y - 12z = -11$
Multiply equation (4) by –1 and add to equation (5).
$-1(y + z) = -1(2)$
$y - 12z = -11$

$-y - z = -2$
$y - 12z = -11$

$-13z = -13$
$z = 1$
Replace z by 1 in equation (4).
$y + z = 2$
$y + 1 = 2$
$y = 1$
Replace y by 1 and z by 1 in equation (1).
$2x - 3y + 7z = 0$
$2x - 3(1) + 7(1) = 0$
$2x - 3 + 7 = 0$
$2x + 4 = 0$
$2x = -4$
$x = -2$
The solution is $(-2, 1, 1)$.

41. (1) $2x + y - z = 5$

(2) $x + 3y + z = 14$

(3) $3x - y + 2z = 1$

Eliminate z. Add equations (1) and (2).

$2x + y - z = 5$

$x + 3y + z = 14$

(4) $3x + 4y = 19$

Multiply equation (1) by 2 and add to equation (3).

$2(2x + y - z) = 2(5)$

$3x - y + 2z = 1$

$4x + 2y - 2z = 10$

$3x - y + 2z = 1$

(5) $7x + y = 11$

Multiply equation (5) by –4 and add to equation (4).

$3x + 4y = 19$

$-4(7x + y) = -4(11)$

$3x + 4y = 19$

$-28x - 4y = -44$

$-25x = -25$

$x = 1$

Replace x by 1 in equation (5).

$7x + y = 11$

$7(1) + y = 11$

$7 + y = 11$

$y = 4$

Replace x by 1 and y by 4 in equation (1).

$2x + y - z = 5$

$2(1) + 4 - z = 5$

$2 + 4 - z = 5$

$6 - z = 5$

$-z = -1$

$z = 1$

The solution is $(1, 4, 1)$.

43. (1) $5x + 3y - z = 5$

(2) $3x - 2y + 4z = 13$

(3) $4x + 3y + 5z = 22$

Eliminate z. Multiply equation (1) by 4 and add to equation (2).

$4(5x + 3y - z) = 4(5)$

$3x - 2y + 4z = 13$

$20x + 12y - 4z = 20$

$3x - 2y + 4z = 13$

(4) $23x + 10y = 33$

Multiply equation (1) by 5 and add to equation (3).

$5(5x + 3y - z) = 5(5)$

$4x + 3y + 5z = 22$

$25x + 15y - 5z = 25$

$4x + 3y + 5z = 22$

(5) $29x + 18y = 47$

Multiply equation (4) by –18 and equation (5) by 10. Then add the equations.

$-18(23x + 10y) = -18(33)$

$10(29x + 18y) = 10(47)$

$-414x - 180y = -594$

$290x + 180y = 470$

$-124x = -124$

$x = 1$

Replace x by 1 in equation (4).

$23x + 10y = 33$

$23(1) + 10y = 33$

$23 + 10y = 33$

$10y = 10$

$y = 1$

Replace x by 1 and y by 1 in equation (1).

$5x + 3y - z = 5$

$5(1) + 3(1) - z = 5$

$5 + 3 - z = 5$

$8 - z = 5$

$-z = -3$

$z = 3$

The solution is $(1, 1, 3)$.

45. Strategy

Let p represent the rate of the plane in calm conditions and let w represent the rate of the wind. Using these variables and the equation $d = rt$, write equations for the distance traveled by the plane with and against the wind. With the wind, the rate of the plane is $p + w$. Against the wind, the rate of the plane is $p - w$.

Solution

$$2(p + w) = 600$$
$$3(p - w) = 600$$
$$p + w = 300$$
$$p - w = 200$$
$$2p = 500$$
$$p = 250$$

$$2(250 + w) = 600$$
$$500 + 2w = 600$$
$$2w = 100$$
$$w = 50$$

The rate of the plane in calm air is 250 mph and the rate of the wind is 50 mph.

47. Strategy

Let x represent the rate of the boat in calm water and y represent the rate of the current. Then
Rate of boat with current: $x + y$
Rate of boat against current: $x - y$
The distance traveled with the current is 88 kilometers. The distance traveled against the current is 64 kilometers. Use the equation $d = rt$ to express the distances traveled with and against the current as the two equations of a system.

Solution

$$4(x + y) = 88$$
$$4(x - y) = 64$$

$$\frac{1}{4} \cdot 4(x + y) = \frac{1}{4} \cdot 88$$
$$\frac{1}{4} \cdot 4(x - y) = \frac{1}{4} \cdot 64$$

$$x + y = 22$$
$$x - y = 16$$

$$2x = 38$$
$$x = 19$$

$$x + y = 22$$
$$19 + y = 22$$
$$y = 3$$

The rate of the boat in calm water is 19 kilometers per hour. The rate of the current is 3 kilometers per hour.

49. Strategy

Let x represent the rate of the boat in calm water and y represent the rate of the current. Then
Rate of boat with current: $x + y$
Rate of boat against current: $x - y$
The distance traveled with the current is 54 miles. The distance traveled against the current is 54 miles. Use the equation $d = rt$ to express the distances traveled with and against the current as the two equations of a system.

Solution

$$3(x + y) = 54$$
$$3.6(x - y) = 54$$

$$\frac{1}{3} \cdot 3(x + y) = \frac{1}{3} \cdot 54$$
$$\frac{1}{3.6} \cdot 3.6(x - y) = \frac{1}{3.6} \cdot 54$$

$$x + y = 18$$
$$x - y = 15$$

$$2x = 33$$
$$x = 16.5$$

$$x + y = 18$$
$$16.5 + y = 18$$
$$y = 1.5$$

The rate of the boat in calm water is 16.5 mph. The rate of the current is 1.5 mph.

51. Strategy

Let x represent the percent concentration of the resulting alloy.

Solution
$$0.70(25) + 0.15(50) = x(25 + 50)$$
$$17.5 + 7.5 = 75x$$
$$25 = 75x$$
$$0.33\overline{3} = x$$

The percent concentration of the resulting alloy is $33\frac{1}{3}\%$.

53. Strategy

Let x represent the number of milliliters of 3% peroxide solution and let y represent the number of milliliters of 12% peroxide solution. The total of the two solutions is 50 milliliters. This gives us the equation $x + y = 50$. The quantity of peroxide in each type of solution is $0.03x$ and $0.12y$. The quantity of peroxide in the resulting solution is $0.084(50) = 4.2$ milliliters. This gives us $0.03x + 0.12y = 4.2$.

Solution

$$-0.12(x + y) = -0.12(50)$$
$$0.03x + 0.12y = 4.2$$

$$-0.12x - 0.12y = -6$$
$$0.03x + 0.12y = 4.2$$

$$-0.09x = -1.8$$
$$x = 20$$

$$20 + y = 50$$
$$y = 30$$

The mixture should be made with 20 milliliters of 3% solution and 30 milliliters of 12% solution.

55. Strategy

Let x represent the number of grams of 25% gold alloy and let y represent the number of grams of 100% gold alloy (pure gold). The resulting alloy is 120 grams. This gives us the equation $x + y = 120$. The quantity of gold in each type of alloy is $0.25x$ and y. The quantity of gold in the resulting alloy is $0.75(120) = 90$ grams. This gives us $0.25x + y = 90$.

Solution

$$-1(x + y) = -1(120)$$
$$0.25x + y = 90$$

$$-x - y = -120$$
$$0.25x + y = 90$$

$$-0.75x = -30$$
$$x = 40$$

$$40 + y = 120$$
$$y = 80$$

The goldsmith should use 40 grams of the 25% alloy and 80 grams of the pure gold.

57. Strategy

Cost of a Model II computer: x
Cost of a Model VI computer: y
Cost of a Model IX computer: z
The bill for the first shipment was $114,000.
The bill for the second shipment was $72,000.
The bill for the third shipment was $81,000.

$$4x + 6y + 10z = 114,000$$
$$8x + 3y + 5z = 72,000$$
$$2x + 9y + 5z = 81,000$$

Solution

$$4x + 6y + 10z = 114,000$$
$$8x + 3y + 5z = 72,000$$
$$2x + 9y + 5z = 81,000$$

$$4x + 6y + 10z = 114,000$$
$$-2(8x + 3y + 5z) = -2(72,000)$$

$$4x + 6y + 10z = 114,000$$
$$-16x - 6y - 10z = -144,000$$

$$-12x = -30,000$$
$$x = 2500$$

$$4x + 6y + 10z = 114,000$$
$$-2(2x + 9y + 5z) = -2(81,000)$$

$$4x + 6y + 10z = 114,000$$
$$-4x - 18y - 10z = 162,000$$

$$-12y = -48,000$$
$$y = 4000$$

The manufacturer charges $4000 for a Model VI computer.

59. Strategy
Amount earning 9% interest: x
Amount earning 7% interest: y
Amount earning 5% interest: z
The total amount deposited is $18,000.
The total interest earned is $1340.
$$x + y + z = 18,000$$
$$x = 2z$$
$$0.09x + 0.07y + 0.05z = 1340$$

Solution
$$x + y + z = 18,000$$
$$x = 2z$$
$$0.09x + 0.07y + 0.05z = 1340$$

$$x + y + z = 18,000$$
$$2z + y + z = 18,000$$
$$3z + y = 18,000$$

$$0.09x + 0.07y + 0.05z = 1340$$
$$0.09(2z) + 0.07y + 0.05z = 1340$$
$$0.18z + 0.07y + 0.05z = 1340$$
$$0.23z + 0.07y = 1340$$

$$0.23z + 0.07y = 1340$$
$$-0.07(3z + y) = -0.07(18,000)$$

$$0.23z + 0.07y = 1340$$
$$-0.21z - 0.07y = -1260$$
$$0.02z = 80$$
$$z = 4000$$

$$x = 2z$$
$$x = 2(4000)$$
$$x = 8000$$

$$x + y + z = 18,000$$
$$8000 + y + 4000 = 18,000$$
$$12,000 + y = 18,000$$
$$y = 6000$$

The amounts deposited in each account are $8000 at 9% interest, $6000 at 7% interest, and $4000 at 5% interest.

61. Strategy
Amount invested at 9%: x
Amount invested at 12%: y
Amount invested at 8%: z
The total amount invested is $33,000.
$$x + y + z = 33,000$$
$$0.09x + 0.12y + 0.08z = 3290$$
$$y = x + z - 5000$$

Solution
$$x + y + z = 33,000$$
$$x + (x + z - 5000) + z = 33,000$$
$$2x + 2z - 5000 = 33,000$$
$$2x + 2z = 38,000$$

$$0.09x + 0.12y + 0.08z = 3290$$
$$0.09x + 0.12(x + z - 5000) + 0.08z = 3290$$
$$0.09x + 0.12x + 0.12z - 600 + 0.08z = 3290$$
$$0.21x + 0.2z - 600 = 3290$$
$$0.21x + 0.2z = 3890$$

$$2x + 2z = 38,000$$
$$-10(0.21x + 0.2z) = -10(3890)$$

$$2x + 2z = 38,000$$
$$-2.1x - 2z = -38,900$$
$$-0.1x = -900$$
$$x = 9000$$

$$2x + 2z = 38,000$$
$$2(9000) + 2z = 38,000$$
$$18,000 + 2z = 38,000$$
$$2z = 20,000$$
$$z = 10,000$$

$$y = x + z - 5000$$
$$y = 9000 + 10,000 - 5000$$
$$y = 14,000$$

The amounts invested are $9000 at 9% interest, $14,000 at 12% interest, and $10,000 at 8% interest.

63. Strategy

x = number of 100 g portions of Food Type I
y = number of 100 g portions of Food Type II
z = number of 100 g portions of Food Type III.
The information from the problem gives us a system of three equations in three unknowns for the first diet:

$$60x + 10y + 70z = 220$$
$$10x + 4y = 18$$
$$20x + 60y + 10z = 160$$

The information from the problem gives us a system of three equations in three unknowns for the second diet:

$$60x + 10y + 70z = 210$$
$$10x + 4y = 28$$
$$20x + 60y + 10z = 170$$

Solution
First diet:

$$60x + 10y + 70z = 220$$
$$10x + 4y = 18$$
$$20x + 60y + 10z = 160$$

$$60x + 10y + 70z = 220$$
$$-7(20x + 60y + 10z) = -7(160)$$

$$60x + 10y + 70z = 220$$
$$-140x - 420y - 70z = -1120$$

$$-80x - 410y = -900$$

$$10x + 4y = 18$$
$$10x = -4y + 18$$
$$x = -0.4y + 1.8$$

$$-80x - 410y = -900$$
$$-80(-0.4y + 1.8) - 410y = -900$$
$$32y - 144 - 410y = -900$$
$$-378y = -756$$
$$y = 2$$

$$x = -0.4(2) + 1.8 = 1$$
$$20x + 60y + 10z = 160$$
$$20(1) + 60(2) + 10z = 160$$
$$20 + 120 + 10z = 160$$
$$10z = 20$$
$$z = 2$$

The first diet, 100 grams of Food Type I, 200 grams of Food Type II, and 200 grams of Food Type III are required.

Second diet:

$$60x + 10y + 70z = 210$$
$$10x + 4y = 28$$
$$20x + 60y + 10z = 170$$

$$60x + 10y + 70z = 210$$
$$-7(20x + 60y + 10z) = -7(170)$$

$$60x + 10y + 70z = 210$$
$$-140x - 420y - 70z = -1190$$

$$-80x - 410y = -980$$

$$10x + 4y = 28$$
$$10x = -4y + 28$$
$$x = -0.4y + 2.8$$

$$-80x - 410y = -980$$
$$-80(-0.4y + 2.8) - 410y = -980$$
$$32y - 224 - 410y = -980$$
$$-378y = -756$$
$$y = 2$$

$$x = -0.4(2) + 2.8 = 2$$
$$20x + 60y + 10z = 170$$
$$20(2) + 60(2) + 10z = 170$$
$$40 + 120 + 10z = 170$$
$$10z = 10$$
$$z = 1$$

The second diet, 200 grams of Food Type I, 200 grams of Food Type II, and 100 grams of Food Type III are required.

Applying Concepts 5.2

65. $Ax - 4y = 9$
$4x + By = -1$

Because $(-1, -3)$ is the solution of the system, substitute -1 for x and -3 for y in the system of equations. Then solve for the values of A and B.

$$A(-1) - 4(-3) = 9$$
$$4(-1) + B(-3) = -1$$

$$-A + 12 = 9$$
$$-A = -3$$
$$A = 3$$

$$-4 - 3B = -1$$
$$-3B = 3$$
$$B = -1$$

The value of A is 3 and the value of B is -1.

67. Because the graphs all intersect at the same point, the point of intersection of the graphs of the first two equations is a solution of the third equation.

$$3x - 2y = -2$$
$$2x - y = 0$$

$$3x - 2y = -2$$
$$-2(2x - y) = -2(0)$$

$$3x - 2y = -2$$
$$-4x + 2y = 0$$
$$\overline{-x = -2}$$
$$x = 2$$

$$2(2) - y = 0$$
$$4 - y = 0$$
$$-y = -4$$
$$y = 4$$

A solution of the third equation is $(2, 4)$.
Substitute 2 for x and 4 for y in the equation and solve for A:

$$Ax + y = 8$$
$$A(2) + 4 = 8$$
$$2A + 4 = 8$$
$$2A = 4$$
$$A = 2$$

69. (1) $\quad 2x + y - z = 13$
(2) $\quad x - 2y + z = -4$

Eliminate z by adding (1) and (2):

$$2x + y - z = 13$$
$$x - 2y + z = -4$$
$$\overline{3x - y = 9}$$

$$3x = y + 9$$
$$x = \frac{1}{3}y + 3$$

Now let $y = 3$:

$$x = \frac{1}{3}y + 3 = \frac{1}{3}(3) + 3 = 1 + 3 = 4$$

Eliminate x by multiplying (2) by -2 and adding to (1):

$$2x + y - z = 13$$
$$-2x + 4y - 2z = 8$$
$$\overline{5y - 3z = 21}$$

$$5y - 21 = 3z$$
$$\frac{5}{3}y - 7 = z$$

Let $y = 3$:

$$z = \frac{5}{3}y - 7 = \frac{5}{3}(3) - 7 = 5 - 7 = -2$$

The value of $(x - z)$ is $4 - (-2) = 4 + 2 = 6$.

71. (1) $\quad x - 3y - 2z = A^2$
(2) $\quad 2x - 5y + Az = 9$
(3) $\quad 2x - 8y + z = 18$

Eliminate x by multiplying (1) by -2 and adding to (2):

$$-2(x - 3y - 2z) = -2A^2$$

$$-2x + 6y + 4z = -2A^2$$
$$2x - 5y + Az = 9$$
$$\overline{y + (A + 4)z = 9 - 2A^2} \quad (4)$$

Eliminate x by multiplying (3) by -1 and adding to (2):

$$-1(2x - 8y + z) = -1(18)$$

$$-2x + 8y - z = -18$$
$$2x - 5y + Az = 9$$
$$\overline{3y + (A - 1)z = -9} \quad (5)$$

Solve (4) for y and substitute into (5):

$$y + (A + 4)z = 9 - 2A^2$$
$$y = -(A + 4)z + 9 - 2A^2$$
$$3y + (A - 1)z = -9$$
$$3[-(A + 4)z + 9 - 2A^2] + (A - 1)z = -9$$
$$-3(A + 4)z + 27 - 6A^2 + (A - 1)z = -9$$
$$(-2A - 13)z + 27 - 6A^2 = -9$$
$$(-2A - 13)z = -36 - 6A^2$$
$$(2A + 13)z = 6A^2 + 36$$

If the system has a unique solution, then the coefficient of z in this last equation would be anything but 0. Therefore, the system has a unique solution if

$$2A + 13 \neq 0$$
$$2A \neq -13$$
$$A \neq -\frac{13}{2}$$

Section 5.3

1. A matrix is a rectangular array of numbers.

3. 1. Interchange two rows.
   2. Multiply a row by a constant.
   3. Replace a row by the sum of that row and a nonzero multiple of another row.

5. **b** is not in row echelon form.

7. $\begin{bmatrix} 1 & 4 & -1 \\ -3 & -13 & 7 \end{bmatrix}$

$$3R_1 + R_2 \rightarrow \begin{bmatrix} 1 & 4 & -1 \\ 0 & -1 & 4 \end{bmatrix}$$

$$-1R_2 \rightarrow \begin{bmatrix} 1 & 4 & -1 \\ 0 & 1 & -4 \end{bmatrix}$$

9. $\begin{bmatrix} 4 & 2 & -2 \\ 7 & 4 & -1 \end{bmatrix}$

$$\frac{1}{4}R_1 \rightarrow \begin{bmatrix} 1 & \frac{1}{2} & -\frac{1}{2} \\ 7 & 4 & -1 \end{bmatrix}$$

$$-7R_1 + R_2 \rightarrow \begin{bmatrix} 1 & \frac{1}{2} & -\frac{1}{2} \\ 0 & \frac{1}{2} & \frac{5}{2} \end{bmatrix}$$

$$2R_2 \rightarrow \begin{bmatrix} 1 & \frac{1}{2} & -\frac{1}{2} \\ 0 & 1 & 5 \end{bmatrix}$$

11. $\begin{bmatrix} 2 & 5 & -4 \\ 3 & 1 & 2 \end{bmatrix}$

$$\frac{1}{2}R_1 \rightarrow \begin{bmatrix} 1 & \frac{5}{2} & -2 \\ 3 & 1 & 2 \end{bmatrix}$$

$$-3R_1 + R_2 \rightarrow \begin{bmatrix} 1 & \frac{5}{2} & -2 \\ 0 & -\frac{13}{2} & 8 \end{bmatrix}$$

$$-\frac{2}{13}R_2 \rightarrow \begin{bmatrix} 1 & \frac{5}{2} & -2 \\ 0 & 1 & -\frac{16}{13} \end{bmatrix}$$

13. $\begin{bmatrix} 1 & 2 & 2 & -1 \\ -4 & -10 & -1 & 3 \\ 3 & 4 & 2 & -2 \end{bmatrix}$

$$\begin{matrix} 4R_1 + R_2 \rightarrow \\ -3R_1 + R_3 \rightarrow \end{matrix} \begin{bmatrix} 1 & 2 & 2 & -1 \\ 0 & -2 & 7 & -1 \\ 0 & -2 & -3 & 1 \end{bmatrix}$$

$$-\frac{1}{2}R_2 \rightarrow \begin{bmatrix} 1 & 2 & 2 & -1 \\ 0 & 1 & -\frac{7}{2} & \frac{1}{2} \\ 0 & -2 & -3 & 1 \end{bmatrix}$$

$$2R_2 + R_3 \rightarrow \begin{bmatrix} 1 & 2 & 2 & -1 \\ 0 & 1 & -\frac{7}{2} & \frac{1}{2} \\ 0 & 0 & -11 & 2 \end{bmatrix}$$

$$-\frac{1}{11}R_3 \rightarrow \begin{bmatrix} 1 & 2 & 2 & -1 \\ 0 & 1 & -\frac{7}{2} & \frac{1}{2} \\ 0 & 0 & 1 & -\frac{2}{11} \end{bmatrix}$$

15. $\begin{bmatrix} -2 & 6 & -1 & 3 \\ 1 & -2 & 2 & 1 \\ 3 & -6 & 7 & 6 \end{bmatrix}$

$$-\frac{1}{2}R_1 \rightarrow \begin{bmatrix} 1 & -3 & \frac{1}{2} & -\frac{3}{2} \\ 1 & -2 & 2 & 1 \\ 3 & -6 & 7 & 6 \end{bmatrix}$$

$$\begin{matrix} -1R_1 + R_2 \rightarrow \\ -3R_1 + R_3 \rightarrow \end{matrix} \begin{bmatrix} 1 & -3 & \frac{1}{2} & -\frac{3}{2} \\ 0 & 1 & \frac{3}{2} & \frac{5}{2} \\ 0 & 3 & \frac{11}{2} & \frac{21}{2} \end{bmatrix}$$

$$-3R_2 + R_3 \rightarrow \begin{bmatrix} 1 & -3 & \frac{1}{2} & -\frac{3}{2} \\ 0 & 1 & \frac{3}{2} & \frac{5}{2} \\ 0 & 0 & 1 & 3 \end{bmatrix}$$

17. $\begin{bmatrix} 4 & -6 & 9 & 4 \\ 2 & 2 & 1 & -5 \\ 3 & 3 & -5 & 1 \end{bmatrix}$

$\frac{1}{4}R_1 \rightarrow \begin{bmatrix} 1 & -\frac{3}{2} & \frac{9}{4} & 1 \\ 2 & 2 & 1 & -5 \\ 3 & 3 & -5 & 1 \end{bmatrix}$

$\begin{matrix} -2R_1 + R_2 \rightarrow \\ -3R_1 + R_3 \rightarrow \end{matrix} \begin{bmatrix} 1 & -\frac{3}{2} & \frac{9}{4} & 1 \\ 0 & 5 & -\frac{7}{2} & -7 \\ 0 & \frac{15}{2} & -\frac{47}{4} & -2 \end{bmatrix}$

$R_2 \leftrightarrow R_3 \begin{bmatrix} 1 & -\frac{3}{2} & \frac{9}{4} & 1 \\ 0 & \frac{15}{2} & -\frac{47}{4} & -2 \\ 0 & 5 & -\frac{7}{2} & -7 \end{bmatrix}$

$\frac{2}{15}R_2 \rightarrow \begin{bmatrix} 1 & -\frac{3}{2} & \frac{9}{4} & 1 \\ 0 & 1 & -\frac{47}{30} & -\frac{4}{15} \\ 0 & 5 & -\frac{7}{2} & -7 \end{bmatrix}$

$-5R_2 + R_3 \rightarrow \begin{bmatrix} 1 & -\frac{3}{2} & \frac{9}{4} & 1 \\ 0 & 1 & -\frac{47}{30} & -\frac{4}{15} \\ 0 & 0 & \frac{13}{3} & -\frac{17}{3} \end{bmatrix}$

$\frac{3}{13}R_3 \rightarrow \begin{bmatrix} 1 & -\frac{3}{2} & \frac{9}{4} & 1 \\ 0 & 1 & -\frac{47}{30} & -\frac{4}{15} \\ 0 & 0 & 1 & -\frac{17}{13} \end{bmatrix}$

19. Writing the augmented matrix as a system of equations,

$x - 3y + 2z = 4$
$y - 2z = 3$
$z = -1$

Using substitution,

$y - 2(-1) = 3$
$y = 1$
$x - 3(1) + 2(-1) = 4$
$x = 9$

The solution is $(9, 1, -1)$.

21. $2x + y = 3$
$x - 4y = 6$

$\begin{bmatrix} 2 & 1 & 3 \\ 1 & -4 & 6 \end{bmatrix}$

$R_1 \leftrightarrow R_2 \begin{bmatrix} 1 & -4 & 6 \\ 2 & 1 & 3 \end{bmatrix}$

$-2R_1 + R_2 \rightarrow \begin{bmatrix} 1 & -4 & 6 \\ 0 & 9 & -9 \end{bmatrix}$

$\frac{1}{9}R_2 \rightarrow \begin{bmatrix} 1 & -4 & 6 \\ 0 & 1 & -1 \end{bmatrix}$

$x - 4y = 6$
$y = -1$
$x - 4(-1) = 6$
$x + 4 = 6$
$x = 2$

The solution is $(2, -1)$.

23. $2x + 3y = 16$
$x - 4y = -14$

$\begin{bmatrix} 2 & 3 & 16 \\ 1 & -4 & -14 \end{bmatrix}$

$R_1 \leftrightarrow R_2 \begin{bmatrix} 1 & -4 & -14 \\ 2 & 3 & 16 \end{bmatrix}$

$-2R_1 + R_2 \rightarrow \begin{bmatrix} 1 & -4 & -14 \\ 0 & 11 & 44 \end{bmatrix}$

$\frac{1}{11}R_2 \rightarrow \begin{bmatrix} 1 & -4 & -14 \\ 0 & 1 & 4 \end{bmatrix}$

$x - 4y = -14$
$y = 4$
$x - 4(4) = -14$
$x - 16 = -14$
$x = 2$

The solution is $(2, 4)$.

25. $2y = 4 - 3x$
$y = 1 - 2x$

$3x + 2y = 4$
$2x + y = 1$

$\begin{bmatrix} 3 & 2 & | & 4 \\ 2 & 1 & | & 1 \end{bmatrix}$

$\frac{1}{3}R_1 \rightarrow \begin{bmatrix} 1 & \frac{2}{3} & | & \frac{4}{3} \\ 2 & 1 & | & 1 \end{bmatrix}$

$-2R_1 + R_2 \rightarrow \begin{bmatrix} 1 & \frac{2}{3} & | & \frac{4}{3} \\ 0 & -\frac{1}{3} & | & -\frac{5}{3} \end{bmatrix}$

$-3R_2 \rightarrow \begin{bmatrix} 1 & \frac{2}{3} & | & \frac{4}{3} \\ 0 & 1 & | & 5 \end{bmatrix}$

$x + \left(\frac{2}{3}\right)y = \frac{4}{3}$
$y = 5$

$x + \left(\frac{2}{3}\right)(5) = \frac{4}{3}$

$x + \frac{10}{3} = \frac{4}{3}$

$x = -2$

The solution is $(-2, 5)$.

27. $3x - 2y = -8$
$y = \frac{3}{2}x - 2$

$3x - 2y = -8$
$3x - 2y = 4$

$\begin{bmatrix} 3 & -2 & | & -8 \\ 3 & -2 & | & 4 \end{bmatrix}$

$\frac{1}{3}R_1 \rightarrow \begin{bmatrix} 1 & -\frac{2}{3} & | & -\frac{8}{3} \\ 3 & -2 & | & 4 \end{bmatrix}$

$-3R_1 + R_2 \rightarrow \begin{bmatrix} 1 & -\frac{2}{3} & | & -\frac{8}{3} \\ 0 & 0 & | & 12 \end{bmatrix}$

$x - \frac{2}{3}y = -\frac{8}{3}$
$0 = 12$

This is not a true equation. The system of equations is inconsistent.

29. $5x + 2y = 3$
$3x + 4y = 13$

$\begin{bmatrix} 5 & 2 & | & 3 \\ 3 & 4 & | & 13 \end{bmatrix}$

$\frac{1}{5}R_1 \rightarrow \begin{bmatrix} 1 & \frac{2}{5} & | & \frac{3}{5} \\ 3 & 4 & | & 13 \end{bmatrix}$

$-3R_1 + R_2 \rightarrow \begin{bmatrix} 1 & \frac{2}{5} & | & \frac{3}{5} \\ 0 & \frac{14}{5} & | & \frac{56}{5} \end{bmatrix}$

$\frac{5}{14}R_2 \rightarrow \begin{bmatrix} 1 & \frac{2}{5} & | & \frac{3}{5} \\ 0 & 1 & | & 4 \end{bmatrix}$

$x + \left(\frac{2}{5}\right)y = \frac{3}{5}$
$y = 4$

$x + \left(\frac{2}{5}\right)(4) = \frac{3}{5}$

$x + \frac{8}{5} = \frac{3}{5}$

$x = -1$

The solution is $(-1, 4)$.

31. $x - y - z = 0$
$3x - y + 5z = -10$
$x + y - 4z = 12$

$\begin{bmatrix} 1 & -1 & -1 & | & 0 \\ 3 & -1 & 5 & | & -10 \\ 1 & 1 & -4 & | & 12 \end{bmatrix}$

$\begin{matrix} -3R_1 + R_2 \rightarrow \\ -1R_1 + R_3 \rightarrow \end{matrix} \begin{bmatrix} 1 & -1 & -1 & | & 0 \\ 0 & 2 & 8 & | & -10 \\ 0 & 2 & -3 & | & 12 \end{bmatrix}$

$\frac{1}{2}R_2 \rightarrow \begin{bmatrix} 1 & -1 & -1 & | & 0 \\ 0 & 1 & 4 & | & -5 \\ 0 & 2 & -3 & | & 12 \end{bmatrix}$

$-2R_2 + R_3 \rightarrow \begin{bmatrix} 1 & -1 & -1 & | & 0 \\ 0 & 1 & 4 & | & -5 \\ 0 & 0 & -11 & | & -22 \end{bmatrix}$

$-\frac{1}{11}R_3 \rightarrow \begin{bmatrix} 1 & -1 & -1 & | & 0 \\ 0 & 1 & 4 & | & -5 \\ 0 & 0 & 1 & | & 2 \end{bmatrix}$

$x - y - z = 0$
$y + 4z = -5$
$z = -2$

$y + 4(-2) = -5$
$y - 8 = -5$
$y = 3$

$x - 3 - (-2) = 0$
$x - 3 + 2 = 0$
$x - 1 = 0$
$x = 1$

The solution is $(1, 3, -2)$.

33. $2x + y - 5z = 3$
$3x + 2y + z = 15$
$5x - y - z = 5$

$$\begin{bmatrix} 2 & 1 & -5 & | & 3 \\ 3 & 2 & 1 & | & 15 \\ 5 & -1 & -1 & | & 5 \end{bmatrix}$$

$\frac{1}{2}R_1 \rightarrow \begin{bmatrix} 1 & \frac{1}{2} & -\frac{5}{2} & | & \frac{3}{2} \\ 3 & 2 & 1 & | & 15 \\ 5 & -1 & -1 & | & 5 \end{bmatrix}$

$\begin{matrix} -3R_1 + R_2 \rightarrow \\ -5R_1 + R_2 \rightarrow \end{matrix} \begin{bmatrix} 1 & \frac{1}{2} & -\frac{5}{2} & | & \frac{3}{2} \\ 0 & \frac{1}{2} & \frac{17}{2} & | & \frac{21}{2} \\ 0 & -\frac{7}{2} & \frac{23}{2} & | & -\frac{5}{2} \end{bmatrix}$

$2R_2 \rightarrow \begin{bmatrix} 1 & \frac{1}{2} & -\frac{5}{2} & | & \frac{3}{2} \\ 0 & 1 & 17 & | & 21 \\ 0 & -\frac{7}{2} & \frac{23}{2} & | & -\frac{5}{2} \end{bmatrix}$

$-\frac{2}{7}R_2 + R_3 \rightarrow \begin{bmatrix} 1 & \frac{1}{2} & -\frac{5}{2} & | & \frac{3}{2} \\ 0 & 1 & 17 & | & 21 \\ 0 & 0 & 71 & | & 71 \end{bmatrix}$

$\frac{1}{71}R_3 \rightarrow \begin{bmatrix} 1 & \frac{1}{2} & -\frac{5}{2} & | & \frac{3}{2} \\ 0 & 1 & 17 & | & 21 \\ 0 & 0 & 1 & | & 1 \end{bmatrix}$

$x + \left(\frac{1}{2}\right)y - \left(\frac{5}{2}\right)z = \frac{3}{2}$
$y + 17z = 21$
$z = 1$

$y + 17(1) = 21$
$y + 17 = 21$
$y = 4$

$x + \left(\frac{1}{2}\right)(4) - \left(\frac{5}{2}\right)(1) = \frac{3}{2}$
$x + 2 - \frac{5}{2} = \frac{3}{2}$
$x - \frac{1}{2} = \frac{3}{2}$
$x = 2$

The solution is $(2, 4, 1)$.

35. $x - 2y + 3z = 2$
$2x + y + 2z = 5$
$2x - 4y + 6z = -4$

$$\begin{bmatrix} 1 & -2 & 3 & | & 2 \\ 2 & 1 & 2 & | & 5 \\ 2 & -4 & 6 & | & -4 \end{bmatrix}$$

$\begin{matrix} -2R_1 + R_2 \rightarrow \\ -2R_1 + R_3 \rightarrow \end{matrix} \begin{bmatrix} 1 & -2 & 3 & | & 2 \\ 0 & 5 & -4 & | & 1 \\ 0 & 0 & 0 & | & -8 \end{bmatrix}$

$x - 2y + 3z = 2$
$5y - 4z = 1$
$0 = -8$

This is not a true equation. The system of equations is inconsistent.

37. $2x + 3y - 3z = -1$
$2x + 3y + 3z = 3$
$4x - 4y + 3z = 4$

$$\begin{bmatrix} 2 & 3 & -3 & | & -1 \\ 2 & 3 & 3 & | & 3 \\ 4 & -4 & 3 & | & 4 \end{bmatrix}$$

$$\frac{1}{2}R_1 \rightarrow \begin{bmatrix} 1 & \dfrac{3}{2} & -\dfrac{3}{2} & | & -\dfrac{1}{2} \\ 2 & 3 & 3 & | & 3 \\ 4 & -4 & 3 & | & 4 \end{bmatrix}$$

$$\begin{matrix} -2R_1 + R_2 \rightarrow \\ -4R_1 + R_3 \rightarrow \end{matrix} \begin{bmatrix} 1 & \dfrac{3}{2} & -\dfrac{3}{2} & | & -\dfrac{1}{2} \\ 0 & 0 & 6 & | & 4 \\ 0 & -10 & 9 & | & 6 \end{bmatrix}$$

$$R_2 \leftrightarrow R_3 \begin{bmatrix} 1 & \dfrac{3}{2} & -\dfrac{3}{2} & | & -\dfrac{1}{2} \\ 0 & -10 & 9 & | & 6 \\ 0 & 0 & 6 & | & 4 \end{bmatrix}$$

$$\begin{matrix} -\dfrac{1}{10}R_2 \rightarrow \\ \dfrac{1}{6}R_3 \rightarrow \end{matrix} \begin{bmatrix} 1 & \dfrac{3}{2} & -\dfrac{3}{2} & | & -\dfrac{1}{2} \\ 0 & 1 & -\dfrac{9}{10} & | & -\dfrac{3}{5} \\ 0 & 0 & 1 & | & \dfrac{2}{3} \end{bmatrix}$$

$x + \left(\dfrac{3}{2}\right)y - \left(\dfrac{3}{2}\right)z = -\dfrac{1}{2}$

$\qquad y - \left(\dfrac{9}{10}\right)z = -\dfrac{3}{5}$

$\qquad\qquad z = \dfrac{2}{3}$

$y - \left(\dfrac{9}{10}\right)\left(\dfrac{2}{3}\right) = -\dfrac{3}{5}$

$\qquad y - \dfrac{3}{5} = -\dfrac{3}{5}$

$\qquad\qquad y = 0$

$x + \left(\dfrac{3}{2}\right)(0) - \left(\dfrac{3}{2}\right)\left(\dfrac{2}{3}\right) = -\dfrac{1}{2}$

$\qquad\qquad x - 1 = -\dfrac{1}{2}$

$\qquad\qquad\qquad x = \dfrac{1}{2}$

The solution is $\left(\dfrac{1}{2}, 0, \dfrac{2}{3}\right)$.

39. $3x - 2y + 2z = 5$
$6x + 3y - 4z = -1$
$3x - y + 2z = 4$

$$\begin{bmatrix} 3 & -2 & 2 & | & 5 \\ 6 & 3 & -4 & | & -1 \\ 3 & -1 & 2 & | & 4 \end{bmatrix}$$

$$\frac{1}{3}R_1 \rightarrow \begin{bmatrix} 1 & -\dfrac{2}{3} & \dfrac{2}{3} & | & \dfrac{5}{3} \\ 6 & 3 & -4 & | & -1 \\ 3 & -1 & 2 & | & 4 \end{bmatrix}$$

$$\begin{matrix} -6R_1 + R_2 \rightarrow \\ -3R_1 + R_3 \rightarrow \end{matrix} \begin{bmatrix} 1 & -\dfrac{2}{3} & \dfrac{2}{3} & | & \dfrac{5}{3} \\ 0 & 7 & -8 & | & -11 \\ 0 & 1 & 0 & | & -1 \end{bmatrix}$$

$$R_2 + R_3 \rightarrow \begin{bmatrix} 1 & -\dfrac{2}{3} & \dfrac{2}{3} & | & \dfrac{5}{3} \\ 0 & 1 & 0 & | & -1 \\ 0 & 7 & -8 & | & -11 \end{bmatrix}$$

$$-7R_2 + R_3 \rightarrow \begin{bmatrix} 1 & -\dfrac{2}{3} & \dfrac{2}{3} & | & \dfrac{5}{3} \\ 0 & 1 & 0 & | & -1 \\ 0 & 0 & -8 & | & -4 \end{bmatrix}$$

$$-\frac{1}{8}R_3 \rightarrow \begin{bmatrix} 1 & -\dfrac{2}{3} & \dfrac{2}{3} & | & \dfrac{5}{3} \\ 0 & 1 & 0 & | & -1 \\ 0 & 0 & 1 & | & \dfrac{1}{2} \end{bmatrix}$$

$x - \left(\dfrac{2}{3}\right)y + \left(\dfrac{2}{3}\right)z = \dfrac{5}{3}$

$\qquad\qquad y = -1$

$\qquad\qquad z = \dfrac{1}{2}$

$x - \left(\dfrac{2}{3}\right)(-1) + \left(\dfrac{2}{3}\right)\left(\dfrac{1}{2}\right) = \dfrac{5}{3}$

$\qquad x + \dfrac{2}{3} + \dfrac{1}{3} = \dfrac{5}{3}$

$\qquad\qquad x + 1 = \dfrac{5}{3}$

$\qquad\qquad\qquad x = \dfrac{2}{3}$

The solution is $\left(\dfrac{2}{3}, -1, \dfrac{1}{2}\right)$.

41. $3y - 2z = -9$
$2x + 3z = 13$
$3x - y = 7$

$$\begin{bmatrix} 0 & 3 & -2 & | & -9 \\ 2 & 0 & 3 & | & 13 \\ 3 & -1 & 0 & | & 7 \end{bmatrix}$$

$-R_2 + R_3 \rightarrow R_3 \begin{bmatrix} 0 & 3 & -2 & | & -9 \\ 2 & 0 & 3 & | & 13 \\ 1 & -1 & -3 & | & -6 \end{bmatrix}$

$R_1 \leftrightarrow R_3 \begin{bmatrix} 1 & -1 & -3 & | & -6 \\ 2 & 0 & 3 & | & 13 \\ 0 & 3 & -2 & | & -9 \end{bmatrix}$

$-2R_1 + R_2 \rightarrow \begin{bmatrix} 1 & -1 & -3 & | & -6 \\ 0 & 2 & 9 & | & 25 \\ 0 & 3 & -2 & | & -9 \end{bmatrix}$

$-R_2 + R_3 \rightarrow \begin{bmatrix} 1 & -1 & -3 & | & -6 \\ 0 & 2 & 9 & | & 25 \\ 0 & 1 & -11 & | & -34 \end{bmatrix}$

$R_2 \leftrightarrow R_3 \begin{bmatrix} 1 & -1 & -3 & | & -6 \\ 0 & 1 & -11 & | & -34 \\ 0 & 2 & 9 & | & 25 \end{bmatrix}$

$-2R_2 + R_3 \rightarrow \begin{bmatrix} 1 & -1 & -3 & | & -6 \\ 0 & 1 & -11 & | & -34 \\ 0 & 0 & 31 & | & 93 \end{bmatrix}$

$\frac{1}{31}R_3 \rightarrow \begin{bmatrix} 1 & -1 & -3 & | & -6 \\ 0 & 1 & -11 & | & -34 \\ 0 & 0 & 1 & | & 3 \end{bmatrix}$

$z = 3$
$y - 11(3) = -34$
$y = -1$
$x - (-1) - 3(3) = -6$
$x = 2$
The solution is $(2, -1, 3)$.

43. $2y - 5z = 12$
$3x + y - 4z = 9$
$2x - 5z = 10$

$$\begin{bmatrix} 0 & 2 & -5 & | & 12 \\ 3 & 1 & -4 & | & 9 \\ 2 & 0 & -5 & | & 10 \end{bmatrix}$$

$-R_3 + R_2 \rightarrow \begin{bmatrix} 0 & 2 & -5 & | & 12 \\ 1 & 1 & 1 & | & -1 \\ 2 & 0 & -5 & | & 10 \end{bmatrix}$

$R_1 \leftrightarrow R_2 \begin{bmatrix} 1 & 1 & 1 & | & -1 \\ 0 & 2 & -5 & | & 12 \\ 2 & 0 & -5 & | & 10 \end{bmatrix}$

$-2R_1 + R_3 \rightarrow \begin{bmatrix} 1 & 1 & 1 & | & -1 \\ 0 & 2 & -5 & | & 12 \\ 0 & -2 & -7 & | & 12 \end{bmatrix}$

$R_2 + R_3 \rightarrow \begin{bmatrix} 1 & 1 & 1 & | & -1 \\ 0 & 2 & -5 & | & 12 \\ 0 & 0 & -12 & | & 24 \end{bmatrix}$

$\frac{1}{2}R_2 \rightarrow$
$-\frac{1}{12}R_3 \rightarrow \begin{bmatrix} 1 & 1 & 1 & | & -1 \\ 0 & 1 & -\frac{5}{2} & | & 6 \\ 0 & 0 & 1 & | & -2 \end{bmatrix}$

$z = -2$
$y - \frac{5}{2}(-2) = 6$
$y = 1$
$x + 1 + (-2) = -1$
$x = 0$
The solution is $(0, 1, -2)$.

45.
$$ax + by + c = z$$
$$(1,-1,5) \quad 1a - 1b + c = 5$$
$$(2,-2,9) \quad 2a - 2b + c = 9$$
$$(-3,-1,-1) \quad -3a - 1b + c = -1$$

$$\begin{bmatrix} 1 & -1 & 1 & | & 5 \\ 2 & -2 & 1 & | & 9 \\ -3 & -1 & 1 & | & -1 \end{bmatrix}$$

$$\begin{matrix} -2R_1 + R_2 \to \\ 3R_1 + R_2 \to \end{matrix} \begin{bmatrix} 1 & -1 & 1 & | & 5 \\ 0 & 0 & -1 & | & -1 \\ 0 & -4 & 4 & | & 14 \end{bmatrix}$$

$$R_2 \leftrightarrow R_3 \begin{bmatrix} 1 & -1 & 1 & | & 5 \\ 0 & -4 & 4 & | & 14 \\ 0 & 0 & -1 & | & -1 \end{bmatrix}$$

$$\begin{matrix} -\frac{1}{4}R_2 \to \\ -R_3 \to \end{matrix} \begin{bmatrix} 1 & -1 & 1 & | & 5 \\ 0 & 1 & -1 & | & -\frac{7}{2} \\ 0 & 0 & 1 & | & 1 \end{bmatrix}$$

$$c = 1$$
$$b - (1) = -\frac{7}{2}$$
$$b = -\frac{5}{2}$$
$$a - \left(-\frac{5}{2}\right) + 1 = 5$$
$$a = \frac{3}{2}$$

The solution is $z = \frac{3}{2}x - \frac{5}{2}y + 1$.

47.
$$ax^2 + bx + c = y$$
$$(3, -4): \quad a(3)^2 + b(3) + c = -4$$
$$(2, -2): \quad a(2)^2 + b(2) + c = -2$$
$$(1, -2): \quad a(1)^2 + b(1) + c = -2$$

$$9a + 3b + c = -4$$
$$4a + 2b + c = -2$$
$$a + b + c = -2$$

$$\begin{bmatrix} 9 & 3 & 1 & | & -4 \\ 4 & 2 & 1 & | & -2 \\ 1 & 1 & 1 & | & -2 \end{bmatrix}$$

$$R_1 \leftrightarrow R_3 \begin{bmatrix} 1 & 1 & 1 & | & -2 \\ 4 & 2 & 1 & | & -2 \\ 9 & 3 & 1 & | & -4 \end{bmatrix}$$

$$\begin{matrix} -4R_1 + R_2 \to \\ -9R_1 + R_3 \to \end{matrix} \begin{bmatrix} 1 & 1 & 1 & | & -2 \\ 0 & -2 & -3 & | & 6 \\ 0 & -6 & -8 & | & 14 \end{bmatrix}$$

$$-3R_2 + R_3 \to \begin{bmatrix} 1 & 1 & 1 & | & -2 \\ 0 & -2 & -3 & | & 6 \\ 0 & 0 & 1 & | & -4 \end{bmatrix}$$

$$-\frac{1}{2}R_2 \to \begin{bmatrix} 1 & 1 & 1 & | & -2 \\ 0 & 1 & \frac{3}{2} & | & -3 \\ 0 & 0 & 1 & | & -4 \end{bmatrix}$$

$$c = -4$$
$$b + \frac{3}{2}(-4) = -3$$
$$b = 3$$
$$a + (3) + (-4) = -2$$
$$a = -1$$

The solution is $y = -x^2 + 3x - 4$.

49. Strategy
The sum of d_1 and d_3 is equal to the length of the rod, which is 20 in.
$w_1 = 3$, $w_2 = 2$, and $w_3 = 3$ so the equation that ensures the mobile will balance is
$3d_1 + 2d_2 = 3d_3$
$d_1 + d_3 = 20$
$d_3 = 2d_2$

Solution
$d_1 + d_3 = 20$
$d_1 + 2d_2 = 20$
$d_1 = 20 - 2d_2$

$3d_1 + 2d_2 = 3d_3$
$3d_1 + 2d_2 = 3(2d_2)$
$3d_1 + 2d_2 = 6d_2$
$3d_1 = 4d_2$
$d_1 = \dfrac{4}{3}d_2$

$20 - 2d_2 = \dfrac{4}{3}d_2$
$20 = \dfrac{10}{3}d_2$
$d_2 = 6$

$d_3 = 2d_2$
$d_3 = 2(6)$
$d_3 = 12$

$d_1 + d_3 = 20$
$d_1 + 12 = 20$
$d_1 = 8$
The distances are $d_1 = 8$ in., $d_2 = 6$ in., and $d_3 = 12$ in.

51. a. Rabbits do not prey on hawks.

    b. Snakes prey on rabbits.

    c. A coyote is not prey for hawks, rabbits, snakes or coyotes.

    d. A rabbit does not prey on hawks, rabbits, snakes or coyotes.

53. Strategy
Substitute 3 for x, -2 for y, and 4 for z in the equations. Solve for A, B, and C.

Solution
$Ax + 3y + 2z = 8$
$A(3) + 3(-2) + 2(4) = 8$
$3A - 6 + 8 = 8$
$3A + 2 = 8$
$3A = 6$
$A = 2$

$2x + By - 3z = -12$
$2(3) + B(-2) - 3(4) = -12$
$6 - 2B - 12 = -12$
$-2B - 6 = -12$
$-2B = -6$
$B = 3$

$3x - 2y + Cz = 1$
$3(3) - 2(-2) + C(4) = 1$
$9 + 4 + 4C = 1$
$4C + 13 = 1$
$4C = -12$
$C = -3$
The value of A is 2. The value of B is 3. The value of C is -3.

55. (1) $\dfrac{1}{x} + \dfrac{2}{y} = 3$

    (2) $\dfrac{1}{x} - \dfrac{3}{y} = -2$

Clear the fractions.
$xy\left(\dfrac{1}{x} + \dfrac{2}{y}\right) = xy \cdot 3$

$xy\left(\dfrac{1}{x} - \dfrac{3}{y}\right) = xy \cdot (-2)$

$y + 2x = 3xy$
$y - 3x = -2xy$

Eliminate y.
$y + 2x = 3xy$
$-y + 3x = 2xy$
$5x = 5xy$
$y = 1$

Substitute y into equation (2).
$\dfrac{1}{x} - \dfrac{3}{y} = -2$
$\dfrac{1}{x} - \dfrac{3}{1} = -2$
$\dfrac{1}{x} = 1$
$x = 1$
The solution is $(1, 1)$.

57. a. A plane is parallel to the yz-plane passing through $x = 3$.

b. A plane parallel to the xz-plane passing through $y = 4$.

c. A plane parallel to the xy-plane passing through $x = 2$.

d. A plane perpendicular to the xy-plane along the line $y = x$ in the xy-plane.

Section 5.4

1. Graph each inequality. Then determine the intersection of the solution sets of the individual inequalities.

3. It must be a solution of every inequality in the system.

5. Check the ordered pair $(5, 1)$ in the system of inequalities

$$\begin{array}{c|c} 2(5) - 1 & 4 \\ 10 - 1 & 4 \\ 9 & 4 \end{array}$$

$9 > 4$
The ordered pair $(5, 1)$ is not a solution.

Check the ordered pair $(-3, -5)$ in the system of inequalities.

$$\begin{array}{c|c} 2(-3) - (-5) & 4 \\ -6 + 5 & 4 \\ -1 & 4 \end{array} \qquad \begin{array}{c|c} -3 - 3(-5) & 6 \\ -3 + 15 & 6 \\ 12 & 6 \end{array}$$

$-1 < 4$ and $12 \geq 6$
The ordered pair $(-3, -5)$ is a solution.

7. $y \leq x - 3$
$y \leq -x + 5$

9. $y > 3x - 3$
$y \geq -2x + 2$

11. Solve each inequality for y.

$$\begin{array}{ll} 2x + y \geq -2 & 6x + 3y \leq 6 \\ \quad y \geq -2x - 2 & \quad 3y \leq -6x + 6 \\ & \quad y \leq -2x + 2 \end{array}$$

13. Solve each inequality for y.

$$\begin{array}{ll} 3x - 2y < 6 & y \leq 3 \\ \quad -2y < -3x + 6 & \\ \quad y > \dfrac{3}{2}x - 3 & \end{array}$$

15. Solve the inequality for y.

$$\begin{array}{ll} y > 2x - 6 & x + y < 0 \\ & \quad y < -x \end{array}$$

17. Solve each inequality for the variable.

$$\begin{array}{ll} x + 1 \geq 0 & y - 3 \leq 0 \\ \quad x \geq -1 & \quad y \leq 3 \end{array}$$

19. Solve each inequality for y.

$$\begin{array}{ll} 2x + y \geq 4 & 3x - 2y < 6 \\ \quad y \geq -2x + 4 & \quad -2y < -3x + 6 \\ & \quad y > \dfrac{3}{2}x - 3 \end{array}$$

21. Solve each inequality for y.

$$\begin{array}{ll} x - 2y \leq 6 & 2x + 3y \leq 6 \\ \quad -2y \leq -x + 6 & \quad 3y \leq -2x + 6 \\ \quad y \geq \dfrac{1}{2}x - 3 & \quad y \leq -\dfrac{2}{3}x + 2 \end{array}$$

23. Solve each inequality for y.

$$x - 2y \le 4 \qquad 3x + 2y \le 8$$
$$-2y \le -x + 4 \qquad 2y \le -3x + 8$$
$$y \ge \frac{1}{2}x - 2 \qquad y \le -\frac{3}{2}x + 4$$

$$y \ge \frac{1}{2}x - 2$$
$$y \le -\frac{3}{2}x + 4$$
$$x > -1$$

25. Solve each inequality for y.

$$2x + 3y \le 15 \qquad 3x - y \le 6$$
$$3y \le -2x + 15 \qquad -y \le -3x + 6$$
$$y \le -\frac{2}{3}x + 5 \qquad y \ge 3x - 6$$

$$y \le -\frac{2}{3}x + 5$$
$$y \ge 3x - 6$$
$$y \ge 0$$

27. Solve each inequality for y.

$$x - y \le 5 \qquad 2x - y \ge 6 \qquad y \ge 0$$
$$-y \le -x + 5 \qquad -y \ge -2x + 6$$
$$y \ge x - 5 \qquad y \le 2x - 6$$

29. Solve each inequality for y.

$$2x - y \le 4 \qquad 3x + y < 1 \qquad y \le 0$$
$$-y \le -2x + 4 \qquad y < 1 - 3x$$
$$y \ge 2x - 4$$

31. $y \ge -2$
$x \ge 1$

33. $y > x$
$y < -x + 2$

Chapter Review Exercises

1. (1) $\quad 2x - 6y = 15$
(2) $\qquad x = 4y + 8$

Substitute $4y + 8$ for x in equation (1).

$$2(4y + 8) - 6y = 15$$
$$8y + 16 - 6y = 15$$
$$2y + 16 = 15$$
$$2y = -1$$
$$y = -\frac{1}{2}$$

Replace y in equation (2).

$$x = 4y + 8$$
$$x = 4\left(-\frac{1}{2}\right) + 8$$
$$= -2 + 8$$
$$= 6$$

The solution is $\left(6, -\frac{1}{2}\right)$.

2. (1) $\quad 3x + 2y = 2$
(2) $\qquad x + y = 3$

Eliminate y. Multiply equation (2) by -2 and add to equation (1).

$$3x + 2y = 2$$
$$-2(x + y) = 3(-2)$$

$$3x + 2y = 2$$
$$-2x - 2y = -6$$

Add the equations.

$$x = -4$$

Replace x in equation (2).

$$x + y = 3$$
$$-4 + y = 3$$
$$y = 7$$

The solution is $(-4, 7)$.

3. Solve the equations for y,

$$x + y = 3 \qquad 3x - 2y = -6$$
$$y = -x + 3 \qquad -2y = -3x - 6$$
$$y = \frac{3}{2}x + 3$$

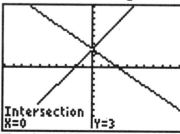

The solution is $(0, 3)$.

4. (1) $2x - y = 4$
  (2) $y = 2x - 4$
Substitute $2x - 4$ for y in equation (1).
$2x - (2x - 4) = 4$
$2x - 2x + 4 = 4$
$\qquad\quad 4 = 4$
This is a true equation. The equations are dependent. The solutions are the ordered pairs $(x, 2x - 4)$.

5. (1) $5x - 15y = 30$
  (2) $x - 3y = 6$
Eliminate x. Multiply equation (2) by -5 and add to equation (1).
$5x - 15y = 30$
$-5(x - 3y) = 6(-5)$

$5x - 15y = 30$
$-5x + 15y = -30$
Add the equations.
$0 = 0$
This is a true equation. The equations are dependent. The solutions are the ordered pairs $\left(x, \dfrac{1}{3}x - 2\right)$.

6. (1) $3x - 4y - 2z = 17$
  (2) $4x - 3y + 5z = 5$
  (3) $5x - 5y + 3z = 14$
Eliminate z. Multiply equation (1) by 5 and equation (2) by 2 and add the new equations.
$5(3x - 4y - 2z) = 17(5)$
$2(4x - 3y + 5z) = 5(2)$

$15x - 20y - 10z = 85$
$8x - 6y + 10z = 10$

  (4) $23x - 26y = 95$
Multiply equation (1) by 3 and equation (3) by 2 and add the new equations.
$3(3x - 4y - 2z) = (17)3$
$2(5x - 5y + 3z) = (14)2$

$9x - 12y - 6z = 51$
$10x - 10y + 6z = 28$

  (5) $19x - 22y = 79$
Multiply equation (4) by -11 and equation (5) by 13 and add the new equations.
$-11(23x - 26y) = 95(-11)$
$13(19x - 22y) = 79(13)$

$-253x + 286y = -1045$
$247x - 286y = 1027$

$\qquad\quad -6x = -18$
$\qquad\qquad x = 3$
Substitute x for 3 in equation (4).
$23x - 26y = 95$
$23(3) - 26y = 95$
$69 - 26y = 95$
$-26y = 26$
$y = -1$
Substitute x by 3 and y by -1 in equation (1).
$3x - 4y - 2z = 17$
$3(3) - 4(-1) - 2z = 17$
$9 + 4 - 2z = 17$
$-2z = 4$
$z = -2$
The solution is $(3, -1, -2)$.

7. Solve the equations for y,
$\quad 2x - 3y = -6 \qquad 2x - y = 2$
$\qquad -3y = -2x - 6 \qquad y = 2x - 2$
$\qquad\quad y = \dfrac{2}{3}x + 2$

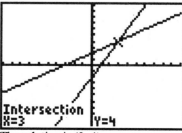

The solution is $(3, 4)$.

8. $\begin{bmatrix} 2 & -3 & -1 & | & 1 \\ 3 & 0 & -4 & | & -2 \\ 0 & 4 & -5 & | & 0 \end{bmatrix}$

9. $\quad x + 3y = -2$
$\quad 2x - y + z = 0$
$\quad 3x + 2y - 5z = 4$

10. $\begin{bmatrix} 3 & 6 & -3 & 9 \\ -3 & -5 & 1 & 4 \\ 2 & 3 & 5 & 2 \end{bmatrix}$

$\frac{1}{3}R_1 \to \begin{bmatrix} 1 & 2 & -1 & 3 \\ -3 & -5 & 1 & 4 \\ 2 & 3 & 5 & 2 \end{bmatrix}$

$\begin{matrix} 3R_1 + R_2 \to \\ -2R_1 + R_3 \to \end{matrix} \begin{bmatrix} 1 & 2 & -1 & 3 \\ 0 & 1 & -2 & 13 \\ 0 & -1 & 7 & -4 \end{bmatrix}$

$R_2 + R_3 \to \begin{bmatrix} 1 & 2 & -1 & 3 \\ 0 & 1 & -2 & 13 \\ 0 & 0 & 5 & 9 \end{bmatrix}$

$\frac{1}{5}R_3 \to \begin{bmatrix} 1 & 2 & -1 & 3 \\ 0 & 1 & -2 & 13 \\ 0 & 0 & 1 & \frac{9}{5} \end{bmatrix}$

11. $\quad 2x + 5y = -1$
$\quad 3x - 4y = 10$

$\begin{bmatrix} 2 & 5 & | & -1 \\ 3 & -4 & | & 10 \end{bmatrix}$

$\frac{1}{2}R_2 \to \begin{bmatrix} 1 & \frac{5}{2} & | & -\frac{1}{2} \\ 3 & -4 & | & 10 \end{bmatrix}$

$-3R_1 + R_2 \to \begin{bmatrix} 1 & \frac{5}{2} & | & -\frac{1}{2} \\ 0 & -\frac{23}{2} & | & \frac{23}{2} \end{bmatrix}$

$-\frac{2}{23}R_2 \to \begin{bmatrix} 1 & \frac{5}{2} & | & -\frac{1}{2} \\ 0 & 1 & | & -1 \end{bmatrix}$

$x + \frac{5}{2}y = -\frac{1}{2}$
$y = -1$
$x + \frac{5}{2}(-1) = -\frac{1}{2}$
$x = 2$
The solution is $(2, -1)$.

12. $\quad 3x + 2y = 5$
$\quad 4x + 5y = 2$

$\begin{bmatrix} 3 & 2 & | & 5 \\ 4 & 5 & | & 2 \end{bmatrix}$

$\frac{1}{3}R_1 \to \begin{bmatrix} 1 & \frac{2}{3} & | & \frac{5}{3} \\ 4 & 5 & | & 2 \end{bmatrix}$

$-4R_1 + R_2 \to \begin{bmatrix} 1 & \frac{2}{3} & | & \frac{5}{3} \\ 0 & \frac{7}{3} & | & -\frac{14}{3} \end{bmatrix}$

$\frac{3}{7}R_2 \to \begin{bmatrix} 1 & \frac{2}{3} & | & \frac{5}{3} \\ 0 & 1 & | & -2 \end{bmatrix}$

$x + \frac{2}{3}y = \frac{5}{3}$
$y = -2$
$x + \frac{2}{3}(-2) = \frac{5}{3}$
$x = 3$
The solution is $(3, -2)$.

13. $\quad x + 3y + z = 6$
$\quad 2x + y - z = 12$
$\quad x + 2y - z = 13$

$\begin{bmatrix} 1 & 3 & 1 & | & 6 \\ 2 & 1 & -1 & | & 12 \\ 1 & 2 & -1 & | & 13 \end{bmatrix}$

$\begin{matrix} -2R_1 + R_2 \to \\ -R_1 + R_3 \to \end{matrix} \begin{bmatrix} 1 & 3 & 1 & | & 6 \\ 0 & -5 & -3 & | & 0 \\ 0 & -1 & -2 & | & 7 \end{bmatrix}$

$R_2 \leftrightarrow R_3 \begin{bmatrix} 1 & 3 & 1 & | & 6 \\ 0 & -1 & -2 & | & 7 \\ 0 & -5 & -3 & | & 0 \end{bmatrix}$

$-1R_2 \to \begin{bmatrix} 1 & 3 & 1 & | & 6 \\ 0 & 1 & 2 & | & -7 \\ 0 & -5 & -3 & | & 0 \end{bmatrix}$

$5R_2 + R_3 \to \begin{bmatrix} 1 & 3 & 1 & | & 6 \\ 0 & 1 & 2 & | & -7 \\ 0 & 0 & 7 & | & -35 \end{bmatrix}$

$\frac{1}{7}R_3 \to \begin{bmatrix} 1 & 3 & 1 & | & 6 \\ 0 & 1 & 2 & | & -7 \\ 0 & 0 & 1 & | & -5 \end{bmatrix}$

$z = -5$
$y + 2z = -7$
$y + 2(-5) = -7$
$y - 10 = -7$
$y = 3$
$x + 3y + z = 6$
$x + 3(3) + (-5) = 6$
$x + 9 - 5 = 6$
$x + 4 = 6$
$x = 2$
The solution is $(2, 3, -5)$.

14.
$$x + y + z = 0$$
$$x + 2y + 3z = 5$$
$$2x + y + 2z = 3$$

$$\begin{bmatrix} 1 & 1 & 1 & | & 0 \\ 1 & 2 & 3 & | & 5 \\ 2 & 1 & 2 & | & 3 \end{bmatrix}$$

$$\begin{matrix} -R_1 + R_2 \to \\ -2R_1 + R_3 \to \end{matrix} \begin{bmatrix} 1 & 1 & 1 & | & 0 \\ 0 & 1 & 2 & | & 5 \\ 0 & -1 & 0 & | & 3 \end{bmatrix}$$

$$R_2 + R_3 \to \begin{bmatrix} 1 & 1 & 1 & | & 0 \\ 0 & 1 & 2 & | & 5 \\ 0 & 0 & 2 & | & 8 \end{bmatrix}$$

$$\frac{1}{2}R_3 \to \begin{bmatrix} 1 & 1 & 1 & | & 0 \\ 0 & 1 & 2 & | & 5 \\ 0 & 0 & 1 & | & 4 \end{bmatrix}$$

$$z = 4$$
$$y + 2z = 5$$
$$y + 2(4) = 5$$
$$y + 8 = 5$$
$$y = -3$$

$$x + y + z = 0$$
$$x + (-3) + 4 = 0$$
$$x + 1 = 0$$
$$x = -1$$

The solution is $(-1, -3, 4)$.

15. Solve each inequality for y.

$$\begin{matrix} x + 3y \le 6 & \qquad & 2x - y \ge 4 \\ 3y \le -x + 6 & & -y \ge -2x + 4 \\ y \le -\dfrac{1}{3}x + 2 & & y \le 2x - 4 \end{matrix}$$

16. Solve each inequality for y.

$$\begin{matrix} 2x + 4y \ge 8 & \qquad & x + y \le 3 \\ 4y \ge -2x + 8 & & y \le -x + 3 \\ y \ge -\dfrac{1}{2}x + 2 & & \end{matrix}$$

17. Strategy

To find the rate of the cabin cruiser in calm water and the rate of the current, let x represent the rate of the cabin cruiser in calm water and y represent the rate of the current. Then

Rate of cruiser with current: $x + y$
Rate of cruiser against current: $x - y$
The distance traveled with the current is 60 miles. The distance traveled against the current is 60 miles. Use the equation $d = rt$ to express the distances traveled with and against the current as the two equations of a system.

Solution
$$3(x + y) = 60$$
$$5(x - y) = 60$$

$$\frac{1}{3} \cdot 3(x + y) = \frac{1}{3}(60)$$

$$\frac{1}{5} \cdot 5(x - y) = \frac{1}{5}(60)$$

$$x + y = 20$$
$$x - y = 12$$

$$2x = 32$$
$$x = 16$$

$$x + y = 20$$
$$16 + y = 20$$
$$y = 4$$

The rate of the cabin cruiser in calm water is 16 mph. The rate of the current is 4 mph.

18. Strategy

To find the rate of the plane in calm air and the rate of the wind, let x represent the rate of the plane in calm air and y represent the rate of the wind. Then

Rate of plane with wind: $x + y$

Rate of plane against wind: $x - y$

The distance traveled with the wind is 600 miles. The time it takes to travel against the wind for the same distance is 4 h. Use the equation $d = rt$ to express the distances traveled with and against the wind as the two equations of a system.

Solution

$3(x + y) = 600$
$4(x - y) = 600$

$\frac{1}{3} \cdot 3(x + y) = \frac{1}{3} \cdot 600$
$\frac{1}{4} \cdot 4(x - y) = \frac{1}{4} \cdot 600$

$x + y = 200$
$x - y = 150$

$2x = 350$
$x = 175$

$x + y = 200$
$175 + y = 200$
$y = 25$

The rate of the plane in calm air is 170 mph. The rate of the wind is 25 mph.

19. Strategy

To find the number of children who attended on Friday evening, let x represent the number of children's tickets sold Friday and y represent the number of adult's tickets sold Friday. The cost of a child's ticket is $5 and the cost of an adult's ticket is $8. The receipts on Friday were $2500, so one equation is $5x + 8y = 2500$. The number of children attending on Saturday was $3x$ and the number of adults attending was $\frac{1}{2}y$. The receipts on Saturday were $2500, so another equation is $5(3x) + 8\left(\frac{1}{2}y\right) = 2500$.

Solution

$5x + 8y = 2500$
$15x + 4y = 2500$

$5x + 8y = 2500$
$-2(15x + 4y) = -2(2500)$

$5x + 8y = 2500$
$-30x - 8y = -5000$

$-25x = -2500$
$x = 100$

The number of children attending on Friday was 100.

20. Strategy

Amount of meat to cook: x

Amount of potatoes to cook: y

Amount of green beans to cook: z

Calories	Amount	Calories	Total Calories
Meat	x	50	$50x$
Potatoes	y	9	$9y$
Beans	z	12	$12z$

Protein	Amount	Protein	Total Protein
Meat	x	20	$20x$
Potatoes	y	1	$1y$
Beans	z	2	$2z$

Sodium	Amount	Sodium	Total Sodium
Meat	x	16	$16x$
Potatoes	y	3	$3y$
Beans	z	17	$17z$

The chef wants the meal to contain 243 cal, 73 g of protein and 131 mg of sodium.

$50x + 9y + 12z = 243$
$20x + 1y + 2z = 73$
$16x + 3y + 17z = 131$

Solution

$50x + 9y + 12z = 243$
$20x + 1y + 2z = 73$
$16x + 3y + 17z = 131$

$50x + 9y + 12z = 243$
$-9(20x + 1y + 2z) = -9(73)$

$50x + 9y + 12z = 243$
$-180x - 9y - 18z = -657$

$-130x - 6z = -414$

$50x + 9y + 12z = 243$
$-3(16x + 3y + 17z) = -3(131)$

$50x + 9y + 12z = 243$
$-48x - 9y - 51z = -393$

$2x - 39z = -150$

$-130x - 6z = -414$
$65(2x - 39z) = 65(-150)$

$-130x - 6z = -414$
$130x - 2535z = -9750$
$-2541z = -10{,}164$
$\dfrac{-2541z}{-2541} = \dfrac{-10{,}164}{-2541}$
$z = 4$

$2x - 39z = -150$
$2x - 39(4) = -150$
$2x - 156 = -150$
$2x = 6$
$x = 3$

$20x + 1y + 2z = 73$
$20(3) + y + 2(4) = 73$
$60 + y + 8 = 73$
$y = 5$

3 oz of meat, 5 oz of potatoes, and 4 oz of green beans should be prepared.

Chapter Test

1. (1) $3x + 2y = 4$

    (2) $\qquad x = 2y - 1$

Substitute $2y - 1$ for x in equation (1).

$3(2y - 1) + 2y = 4$

$6y - 3 + 2y = 4$

$8y = 7$

$y = \dfrac{7}{8}$

Substitute into equation (2).

$x = 2y - 1$

$x = 2\left(\dfrac{7}{8}\right) - 1$

$x = \dfrac{7}{4} - 1 = \dfrac{3}{4}$

The solution is $\left(\dfrac{3}{4}, \dfrac{7}{8}\right)$.

2. (1) $4x - 6y = 5$

    (2) $6x - 9y = 4$

Multiply equation (1) by -3. Multiply equation (2) by 2. Add the new equations.

$-3(4x - 6y) = -3(5)$

$2(6x - 9y) = 2(4)$

$-12x + 18y = -15$

$12x - 18y = 8$

$0 = -7$

This is not a true equation. The system of equations is inconsistent and therefore has no solution.

3. (1) $3x + y = 7$

    (2) $3x - y = 3$

Solve equation (1) for y.

$3x + y = 7$

$y = -3x + 7$

Substitute $-3x + 7$ for y into equation (2).

$2x - (-3x + 7) = 3$

$2x + 3x - 7 = 3$

$5x = 10$

$x = 2$

Substitute into equation (1).

$y = -3x + 7$

$y = -3(2) + 7 = -6 + 7 = 1$

The solution is $(2, 1)$.

4. (1) $5x + 2y = -23$

    (2) $2x + y = -10$

Solve equation (2) for y.

$2x + y = -10$

$y = -2x - 10$

Substitute $-2x - 10$ for y in equation (1).

$5x + 2y = -23$

$5x + 2(-2x - 10) = -23$

$5x - 4x - 20 = -23$

$x - 20 = -23$

$x = -3$

Substitute into equation (2).

$2x + y = -10$

$2(-3) + y = -10$

$-6 + y = -10$

$y = -4$

The solution is $(-3, -4)$.

5. (1) $4x - 12y = 12$

    (2) $x - 3y = 3$

Eliminate x. Multiply equation (2) by -4 and add to equation (1).

$4x - 12y = 12$

$-4(x - 3y) = 3(-4)$

$4x - 12y = 12$

$-4x + 12y = -12$

Add the equations.

$0 = 0$

This is a true equation. The equations are dependent. The solutions are the ordered pairs $\left(x, \dfrac{1}{3}x - 1\right)$.

6.

(1) $3x + 2y + 2z = 2$
(2) $x - 2y - z = 1$
(3) $2x - 3y - 3z = -3$

Eliminate z. Multiply equation (2) by 2 and add to equation (1).

$3x + 2y + 2z = 2$
$2(x - 2y - z) = 1(2)$

$3x + 2y + 2z = 2$
$2x - 4y - 2z = 2$

(4) $5x - 2y = 4$

Multiply equation (2) by –3 and add to equation (3).

$-3(x - 2y - z) = 1(-3)$
$2x - 3y - 3x = -3$

$-3x + 6y + 3z = -3$
$2x - 3y - 3x = -3$

(5) $-x + 3y = -6$

Multiply equation (5) by 5 and add to equation (5).

$5x - 2y = 4$
$5(-x + 3y) = 5(-6)$

$5x - 2y = 4$
$-5x + 15y = -30$

$13y = -26$
$y = -2$

Substitute y for –2 in equation (5).

$-x + 3y = -6$
$-x + 3(-2) = -6$
$-x - 6 = -6$
$-x = 0$
$x = 0$

Substitute x by 0 and y by –2 in equation (2).

$x - 2y - z = 1$
$0 - 2(-2) - z = 1$
$4 - z = 1$
$-z = -3$
$z = 3$

The solution is (0, –2, 3).

7. Solve the equations for y,

$x - 2y = -5 \qquad 3x + 4y = -15$
$-2y = -x - 5 \qquad 4y = -3x - 15$
$y = \dfrac{1}{2}x + \dfrac{5}{2} \qquad y = -\dfrac{3}{4}x - \dfrac{15}{4}$

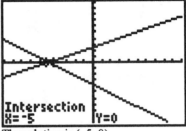

Intersection
X=-5   Y=0

The solution is (–5, 0).

8. $\begin{bmatrix} 3 & -1 & 2 & | & 4 \\ 1 & 4 & 0 & | & -1 \\ 0 & 5 & -1 & | & 3 \end{bmatrix}$

9. $2x - y + 3z = 4$
$x + 5y - 2z = 6$
$-3x - 4z = 1$

10. $\begin{bmatrix} 2 & 3 & -2 \\ 4 & 1 & 1 \end{bmatrix}$

$\dfrac{1}{2}R_1 \rightarrow \begin{bmatrix} 1 & \dfrac{3}{2} & -1 \\ 4 & 1 & 1 \end{bmatrix}$

$-4R_1 + R_2 \rightarrow \begin{bmatrix} 1 & \dfrac{3}{2} & -1 \\ 0 & -5 & 5 \end{bmatrix}$

$-\dfrac{1}{5}R_3 \rightarrow \begin{bmatrix} 1 & \dfrac{3}{2} & -1 \\ 0 & 1 & -1 \end{bmatrix}$

11. $3x + 4y = -2$
$2x + 5y = 1$

$\begin{bmatrix} 3 & 4 & | & -2 \\ 2 & 5 & | & 1 \end{bmatrix}$

$-1R_2 + R_1 \rightarrow \begin{bmatrix} 1 & -1 & | & -3 \\ 2 & 5 & | & 1 \end{bmatrix}$

$-2R_1 + R_2 \rightarrow \begin{bmatrix} 1 & -1 & | & -3 \\ 0 & 7 & | & 7 \end{bmatrix}$

$\dfrac{1}{7}R_2 \rightarrow \begin{bmatrix} 1 & -1 & | & -3 \\ 0 & 1 & | & 1 \end{bmatrix}$

$x - y = -3$
$y = 1$
$x - 1 = -3$
$x = -2$

The solution is (–2, 1).

12. $x - y = 3$
$2x + y = -4$

$$\begin{bmatrix} 1 & -1 & | & 3 \\ 2 & 1 & | & -4 \end{bmatrix}$$

$-2R_1 + R_2 \rightarrow \begin{bmatrix} 1 & -1 & | & 3 \\ 0 & 3 & | & -10 \end{bmatrix}$

$\dfrac{1}{3}R_2 \rightarrow \begin{bmatrix} 1 & -1 & | & 3 \\ 0 & 1 & | & -\dfrac{10}{3} \end{bmatrix}$

$x - y = 3$

$y = -\dfrac{10}{3}$

$x - \left(-\dfrac{10}{3}\right) = 3$

$x = -\dfrac{1}{3}$

The solution is $\left(-\dfrac{1}{3}, -\dfrac{10}{3}\right)$.

13. $x - y - z = 5$
$2x + z = 2$
$3y - 2z = 1$

$$\begin{bmatrix} 1 & -1 & -1 & | & 5 \\ 2 & 0 & 1 & | & 2 \\ 0 & 3 & -2 & | & 1 \end{bmatrix}$$

$-2R_1 + R_2 \rightarrow \begin{bmatrix} 1 & -1 & -1 & | & 5 \\ 0 & 2 & 3 & | & -8 \\ 0 & 3 & -2 & | & 1 \end{bmatrix}$

$R_2 \leftrightarrow R_3 \begin{bmatrix} 1 & -1 & -1 & | & 5 \\ 0 & 3 & -2 & | & 1 \\ 0 & 2 & 3 & | & -8 \end{bmatrix}$

$-1R_3 + R_2 \rightarrow \begin{bmatrix} 1 & -1 & -1 & | & 5 \\ 0 & 1 & -5 & | & 9 \\ 0 & 2 & 3 & | & -8 \end{bmatrix}$

$-2R_2 + R_3 \rightarrow \begin{bmatrix} 1 & -1 & -1 & | & 5 \\ 0 & 1 & -5 & | & 9 \\ 0 & 0 & 13 & | & -26 \end{bmatrix}$

$\dfrac{1}{13}R_3 \rightarrow \begin{bmatrix} 1 & -1 & -1 & | & 5 \\ 0 & 1 & -5 & | & 9 \\ 0 & 0 & 1 & | & -2 \end{bmatrix}$

$x - y - z = 5$
$y - 5z = 9$
$z = -2$

$y - 5z = 9$
$y - 5(-2) = 9$
$y + 10 = 9$
$y = -1$

$x - y - z = 5$
$x - (-1) - (-2) = 5$
$x + 1 + 2 = 5$
$x + 3 = 5$
$x = 2$

The solution is $(2, -1, -2)$.

14.
(1) $x - y + z = 2$
(2) $2x - y - z = 1$
(3) $x + 2y - 3z = -4$

Eliminate z. Add equation (1) and equation (2).
$x - y + z = 2$
$2x - y - z = 1$

(4) $3x - 2y = 3$

Multiply equation (1) by 3 and add to equation (3).
$3(x - y + z) = 3(2)$
$x + 2y - 3z = -4$

$3x - 3y + 3z = 6$
$x + 2y - 3z = -4$

(5) $4x - y = 2$

Multiply equation (5) by -2 and add to equation (4).
$3x - 2y = 3$
$-2(4x - y) = -2(2)$

$3x - 2y = 3$
$-8x + 2y = -4$

$-5x = -1$
$x = \dfrac{1}{5}$

Substitute x in equation (5).
$4x - y = 2$

$4\left(\dfrac{1}{5}\right) - y = 2$

$\dfrac{4}{5} - y = 2$

$-y = \dfrac{6}{5}$

$y = -\dfrac{6}{5}$

Substitute x and y in equation (1).
$x - y + z = 2$

$\dfrac{1}{5} - \left(-\dfrac{6}{5}\right) + z = 2$

$\dfrac{7}{5} + z = 2$

$z = \dfrac{3}{5}$

The solution is $\left(\dfrac{1}{5}, -\dfrac{6}{5}, \dfrac{3}{5}\right)$.

15. Solve each inequality for y.

$$3x - 2y \geq 4 \qquad x + y < 3$$
$$-2y \geq -3x + 4 \qquad y < -x + 3$$
$$y \leq \frac{3}{2}x - 2$$

16. Solve each inequality for y.

$$x + y > 2 \qquad 2x - y < -1$$
$$y > -x + 2 \qquad -y < -2x - 1$$
$$y > 1 + 2x$$

17. Strategy

To find the rate of the plane in calm air and the rate of the wind, let x represent the rate of the plane in calm air and y represent the rate of the wind. Then
Rate of plane with wind: $x + y$
Rate of plane against wind: $x - y$
The distance traveled with the wind is 350 miles. The time it takes to travel against the wind for the same distance is 2.8 h. Use the equation $d = rt$ to express the distances traveled with and against the wind as the two equations of a system.

Solution

$$2(x + y) = 350$$
$$2.8(x - y) = 350$$

$$\frac{1}{2} \cdot 2(x + y) = \frac{1}{2} \cdot 350$$
$$\frac{1}{2.8} \cdot 2.8(x - y) = \frac{1}{2.8} \cdot 350$$

$$x + y = 175$$
$$x - y = 125$$

$$2x = 300$$
$$x = 150$$

$$x + y = 175$$
$$150 + y = 175$$
$$y = 25$$

The rate of the plane in calm air is 150 mph. The rate of the wind is 25 mph.

18. Strategy

To find the cost per yard of the cotton and wool, let x represent the cost per yard of cotton and y represent the cost per yard of wool. The manufacturer purchased 60 yards of cotton and 90 yards of wool for $1800, so one equation is $60x + 90y = 1800$. Another purchase was 80 yards of cotton and 20 yards of wool for $1000, so the other equation is $80x + 20y = 1000$.

Solution

$$-4(60x + 90y) = -4(1800)$$
$$3(80x + 20y) = 3(1000)$$

$$-240x - 360y = -7200$$
$$240x + 60y = 3000$$

$$-300y = -4200$$
$$y = 14$$

$$60x + 90(14) = 1800$$
$$60x + 1260 = 1800$$
$$60x = 540$$
$$x = 9$$

The cost per yard of cotton is $9.00. The cost per yard of wool is $14.00.

19. Strategy

To find the rate of the motorboat in calm water and the rate of the current, let x represent the rate of the motorboat in calm water and y represent the rate of the current. Then
Rate of boat with current: $x + y$
Rate of boat against current: $x - y$
The distance traveled with the current is 80 miles. The distance traveled against the current is 80 miles. Use the equation $d = rt$ to express the distances traveled with and against the current as the two equations of a system.

Solution

$$4(x + y) = 80$$
$$5(x - y) = 80$$

$$\frac{1}{4} \cdot 4(x + y) = \frac{1}{4}(80)$$
$$\frac{1}{5} \cdot 5(x - y) = \frac{1}{5}(80)$$

$$x + y = 20$$
$$x - y = 16$$

$$2x = 36$$
$$x = 18$$

$$x + y = 20$$
$$18 + y = 20$$
$$y = 2$$

The rate of the motorboat in calm water is 18 mph. The rate of the current is 2 mph.

20. One red = 1 green + 1 blue
Five green = 1 red + 1 blue
One yellow = 1 red + 1 green.
Let r = weight of red block, g = weight of green block, b = weight of blue block, and y = weight of yellow block.
(1) $\quad r = g + b$
(2) $\quad 5g = r + b$
(3) $\quad y = r + g$

Eliminate r, substitute (1) into (2) and solve for b
$5g = g + b + b$
$5g = g + 2b$
$4g = 2b$
$2g = b$
Since b weighs 4 lb, we can solve for g.
$2g = 4$
$g = 2$
Solve equation (1) for r
$r = g + b$
$r = 2 + 4 = 6$
Solve equation (3) for y
$y = r + g$
$y = 6 + 2 = 8$
The yellow block weighs 8 lb.

Cumulative Review Exercises

1. Strategy
To find the units digit of the product of all the positive prime numbers less than 100, look for a pattern by multiplying the first 3 prime numbers, then 4, then 5, etc.

Solution
$2 \times 3 \times 5 = 30$
$2 \times 3 \times 5 \times 7 = 210$
$2 \times 3 \times 5 \times 7 \times 11 = 2310$
$2 \times 3 \times 5 \times 7 \times 11 \times 13 = 30{,}030$
$2 \times 3 \times 5 \times 7 \times 11 \times 13 \times 17 = 510{,}510$
Notice that the product of the first 3 prime numbers has a units digit of 0, that the product of the first 4 prime numbers has a units digit of 0, etc. From this pattern, we guess that the product of all the positive prime numbers less than 100 has a units digit of 0.

2. Strategy
To find the least number of votes cast in the election, try finding 94% and 100% of successively larger numbers until we find a number having a value of 94% that is less than the number minus one.

Solution
$0.94(10) = 9.40$	$1.00(10) = 10$
$0.94(11) = 10.34$	$1.00(11) = 11$
$0.94(12) = 11.28$	$1.00(12) = 12$
$0.94(13) = 12.22$	$1.00(13) = 13$
$0.94(14) = 13.16$	$1.00(14) = 14$
$0.94(15) = 14.10$	$1.00(15) = 15$
$0.94(16) = 15.04$	$1.00(16) = 16$
$0.94(17) = 15.98$	$1.00(17) = 17$

When reaching the number 17, it is determined for the first time a number having at least 94% a value which is less than the number (17) itself. Therefore, the least number of votes cast is 17.

3. $1 + 3 = 4 = 2^2$
$1 + 3 + 5 = 9 = 3^2$
$1 + 3 + 5 + 7 = 16 = 4^2$
$1 + 3 + 5 + 7 + 9 = 25 = 5^2$
The sums follow the pattern of successive perfect squares. In fact, each number is the square of the number of odd consecutive integers added. Using this pattern, it can be reasoned that
$1 + 3 + 5 + 7 + 9 + 11 = 6^2 = 36$.

4. The conclusion is based on a principle. Therefore, it is an example of deductive reasoning.

5. $g(x) = x^2 - 4x$
$g(-3) = (-3)^2 - 4(-3) = 9 + 12 = 21$
$g(-2) = (-2)^2 - 4(-2) = 4 + 8 = 12$
$g(-1) = (-1)^2 - 4(-1) = 1 + 4 = 5$
$g(0) = (0)^2 - 4(0) = 0$
$g(1) = (1)^2 - 4(1) = 1 - 4 = -3$
$g(2) = (2)^2 - 4(2) = 4 - 8 = -4$
$g(3) = (3)^2 - 4(3) = 9 - 12 = -3$
The range is $\{-4, -3, 0, 5, 12, 21\}$.

6. $H(x) = 2x^2 - 4x + 1$

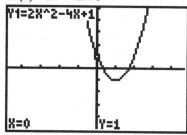

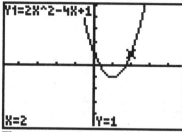

The two x-coordinates are 0 and 2.

7. $G(x) = x^3 + 5x^2 + 2x - 8$

$G(0) = (0)^3 + 5(0)^2 + 2(0) - 8 = -8$

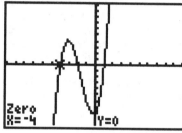

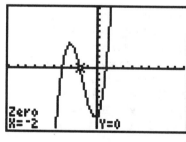

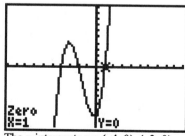

The x-intercepts are $(-4, 0)$, $(-2, 0)$ and $(1, 0)$.
The y-intercept is $(0, -8)$.

8. The input-output table is shown below.

s	3.50s + 750	F
1500	3.50(1500) + 750	6000
1600	3.50(1600) + 750	6350
1700	3.50(1700) + 750	6700
1800	3.50(1800) + 750	7050
1900	3.50(1900) + 750	7400
2000	3.50(2000) + 750	7750
2100	3.50(2100) + 750	8100

9. $3n = 4(n - 3) - (2n + 1)$
$3n = 4n - 12 - 2n - 1$
$3n = 2n - 13$
$n = -13$

10. $3(2t - 1) \geq 5t - 3(t + 9)$
$6t - 3 \geq 5t - 3t - 27$
$6t - 3 \geq 2t - 27$
$4t - 3 \geq -27$
$4t \geq -24$
$t \geq -6$
$[-6, \infty)$

11. $7 < 4x - 5 < 19$
$12 < 4x < 24$
$3 < x < 6$
$\{x \mid 3 < x < 6\}$

12. $|6 - 3x| - 5 = -2$
$|6 - 3x| = 3$

$6 - 3x = 3$ or $6 - 3x = -3$
$-3x = -3$ $-3x = -9$
$x = 1$ $x = 3$
The solutions are 1 and 3.

13. $(x_1, y_1) = (3, -2), (x_2, y_2) = (-1, 2)$
$m = \dfrac{y_2 - y_1}{x_2 - x_1} = \dfrac{2 - (-2)}{-1 - 3} = \dfrac{4}{-4} = -1$
$y - y_1 = m(x - x_1)$
$y - (-2) = -1(x - 3)$
$y + 2 = -x + 3$
$y = -x + 1$
The equation of the line is $y = -x + 1$.

14. (1) $\quad 4x - y = 11$
(2) $\quad 3x - 5y = 21$

First, solve equation (1) for y.
$$4x - y = 11$$
$$-y = -4x + 11$$
$$y = 4x - 11$$

Now substitute for y in equation (2).
$$3x - 5y = 21$$
$$3x - 5(4x - 11) = 21$$
$$3x - 20x + 55 = 21$$
$$-17x + 55 = 21$$
$$-17x = -34$$
$$x = 2$$

Substitute for x in $y = 4x - 11$:
$$y = 4x - 11$$
$$y = 4(2) - 11$$
$$y = 8 - 11 = -3$$

The solution is $(2, -3)$.

15. (1) $\quad 3x - 5y = -1$
(2) $\quad 4x + 3y = -11$

Eliminate y by multiplying (1) by 3 and (2) by 5
and then adding the resulting equations.
$$3(3x - 5y) = 3(-1)$$
$$5(4x + 3y) = 5(-11)$$

$$9x - 15y = -3$$
$$\underline{20x + 15y = -55}$$
$$29x = -58$$
$$x = -2$$

Substitute for x in equation (1):
$$3x - 5y = -1$$
$$3(-2) - 5y = -1$$
$$-6 - 5y = -1$$
$$-5y = 5$$
$$y = -1$$

The solution is $(-2, -1)$.

16. Solve each equation for y:
$$4x - y = 8 \qquad\qquad 2x + y = 4$$
$$-y = -4x + 8 \qquad\qquad y = -2x + 4$$
$$y = 4x - 8$$

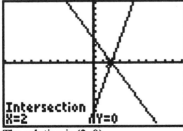

The solution is $(2, 0)$.

17. $\quad x - y + z = 1$
$$2x + 3y - z = 3$$
$$-x + 2y - 4z = 4$$

$$\begin{bmatrix} 1 & -1 & 1 & | & 1 \\ 2 & 3 & -1 & | & 3 \\ -1 & 2 & -4 & | & 4 \end{bmatrix}$$

$$\begin{matrix} -2R_1 + R_2 \to \\ R_1 + R_3 \to \end{matrix} \begin{bmatrix} 1 & -1 & 1 & | & 1 \\ 0 & 5 & -3 & | & 1 \\ 0 & 1 & -3 & | & 5 \end{bmatrix}$$

$$R_2 \leftrightarrow R_3 \begin{bmatrix} 1 & -1 & 1 & | & 1 \\ 0 & 1 & -3 & | & 5 \\ 0 & 5 & -3 & | & 1 \end{bmatrix}$$

$$-5R_2 + R_3 \begin{bmatrix} 1 & -1 & 1 & | & 1 \\ 0 & 1 & -3 & | & 5 \\ 0 & 0 & 12 & | & -24 \end{bmatrix}$$

$$\frac{1}{12}R_3 \to \begin{bmatrix} 1 & -1 & 1 & | & 1 \\ 0 & 1 & -3 & | & 5 \\ 0 & 0 & 1 & | & -2 \end{bmatrix}$$

18. $\quad x - 2y + z = 5$
$$3x - 2y - z = 3$$
$$4x + 5y - 4z = -9$$

$$\begin{bmatrix} 1 & -2 & 1 & | & 5 \\ 3 & -2 & -1 & | & 3 \\ 4 & 5 & -4 & | & -9 \end{bmatrix}$$

$$\begin{matrix} -3R_1 + R_2 \to \\ -4R_1 + R_3 \to \end{matrix} \begin{bmatrix} 1 & -2 & 1 & | & 5 \\ 0 & 4 & -4 & | & -12 \\ 0 & 13 & -8 & | & -29 \end{bmatrix}$$

$$\frac{1}{12}R_2 \to \begin{bmatrix} 1 & -2 & 1 & | & 5 \\ 0 & 1 & -1 & | & -3 \\ 0 & 13 & -8 & | & -29 \end{bmatrix}$$

$$-13R_2 + R_3 \to \begin{bmatrix} 1 & -2 & 1 & | & 5 \\ 0 & 1 & -1 & | & -3 \\ 0 & 0 & 5 & | & 10 \end{bmatrix}$$

$$\frac{1}{5}R_3 \to \begin{bmatrix} 1 & -2 & 1 & | & 5 \\ 0 & 1 & -1 & | & -3 \\ 0 & 0 & 1 & | & 2 \end{bmatrix}$$

$$x - 2y + z = 5$$
$$y - z = -3$$
$$z = 2$$

$$y - z = -3$$
$$y - 2 = -3$$
$$y = -1$$

$$x - 2y + z = 5$$
$$x - 2(-1) + 2 = 5$$
$$x + 2 + 2 = 5$$
$$x + 4 = 5$$
$$x = 1$$

The solution is $(1, -1, 2)$.

19. **a.** The regression line is

```
LinReg
y=ax+b
a=-.3571428571
b=766.7142857
r²=.9873617694
r=-.9936607919
```

$y = -0.3571428571x + 766.71429$.

b. $y = -0.3571428571x + 766.71429$
$y = -0.3571428571(2020) + 766.71429 \approx 45$

The population expected to live in rural areas in 2020 is 45%.

c. The slope is negative; as x increases, y decreases.

20. Strategy
To find the rate of the cruise ship in calm water and the rate of the current, let x represent the rate of the cruise ship in calm water and y represent the rate of the current. Then
Rate of ship with current: $x + y$
Rate of ship against current: $x - y$
The distance traveled with the current is 90 miles. The distance traveled against the current is 90 miles. Use the equation $d = rt$ to express the distances traveled with and against the current as the two equations of a system.

Solution
$$3(x + y) = 90$$
$$4.5(x - y) = 90$$

$$\frac{1}{3} \cdot 3(x + y) = \frac{1}{3} \cdot 90$$
$$\frac{1}{4.5} \cdot 4.5(x - y) = \frac{1}{4.5} \cdot 90$$

$$x + y = 30$$
$$x - y = 20$$

$$2x = 50$$
$$x = 25$$

$$x + y = 30$$
$$25 + y = 30$$
$$y = 5$$

The rate of the cruise ship is 25 mph. The rate of the current is 5 mph.

Chapter 6: Polynomials

Prep Test

1. $-4(3y) = -12y$

2. $(-2)^3 = -8$

3. $-4a - 8b + 7a = 3a - 8b$

4. $3x - 2[y - 4(x+1) + 5]$
   $= 3x - 2[y - 4x - 4 + 5]$
   $= 3x - 2[y - 4x + 1]$
   $= 3x - 2y + 8x - 2$
   $= 11x - 2y - 2$

5. $-(x - y) = -x + y$

Go Figure

There are less than 10 tables. If you seat 5 people at each table, and there are two people at the last table, you may have as many as 47 guests or as few as 7 guests. However, since we also know that if we seat 3 people at each table and have 9 people with nowhere to sit, we know that neither 47 nor 7 is the solution.

The number of guests can be written as the expression $5x + 2$ from the first sentence and $3y + 9$, from the second sentence, where x and y represent the number of tables and are integers less than 10. We want to find the value of the expressions when they are equal.

One way to approach the solution is to use trial and error and try all values of tables until a solution is determined:

$5(9) + 2 = 47$	$3(9) + 9 = 36$
$5(8) + 2 = 42$	$3(8) + 9 = 33$
$5(7) + 2 = 37$	$3(7) + 9 = 30$
$5(6) + 2 = 32$	$3(6) + 9 = 27$
$5(5) + 2 = 27$	

There are 27 guests.

Section 6.1

1. **a.** This is a monomial because it is the product of a number, 32, and variables, a and b.

    b. This is a monomial because it is the product of a number, $\frac{5}{7}$, and a variable, n.

    c. This is not a monomial because there is a variable in the denominator.

3. **a.** The exponent on 6 is positive; it should not be moved to the denominator. $6x^{-3} = \frac{6}{x^3}$

    b. The exponent on x is positive; it should not be moved to the denominator. $xy^{-2} = \frac{x}{y^2}$

    c. The exponent on 8 is positive; it should not be moved to the numerator. $\frac{1}{8a^{-4}} = \frac{a^4}{8}$

    d. The exponent on c is positive; it should not be moved to the numerator. $\frac{1}{b^{-5}c} = \frac{b^5}{c}$

5. $a^4 \cdot a^5 = a^{4+5} = a^9$

7. $z^3 \cdot z \cdot z^4 = z^3 \cdot z^1 \cdot z^4 = z^{3+1+4} = z^8$

9. $(x^3)^5 = x^{3 \cdot 5} = x^{15}$

11. $(x^2 y^3)^6 = x^{2 \cdot 6} y^{3 \cdot 6} = x^{12} y^{18}$

13. $12s^4 t^3 + 5s^4 t^3 = 17s^4 t^3$

15. $27^0 = 1$

17. $\frac{a^8}{a^2} = a^{8-2} = a^6$

19. $(-m^3 n)(m^6 n^2) = (-m^3 \cdot m^6)(n \cdot n^2)$
    $= -m^{3+6} \cdot n^{1+2}$
    $= -m^9 n^3$

21. $(2x)(3x^2)(4x^4) = (2 \cdot 3 \cdot 4)(x \cdot x^2 \cdot x^4)$
    $= 24x^{1+2+4}$
    $= 24x^7$

23. $(-2a^2)^3 = (-2)^{1 \cdot 3} a^{2 \cdot 3}$
    $= (-2)^3 a^6$
    $= -8a^6$

25. $11p^4 q^5 - 7p^4 q^5 = 4p^4 q^5$

27. $(6r^2)(-4r) = (-4 \cdot 6)(r^2 \cdot r)$
$$= -24r^{2+1}$$
$$= -24r^3$$

29. $(2a^3bc^2)^3 = 2^{1 \cdot 3}a^{3 \cdot 3}b^{1 \cdot 3}c^{2 \cdot 3}$
$$= 2^3 a^9 b^3 c^6$$
$$= 8a^9 b^3 c^6$$

31. $\dfrac{m^4 n^7}{m^3 n^5} = m^{4-3}n^{7-5}$
$$= m^1 n^2$$
$$= mn^2$$

33. $(3x)^0 = 1$

35. $\dfrac{-16a^7}{24a^6} = -\dfrac{2a^7}{3a^6} = -\dfrac{2a^{7-6}}{3} = -\dfrac{2a}{3}$

37. $(9mn^4 p)(-3mp^2)$
$$= (-3 \cdot 9)(m \cdot m)(n^4)(p \cdot p^2)$$
$$= (-27)(m^{1+1})(n^4)(p^{1+2})$$
$$= -27m^2 n^4 p^3$$

39. $(-xy^5)(3x^2)(5y^3)$
$$= (3 \cdot 5)(-x \cdot x^2)(y^5 \cdot y^3)$$
$$= -15(x^{1+2})(y^{5+3})$$
$$= -15x^3 y^8$$

41. $\dfrac{x^4}{x^9} = x^{4-9} = x^{-5} = \dfrac{1}{x^5}$

43. $(-2n^2)(-3n^4)^3 = (-2n^2)(-3)^{1 \cdot 3}(n^{4 \cdot 3})$
$$= (-2n^2)(-3)^3 n^{12}$$
$$= (-2n^2)(-27)n^{12}$$
$$= (-2)(-27)n^{2+12}$$
$$= 54n^{14}$$

45. $\dfrac{14x^4 y^6 z^2}{16x^3 y^9 z} = \dfrac{7x^4 y^6 z^2}{8x^3 y^9 z}$
$$= \dfrac{7x^{4-3}y^{6-9}z^{2-1}}{8}$$
$$= \dfrac{7x^1 y^{-3}z^1}{8}$$
$$= \dfrac{7xz}{8y^3}$$

47. $(-2x^3 y^2)^3 (-xy^2)^4$
$$= (-2)^{1 \cdot 3}x^{3 \cdot 3}y^{2 \cdot 3}(-1)^{1 \cdot 4}x^{1 \cdot 4}y^{2 \cdot 4}$$
$$= (-2)^3 x^9 y^6 (-1)^4 x^4 y^8$$
$$= -8x^9 y^6 (1)x^4 y^8$$
$$= -8x^{9+4}y^{6+8}$$
$$= -8x^{13}y^{14}$$

49. $w^{-8} = \dfrac{1}{w^8}$

51. $\dfrac{1}{a^{-5}} = a^5$

53. $4^{-3} = \dfrac{1}{4^3} = \dfrac{1}{64}$

55. $\dfrac{1}{3^{-5}} = 3^5 = 243$

57. $4x^{-7} = \dfrac{4}{x^7}$

59. $\dfrac{2x^{-2}}{y^4} = \dfrac{2}{x^2 y^4}$

61. $x^{-4} \cdot x^4 = x^0 = 1$

63. $\dfrac{x^{-3}}{x^2} = x^{-5} = \dfrac{1}{x^5}$

65. $(3x^{-2})^2 = 3^2 x^{-4} = \dfrac{9}{x^4}$

67. $\dfrac{1}{3x^{-2}} = \dfrac{x^2}{3}$

69. $(x^2 y^{-4})^3 = x^6 y^{-12} = \dfrac{x^6}{y^{12}}$

71. $(3x^{-1}y^{-2})^2 = 3^2 x^{-2}y^{-4} = \dfrac{9}{x^2 y^4}$

73. $(2x^{-1})(x^{-3}) = 2x^{-1+(-3)} = 2x^{-4} = \dfrac{2}{x^4}$

75. $\dfrac{3x^{-2}y^2}{6xy^2} = \dfrac{1x^{-2}y^2}{2xy^2}$
$$= \dfrac{1x^{-2-1}y^{2-2}}{2}$$
$$= \dfrac{1x^{-3}y^0}{2}$$
$$= \dfrac{1}{2x^3}$$

77. $\dfrac{2x^{-1}y^{-4}}{4xy^2} = \dfrac{1x^{-1}y^{-4}}{2xy^2}$
$$= \dfrac{1x^{-1-1}y^{-4-2}}{2}$$
$$= \dfrac{1x^{-2}y^{-6}}{2}$$
$$= \dfrac{1}{2x^2 y^6}$$

79. $(x^{-2}y)^2 (xy)^{-2} = (x^{-4}y^2)(x^{-2}y^{-2})$
$$= x^{-6}y^0$$
$$= \dfrac{1}{x^6}$$

81. $\left(\dfrac{x^2 y^{-1}}{xy}\right)^{-4} = \left(\dfrac{x}{y^2}\right)^{-4} = \dfrac{x^{-4}}{y^{-8}} = \dfrac{y^8}{x^4}$

83. $\left(\dfrac{4a^{-2}b}{8a^3 b^{-4}}\right)^2 = \left(\dfrac{b^5}{2a^5}\right)^2 = \dfrac{b^{10}}{4a^{10}}$

85. The length of line segment AC is the sum of the lengths of segments AB and BC:
$3xy + 8xy = 11xy$.

87. The length of line segment MN is the difference in lengths of segments LN and LM:
$27a^2 b - 12a^2 b = 15a^2 b$

89. The area of a square is the length of a side squared:
$$(8x^2 y)^2 = 8^{1\cdot2} x^{2\cdot2} y^{1\cdot2}$$
$$= 8^2 x^4 y^2$$
$$= 64x^4 y^2$$
The area of the square is $64x^4 y^2$ m^2.

91. The perimeter of the rectangle is the sum of twice the lengths of each side:
$$2(15c^3 a^4) + 2(10c^3 a^4)$$
$$= 30c^3 a^4 + 20c^3 a^4$$
$$= 50c^3 a^4$$
The perimeter of the rectangle is $50c^3 a^4$ mi.

93. The area of the rectangle is the product of the lengths of the sides:
$$(9mn^2)(6mn^2) = (9\cdot6)m^{1+1} n^{2+2}$$
$$= 54m^2 n^4$$
The area is $54m^2 n^4$ km^2.

95. The length of the rectangle is the quotient of the area of the rectangle and the width of the rectangle:
$$\dfrac{24a^3 b^5}{4ab^2} = \dfrac{6a^3 b^5}{1ab^2}$$
$$= \dfrac{6a^{3-1} b^{5-2}}{1}$$
$$= \dfrac{6a^2 b^3}{1}$$
$$= 6a^2 b^3$$
The length of the rectangle is $6a^2 b^3$ yd.

97. The monomial is the quotient of $12a^2 b$ and $4b$:
$\dfrac{12a^2 b}{4b} = \dfrac{3a^2 b}{1b} = \dfrac{3a^2 b^{1-1}}{1} = 3a^2 b^0 = 3a^2$

99. Move the decimal point 6 places to the left. The exponent on 10 is 6:
$2,370,000 = 2.37 \times 10^6$

101. Move the decimal point 4 places to the right. The exponent on 10 is –4:
$0.00045 = 4.5 \times 10^{-4}$

103. Move the decimal point 5 places to the left. The exponent on 10 is 5:
$309,000 = 3.09 \times 10^5$

105. Move the decimal point 7 places to the right. The exponent on 10 is –7:
$0.000000601 = 6.01 \times 10^{-7}$

107. Move the decimal point 10 places to the left. The exponent on 10 is 10:
$57,000,000,000 = 5.7 \times 10^{10}$

109. Move the decimal point 8 places to the right. The exponent on 10 is –8:
$0.000000017 = 1.7 \times 10^{-8}$

111. The exponent on 10 is positive. Move the decimal point 5 places to the right:
$7.1 \times 10^5 = 710,000$

113. The exponent on 10 is negative. Move the decimal point 5 places to the left:
$4.3 \times 10^{-5} = 0.000043$

115. The exponent on 10 is positive. Move the decimal point 8 places to the right:
$6.71 \times 10^8 = 671,000,000$

117. The exponent on 10 is negative. Move the decimal point 6 places to the left:
$7.13 \times 10^{-6} = 0.00000713$

119. The exponent on 10 is positive. Move the decimal point 12 places to the right:
$5 \times 10^{12} = 5,000,000,000,000$

121. The exponent on 10 is negative. Move the decimal point 3 places to the left:
$8.01 \times 10^{-3} = 0.00801$

123. Move the decimal point 10 places to the left. The exponent on 10 is 10:
$16,000,000,000 = 1.6 \times 10^{10}$

125. The dollar amount for Star Wars was $131.7 million. Move the decimal point 8 places to the left. The exponent on 10 is 8:
$131,700,000 = \$1.317 \times 10^8$

127. Move the decimal point 19 places to the right. The exponent on 10 is –19:
0.0000000000000000016
$= 1.6 \times 10^{-19}$

129. Move the decimal point 23 places to the left. The exponent on 10 is 23:
$$602,300,000,000,000,000,000,000$$
$$= 6.023 \times 10^{23}$$

131. Move the decimal point 18 places to the left. The exponent on 10 is 18:
$$3,086,000,000,000,000,000$$
$$= 3.086 \times 10^{18}$$

133. $(1.9 \times 10^{12})(3.5 \times 10^{7}) = (1.9)(3.5) \times 10^{12+7}$
$$= 6.65 \times 10^{19}$$

135. $(2.3 \times 10^{-8})(1.4 \times 10^{-6})$
$$= (2.3)(1.4) \times 10^{-8+(-6)}$$
$$= 3.22 \times 10^{-14}$$

137. $\dfrac{6.12 \times 10^{14}}{1.7 \times 10^{9}} = \left(\dfrac{6.12}{1.7}\right) \times 10^{14-9}$
$$= 3.6 \times 10^{5}$$

139. $\dfrac{5.58 \times 10^{-7}}{3.1 \times 10^{11}} = \left(\dfrac{5.58}{3.1}\right) \times 10^{-7-11}$
$$= 1.8 \times 10^{-18}$$

141. a. (a) $8^{-2} + 2^{-5} = \dfrac{1}{8^2} + \dfrac{1}{2^5}$
$$= \dfrac{1}{64} + \dfrac{1}{32}$$
$$= \dfrac{1}{64} + \dfrac{2}{64}$$
$$= \dfrac{3}{64}$$

b. (b) $9^{-2} + 3^{-3} = \dfrac{1}{9^2} + \dfrac{1}{3^3}$
$$= \dfrac{1}{81} + \dfrac{1}{27}$$
$$= \dfrac{1}{81} + \dfrac{3}{81}$$
$$= \dfrac{4}{81}$$

143. $2^x = 2^{-2} = \dfrac{1}{2^2} = \dfrac{1}{4}$
$$2^x = 2^{-1} = \dfrac{1}{2^1} = \dfrac{1}{2}$$
$$2^x = 2^0 = 1$$
$$2^x = 2^1 = 2$$
$$2^x = 2^2 = 4$$
and
$$2^{-x} = 2^{-(-2)} = 2^2 = 4$$
$$2^{-x} = 2^{-(-1)} = 2^1 = 2$$
$$2^{-x} = 2^{-(0)} = 2^0 = 1$$
$$2^{-x} = 2^{-1} = \dfrac{1}{2^1} = \dfrac{1}{2}$$
$$2^{-x} = 2^{-2} = \dfrac{1}{2^2} = \dfrac{1}{4}$$

145. If $m = n + 1$ and $a \neq 0$, then
$$\dfrac{a^m}{a^n} = \dfrac{a^{n+1}}{a^n} = a^{n+1-n} = a^1 = a$$

Section 6.2

1. a. This is a binomial. It contains two terms, $8x^4$ and $-6x^2$.

   b. This is a trinomial. It contains three terms, $4a^2b^2$, $9ab$, and 10.

   c. This is a monomial. It is one term, $7x^3y^4$. (Note: it is a product of a number and variables. There is no addition or subtraction operation in the expression.)

3. a. Yes. Both $\dfrac{1}{5}x^3$ and $\dfrac{1}{2}x$ are monomials. (Note: the coefficients of variables can be fractions.)

   b. No. A polynomial does not have a variable in the denominator of a fraction.

   c. Yes. Both x and $\sqrt{5}$ are monomials. (Note: the variable is not under a radical sign.)

5. $V(h) = \dfrac{8}{3}\pi h^3$
$$V(2) = \dfrac{8}{3}\pi (2)^3$$
$$= \dfrac{8}{3}\pi (8)$$
$$= \dfrac{64}{3}\pi \approx 67.02$$
The volume of a sand pile that is 2 feet high is 67.02 ft^3.

7. $L(v) = 0.6411v^2$
$$L(30) = 0.6411(30)^2$$
$$= 0.6411(900)$$
$$= 576.99$$
The length of a deep-water wave that has a speed of 30 meters per second is 576.99 m.

9. The value of t before the diver starts the dive is 0:
$$h(t) = -16t^2 + 5t + 50$$
$$h(0) = -16(0)^2 + 5(0) + 50$$
$$= 0 + 0 + 50$$
$$= 50$$
The cliff is 50 ft high.

11. $F(x) = -14.2x^3 + 63.9x^2$
$$F(3) = -14.2(3)^3 + 63.9(3)^2$$
$$= -383.4 + 575.1$$
$$= 191.7$$
The force on the dam is 191.7 lb.

13. $E(x) = 62.4\pi\left(-\dfrac{x^4}{64} + \dfrac{5x^3}{16}\right)$

$E(8) = 62.4\pi\left(-\dfrac{(8)^4}{64} + \dfrac{5(8)^3}{16}\right)$

$= 196.04(-64 + 160)$

$= 18{,}819.4$

The energy required is 18,819 foot-pounds.

15. $(x^2 + 7x) + (-3x^2 - 4x)$

$= (x^2 - 3x^2) + (7x - 4x)$

$= -2x^2 + 3x$

17. $(x^2 - 6x) - (x^2 - 10x)$

$= (x^2 - 6x) + (-x^2 + 10x)$

$= (x^2 - x^2) + (-6x + 10x)$

$= 0 + 4x$

$= 4x$

19. $(4b^2 - 5b) + (3b^2 + 6b - 4)$

$= (4b^2 + 3b^2) + (-5b + 6b) + (-4)$

$= 7b^2 + b - 4$

21. $(2y^2 - 4y) - (-y^2 + 2)$

$= (2y^2 - 4y) + (y^2 - 2)$

$= (2y^2 + y^2) + (-4y) + (-2)$

$= 3y^2 - 4y - 2$

23. $(2a^2 - 7a + 10) + (a^2 + 4a + 7)$

$= (2a^2 + a^2) + (-7a + 4a) + (10 + 7)$

$= 3a^2 - 3a + 17$

25. $(x^2 - 2x + 1) - (x^2 + 5x + 8)$

$= (x^2 - 2x + 1) + (-x^2 - 5x - 8)$

$= (x^2 - x^2) + (-2x - 5x) + (1 - 8)$

$= (0) + (-7x) + (-7)$

$= -7x - 7$

27. $(-2x^3 + x - 1) - (-x^2 + x - 3)$

$= (-2x^3 + x - 1) + (x^2 - x + 3)$

$= -2x^3 + x^2 + (x - x) + (-1 + 3)$

$= -2x^3 + x^2 + (0) + 2$

$= -2x^3 + x^2 + 2$

29. $(x^3 - 7x + 4) + (2x^2 + x - 10)$

$= x^3 + 2x^2 + (-7x + x) + (4 - 10)$

$= x^3 + 2x^2 - 6x - 6$

31. $(5x^3 + 7x - 7) + (10x^2 - 8x + 3)$

$= 5x^3 + 10x^2 + (7x - 8x) + (-7 + 3)$

$= 5x^3 + 10x^2 - x - 4$

33. $(2y^3 + 6y - 2) - (y^3 + y^2 + 4)$

$= (2y^3 + 6y - 2) + (-y^3 - y^2 - 4)$

$= (2y^3 - y^3) - y^2 + 6y + (-2 - 4)$

$= y^3 - y^2 + 6y - 6$

35. $(4y^3 - y - 1) - (2y^2 - 3y + 3)$

$= (4y^3 - y - 1) + (-2y^2 + 3y - 3)$

$= 4y^3 - 2y^2 + (-y + 3y) + (-1 - 3)$

$= 4y^3 - 2y^2 + 2y - 4$

37. To find the length of line segment AC, add the lengths of line segments AB and BC:

$(3x^2 - 4x + 5) + (8x^2 + 6x - 1)$

$= (3x^2 + 8x^2) + (-4x + 6x) + (5 - 1)$

$= 11x^2 + 2x + 4$

39. To find the length of line segment MN, subtract the length of line segment LM from the length of line segment LN:

$(7a^2 + 4a - 3) - (2a^2 + a + 6)$

$= (7a^2 + 4a - 3) + (-2a^2 - a - 6)$

$= (7a^2 - 2a^2) + (4a - a) + (-3 - 6)$

$= 5a^2 + 3a - 9$

41. The perimeter of the rectangle is the sum of all of the lengths of the sides of the rectangle:

$(3d^2 + 5d - 4) + (d^2 + d + 6)$

$\quad + (3d^2 + 5d - 4) + (d^2 + d + 6)$

$= (3d^2 + d^2 + 3d^2 + d^2)$

$\quad + (5d + d + 5d + d) + (-4 + 6 - 4 + 6)$

$= 8d^2 + 12d + 4$

The perimeter is ($8d^2 + 12d + 4$) km.

43. Let $C = 240n + 1200$ and $R = -2n^2 + 400n$. Then

$P = R - C$

$= (-2n^2 + 400n) - (240n + 1200)$

$= (-2n^2 + 400n) + (-240n - 1200)$

$= -2n^2 + (400n - 240n) - 1200$

$= -2n^2 + 160n - 1200$

The company's monthly profit in terms of n is $(-2n^2 + 160n - 1200)$ dollars.

45. To find the polynomial that must be added, subtract $3x^2 - 4x - 2$ from $-x^2 + 2x + 1$:

$(-x^2 + 2x + 1) - (3x^2 - 4x - 2)$

$= (-x^2 + 2x + 1) + (-3x^2 + 4x + 2)$

$= (-x^2 - 3x^2) + (2x + 4x) + (1 + 2)$

$= -4x^2 + 6x + 3$

47. To find the polynomial that must be subtracted, subtract $2x^2 + 2x - 5$ from $6x^2 - 4x - 2$:

$(6x^2 - 4x - 2) - (2x^2 + 2x - 5)$
$= (6x^2 - 4x - 2) + (-2x^2 - 2x + 5)$
$= (6x^2 - 2x^2) + (-4x - 2x) + (-2 + 5)$
$= 4x^2 - 6x + 3$

Applying Concepts 6.2

49. a. Sometimes true

b. Always true

c. Sometimes true

51. a. $(2x^3 + 3x^2 + kx + 5) - (x^3 + 2x^2 + 3x + 7)$
$= x^3 + x^2 + 5x - 2$
To find the value of k, we only use the terms from the equation that are of the same degree.
$kx - 3x = 5x$
$kx = 8x$
$k = 8$

b. $(6x^3 + kx^2 - 2x - 1) - (4x^3 - 3x^2 + 1)$
$= 2x^3 - x^2 - 2x - 2$
To find the value of k, we only use the terms from the equation that are of the same degree.
$kx^2 + 3x^2 = -x^2$
$kx^2 = -4x^2$
$k = -4$

Section 6.3

1. The FOIL method is used to multiply two binomials.

3. $x + 1$ and $x^2 - x + 1$

5. a. Sometimes true

b. Never true

c. Always true

7. The degree of the first term of the quotient is one degree less than the degree of the first term of the dividend.

9. $x^2(3x^4 - 3x^2 - 2)$
$= 3x^6 - 3x^4 - 2x^2$

11. $2y^2(-3y^2 - 6y + 7)$
$= -6y^4 - 12y^3 + 14y^2$

13. $(-a^2 + 3a - 2)(2a - 1)$
$= -a^2(2a - 1) + 3a(2a - 1) - 2(2a - 1)$
$= -2a^3 + a^2 + 6a^2 - 3a - 4a + 2$
$= -2a^3 + 7a^2 - 7a + 2$

15. $(y^3 + 4y^2 - 8)(2y - 1)$
$= y^3(2y - 1) + 4y^2(2y - 1) - 8(2y - 1)$
$= 2y^4 - y^3 + 8y^3 - 4y^2 - 16y + 8$
$= 2y^4 + 7y^3 - 4y^2 - 16y + 8$

17. $(2a - 3)(2a^3 - 3a^2 + 2a - 1)$
$= 2a(2a^3 - 3a^2 + 2a - 1) - 3(2a^3 - 3a^2 + 2a - 1)$
$= 4a^4 - 6a^3 + 4a^2 - 2a - 6a^3 + 9a^2 - 6a + 3$
$= 4a^4 - 12a^3 + 13a^2 - 8a + 3$

19. $(y + 2)(y + 5)$
$= y(y) + y(5) + 2(y) + 2(5)$
$= y^2 + 5y + 2y + 10$
$= y^2 + 7y + 10$

21. $(b - 6)(b + 3)$
$= b(b) + b(3) + (-6)(b) + (-6)(3)$
$= b^2 + 3b - 6b - 18$
$= b^2 - 3b - 18$

23. $(a - 8)(a - 9)$
$= a(a) + a(-9) + (-8)(a) + (-8)(-9)$
$= a^2 - 9a - 8a + 72$
$= a^2 - 17a + 72$

25. $(y + 2)(5y + 1)$
$= y(5y) + y(1) + 2(5y) + 2(1)$
$= 5y^2 + y + 10y + 2$
$= 5y^2 + 11y + 2$

27. $(7x - 2)(x + 4) = 7x^2 + 28x - 2x - 8$
$\qquad\qquad\qquad = 7x^2 + 26x - 8$

29. $(2x - 3)(4x - 7) = 8x^2 - 14x - 12x + 21$
$\qquad\qquad\qquad = 8x^2 - 26x + 21$

31. $(5y - 9)(y + 5) = 5y^2 + 25y - 9y - 45$
$\qquad\qquad\qquad = 5y^2 + 16y - 45$

33. $(5a - 12)(3a - 7)$
$= 15a^2 - 35a - 36a + 84$
$= 15a^2 - 71a + 84$

35. $(x + y)(2x + y) = 2x^2 + xy + 2xy + y^2$
$\qquad\qquad\qquad = 2x^2 + 3xy + y^2$

37. $(3x - 4y)(x - 2y)$
$= 3x^2 - 6xy - 4xy + 8y^2$
$= 3x^2 - 10xy + 8y^2$

39. $(5a - 3b)(2a + 4b)$
$= 10a^2 + 20ab - 6ab - 12b^2$
$= 10a^2 + 14ab - 12b^2$

41. $(y - 5)(y + 5) = y^2 + 5y - 5y - 25$
$\qquad\qquad\qquad = y^2 - 25$

43. $(4x-7)(4x+7)$
$=16x^2+28x-28x-49$
$=16x^2-49$

45. $(y-3)^2=(y-3)(y-3)$
$=y^2-3y-3y+9$
$=y^2-6y+9$

47. $(6x-5)^2=(6x-5)(6x-5)$
$=36x^2-30x-30x+25$
$=36x^2-60x+25$

49. $\dfrac{5y+5}{5}=\dfrac{5y}{5}+\dfrac{5}{5}=y+1$

51. $\dfrac{16b-40}{8}=\dfrac{16b}{8}-\dfrac{40}{8}=2b-5$

53. $\dfrac{6y^2+4y}{y}=\dfrac{6y^2}{y}+\dfrac{4y}{y}=6y+4$

55. $\dfrac{12x^2-7x}{x}=\dfrac{12x^2}{x}-\dfrac{7x}{x}=12x-7$

57. $\dfrac{10y^2-6y}{2y}=\dfrac{10y^2}{2y}-\dfrac{6y}{2y}=5y-3$

59. $\dfrac{3y^2-27y}{-3y}=\dfrac{3y^2}{-3y}-\dfrac{27y}{-3y}=-y+9$

61. $\dfrac{a^3-5a^2+7a}{a}=\dfrac{a^3}{a}-\dfrac{5a^2}{a}+\dfrac{7a}{a}$
$=a^2-5a+7$

63. $\dfrac{a^8-5a^5-3a^3}{a^2}=\dfrac{a^8}{a^2}-\dfrac{5a^5}{a^2}-\dfrac{3a^3}{a^2}$
$=a^6-5a^3-3a$

65. $\dfrac{8x^2y^2-24xy}{8xy}=\dfrac{8x^2y^2}{8xy}-\dfrac{24xy}{8xy}$
$=xy-3$

67.
$$
\begin{array}{r}
x+2 \\
x-3\overline{)x^2-x-6} \\
\underline{x^2-3x} \\
2x-6 \\
\underline{2x-6} \\
0
\end{array}
$$
$(x^2-x-6)\div(x-3)=x+2$

69.
$$
\begin{array}{r}
2y-7 \\
y-3\overline{)2y^2-13y+21} \\
\underline{2y^2-6y} \\
-7y+21 \\
\underline{-7y+21} \\
0
\end{array}
$$
$(2y^2-13y+21)\div(y-3)=2y-7$

71.
$$
\begin{array}{r}
x-2 \\
x+2\overline{)x^2+0x+4} \\
\underline{x^2+2x} \\
-2x+4 \\
\underline{-2x-4} \\
8
\end{array}
$$
$(x^2+4)\div(x+2)=x-2+\dfrac{8}{x+2}$

73.
$$
\begin{array}{r}
3y-5 \\
2y+4\overline{)6y^2+2y+0} \\
\underline{6y^2+12y} \\
-10y+0 \\
\underline{-10y-20} \\
20
\end{array}
$$
$(6y^2+2y)\div(2y+4)=3y-5+\dfrac{20}{2y+4}$

75.
$$
\begin{array}{r}
b-5 \\
b-3\overline{)b^2-8b-9} \\
\underline{b^2-3b} \\
-5b-9 \\
\underline{-5b+15} \\
-24
\end{array}
$$
$(b^2-8b-9)\div(b-3)=b-5-\dfrac{24}{b-3}$

77.
$$
\begin{array}{r}
3x+17 \\
x-4\overline{)3x^2+5x-4} \\
\underline{3x^2-12x} \\
17x-4 \\
\underline{17x-68} \\
64
\end{array}
$$
$(3x^2+5x-4)\div(x-4)=3x+17+\dfrac{64}{x-4}$

79.
$$
\begin{array}{r}
5y+3 \\
2y+3\overline{)10y^2+21y+10} \\
\underline{10y^2+15y} \\
6y+10 \\
\underline{6y+\ 9} \\
1
\end{array}
$$
$(10+21y+10y^2)\div(2y+3)$
$=5y+3+\dfrac{1}{2y+3}$

81.
$$\begin{array}{r} x^2 - 5x + 2 \\ x-1\overline{)x^3 - 6x^2 + 7x - 2} \\ \underline{x^3 - x^2} \\ -5x^2 + 7x \\ \underline{-5x^2 + 5x} \\ 2x - 2 \\ \underline{2x - 2} \\ 0 \end{array}$$

$(x^3 - 6x^2 + 7x - 2) \div (x - 1) = x^2 - 5x + 2$

83.
$$\begin{array}{r} x^2 + 5 \\ x^2-2\overline{)x^4 + 3x^2 - 10} \\ \underline{x^4 - 2x^2} \\ 5x^2 - 10 \\ \underline{5x^2 - 10} \\ 0 \end{array}$$

$(x^4 + 3x^2 - 10) \div (x^2 - 2) = x^2 + 5$

85. The area of a square is the square of the length of a side:

$(3a - 2)^2 = (3a - 2)(3a - 2)$
$\qquad = 9a^2 - 6a - 6a + 4$
$\qquad = 9a^2 - 12a + 4$

The area of the square is $(9a^2 - 12a + 4)$ yd^2.

87. The area of the rectangle is the product of the lengths of its two sides:

$(x - 6)(2x + 3) = 2x^2 + 3x - 12x - 18$
$\qquad\qquad = 2x^2 - 9x - 18$

The area of the rectangle is $(2x^2 - 9x - 18)$ ft^2.

89. $A = \pi r^2$
$\quad = \pi(x - 3)^2$
$\quad = \pi(x - 3)(x - 3)$
$\quad = \pi(x^2 - 3x - 3x + 9)$
$\quad = \pi(x^2 - 6x + 9)$
$\quad = \pi x^2 - 6\pi x + 9\pi$

The area of the circle is $(\pi x^2 - 6\pi x + 9\pi)$ cm^2.

91. To find the volume of the box multiply the length by the width by the height:

$4x(5x + 3)(2x - 1)$
$= (20x^2 + 12x)(2x - 1)$
$= 40x^3 - 20x^2 + 24x^2 - 12x$
$= 40x^3 + 4x^2 - 12x$

The volume of the box is
$(40x^3 + 4x^2 - 12x)$ cm^3.

93. $A = 0.5bh$
$\quad = 0.5(2x + 6)(x - 8)$
$\quad = 0.5(2x^2 - 16x + 6x - 48)$
$\quad = 0.5(2x^2 - 10x - 48)$
$\quad = x^2 - 5x - 24$

The area of the triangle is $(x^2 - 5x - 24)$ in^2.

95. Width $= 4x - 3$ and length $= 2(4x - 3)$:
$A = LW$
$\quad = 2(4x - 3)(4x - 3)$
$\quad = 2(16x^2 - 12x - 12x + 9)$
$\quad = 2(16x^2 - 24x + 9)$
$\quad = 32x^2 - 48x + 18$

The area of the rectangle is
$(32x^2 - 48x + 18)$ cm^2.

97. $A = 10x^2 + 7x - 12$, $L = 5x - 4$

$W = \dfrac{A}{L} = \dfrac{10x^2 + 7x - 12}{5x - 4}$

$$\begin{array}{r} 2x + 3 \\ 5x-4\overline{)10x^2 + 7x - 12} \\ \underline{10x^2 - 8x} \\ 15x - 12 \\ \underline{15x - 12} \\ 0 \end{array}$$

The width is $(2x + 3)$ m.

99. $A = 2x^3 + 6x^2 - 4x - 12$, $b = x + 3$

$h = \dfrac{A}{b} = \dfrac{2x^3 + 6x^2 - 4x - 12}{x + 3}$

$$\begin{array}{r} 2x^2 - 4 \\ x+3\overline{)2x^3 + 6x^2 - 4x - 12} \\ \underline{2x^3 + 6x^2} \\ -4x - 12 \\ \underline{-4x - 12} \\ 0 \end{array}$$

The height of the parallelogram is $(2x^2 - 4)$ m.

101. The length of the field including end zones is $w + 100 + w = 2w + 100$. The width of the field is 30 yards. The area is $30(2w + 100) = (60w + 3000)$ yd^2.

103. The width of the trough is $50 - x - x = 50 - 2x$. The height of the trough is x. Thus the volume is:
$V = 200x(50 - 2x)$
$\quad = 10,000x - 400x^2$

When $x = 10$:
$10,000x - 400x^2 = 10,000(10) - 400(10)^2$
$\qquad\qquad\qquad = 10,000(10) - 400(100)$
$\qquad\qquad\qquad = 100,000 - 40,000$
$\qquad\qquad\qquad = 60,000$

The volume is 60,000 cm^3.

105. To find the polynomial, multiply the quotient by the dividend:

$(3x - 4)(4x + 5) = 12x^2 + 15x - 16x - 20$
$\qquad\qquad\qquad = 12x^2 - x - 20$

107.

$$x-2\overline{)x^3+2x^2-9x+2}$$ with quotient x^2+4x-1

$$\begin{array}{r} x^2+4x-1 \\ x-2\overline{)x^3+2x^2-9x+2} \\ \underline{x^3-2x^2} \\ 4x^2-9x \\ \underline{4x^2-8x} \\ -x+2 \\ \underline{-x+2} \\ 0 \end{array}$$

Another factor of x^3+2x^2-9x+2 is

x^2+4x-1.

109. First find the product:

$(2x-5)(3x+1)=6x^2+2x-15x-5$
$=6x^2-13x-5$

Now add the given polynomials to this result:

$(6x^2-13x-5)+(x^2+2x-3)$
$=(6x^2+x^2)+(-13x+2x)+(-5-3)$
$=7x^2-11x-8$

111. To find the polynomial, multiply the given divisor and quotient:

$\left(x^2-x+8+\dfrac{22}{x-3}\right)(x-3)$

$=x^2(x-3)-x(x-3)+8(x-3)+\dfrac{22}{x-3}(x-3)$

$=x^3-3x^2-x^2+3x+8x-24+22$

$=x^3-4x^2+11x-2$

113.

$$\begin{array}{c|cccc} 3 & 1 & -6 & 11 & -6 \\ & & 3 & -9 & 6 \\ \hline & 1 & -3 & 2 & 0 \end{array}$$

$(x^3-6x^2+11x-6)\div(x-3)=x^2-3x+2$

115.

$$\begin{array}{c|cccc} -1 & 2 & -1 & 6 & 9 \\ & & -2 & 3 & -9 \\ \hline & 2 & -3 & 9 & 0 \end{array}$$

$(2x^3-x^2+6x+9)\div(x+1)=2x^2-3x+9$

117.

$$\begin{array}{c|cccc} -2 & 1 & -3 & 6 & -9 \\ & & -2 & 10 & -32 \\ \hline & 1 & -5 & 16 & -41 \end{array}$$

$(6x-3x^2+x^3-9)\div(x+2)$

$=x^2-5x+16-\dfrac{41}{x+2}$

119.

$$\begin{array}{c|cccc} -1 & 1 & 0 & 1 & -2 \\ & & -1 & 1 & -2 \\ \hline & 1 & -1 & 2 & -4 \end{array}$$

$(x^3+x-2)\div(x+1)=x^2-x+2-\dfrac{4}{x+1}$

121.

$$\begin{array}{c|ccc} 1 & 3 & 0 & -4 \\ & & 3 & 3 \\ \hline & 3 & 3 & -1 \end{array}$$

$(3x^2-4)\div(x-1)=3x+3-\dfrac{1}{x-1}$

123.

$$\begin{array}{c|ccccc} 5 & 2 & -13 & 16 & -9 & 20 \\ & & 10 & -15 & 5 & -20 \\ \hline & 2 & -3 & 1 & -4 & 0 \end{array}$$

$\dfrac{16x^2-13x^3+2x^4-9x+20}{x-5}=2x^3-3x^2+x-4$

125.

$$\begin{array}{c|ccccc} -1 & 3 & 3 & -1 & 3 & 2 \\ & & -3 & 0 & 1 & -4 \\ \hline & 3 & 0 & -1 & 4 & -2 \end{array}$$

$\dfrac{3x^4+3x^3-x^2+3x+2}{x+1}$

$=3x^3-x+4-\dfrac{2}{x+1}$

127.

$$\begin{array}{c|ccccc} 3 & 2 & 0 & -1 & 0 & 2 \\ & & 6 & 18 & 51 & 153 \\ \hline & 2 & 6 & 17 & 51 & 155 \end{array}$$

$\dfrac{2x^4-x^2+2}{x-3}$

$=2x^3+6x^2+17x+51+\dfrac{155}{x-3}$

129. Divide the volume by the height and then by the length to find the width.

$$\begin{array}{c|cccc} -2 & 1 & 11 & 38 & 40 \\ & & -2 & -18 & -40 \\ \hline & 1 & 9 & 20 & 0 \end{array}$$

$$\begin{array}{c|ccc} -5 & 1 & 9 & 20 \\ & & -5 & -20 \\ \hline & 1 & 4 & 0 \end{array}$$

The width is $(x+4)$ in.

131. Divide the polynomial by each of the linear factors to find the other linear factor.

$$
\begin{array}{c|ccccc}
1 & 1 & 1 & -7 & -1 & 6 \\
  &   & 1 & 2 & -5 & -6 \\
\hline
  & 1 & 2 & -5 & -6 & 0 \\
\end{array}
$$

$$
\begin{array}{c|cccc}
2 & 1 & 2 & -5 & -6 \\
  &   & 2 & 8 & 6 \\
\hline
  & 1 & 4 & 3 & 0 \\
\end{array}
$$

$$
\begin{array}{c|ccc}
-3 & 1 & 4 & 3 \\
   &   & -3 & -3 \\
\hline
   & 1 & 1 & 0 \\
\end{array}
$$

The other factor is $(x + 1)$.

Applying Concepts 6.3

133. a. Always true

   b. Always true

135. The length of each side is $20 - x - x = 20 - 2x$. The height of the box is x. Thus the volume is:

$$
\begin{aligned}
V &= x(20 - 2x)(20 - 2x) \\
  &= x(400 - 40x - 40x + 4x^2) \\
  &= x(400 - 80x + 4x^2) \\
  &= 4x^3 - 80x^2 + 400x
\end{aligned}
$$

The volume is $4x^3 - 80x^2 + 400x$ in^3.
No; explanations will vary.

137.
$$
\begin{array}{c|cccc}
2 & 1 & -2 & 1 & k \\
  &   & 2 & 0 & 2 \\
\hline
  & 1 & 0 & 1 & k+2 \\
\end{array}
$$

$$
\begin{aligned}
k + 2 &= 0 \\
k &= -2
\end{aligned}
$$

The remainder is zero when k equals -2.

139.
$$
\begin{array}{c|cccc}
1 & 1 & 0 & k & k-1 \\
  &   & 1 & 1 & k+1 \\
\hline
  & 1 & 1 & k+1 & 2k \\
\end{array}
$$

$$
\begin{aligned}
2k &= 0 \\
k &= 0
\end{aligned}
$$

The remainder is zero when k equals 0.

141.
$$
\begin{array}{c|cccc}
-1 & 3 & -2 & t & -4 \\
   &   & -3 & 5 & -t-5 \\
\hline
   & 3 & -5 & t+5 & -t-9 \\
\end{array}
$$

Because we are given that $x + 1$ is a factor, we know that the remainder is zero. Therefore,

$$
\begin{aligned}
-t - 9 &= 0 \\
-t &= 9 \\
t &= -9
\end{aligned}
$$

143.
$$
\begin{array}{c|ccc}
3 & 1 & -(a+b) & 3b \\
  &   & 3 & 9-3a-3b \\
\hline
  & 1 & 3-(a+b) & 9-3a \\
\end{array}
$$

$$
\begin{aligned}
9 - 3a &= 0 \\
9 &= 3a \\
3 &= a
\end{aligned}
$$

$$
\begin{array}{c|ccc}
3 & a-1 & b & a \\
  &   & 3a-3 & 9a-9+3b \\
\hline
  & a-1 & 3a-3+b & 10a-9+3b \\
\end{array}
$$

$$
\begin{aligned}
10a - 9 + 3b &= 0 \\
10(3) - 9 + 3b &= 0 \\
30 - 9 + 3b &= 0 \\
21 + 3b &= 0 \\
3b &= -21 \\
b &= -7
\end{aligned}
$$

The ordered pair is $(3, -7)$.

Chapter Review Exercises

1. $47a^2b^3c - 23a^2b^3c = 24a^2b^3c$

2.
$$
\begin{aligned}
&(3y^2 - 5y + 8) - (-2y^2 + 5y + 8) \\
&= (3y^2 - 5y + 8) + (2y^2 - 5y - 8) \\
&= (3y^2 + 2y^2) + (-5y - 5y) + (8 - 8) \\
&= 5y^2 - 10y
\end{aligned}
$$

3. $(5xy^2)(-4x^2y^3) = -20x^3y^5$

4. $\dfrac{12x^2}{-3x^{-4}} = -4x^{2-(-4)} = -4x^6$

5.
$$
\begin{aligned}
(2ab^{-3})(3a^{-2}b^4) &= 6a^{1+(-2)}b^{-3+4} \\
&= 6a^{-1}b^1 \\
&= \frac{6b}{a}
\end{aligned}
$$

6.
$$
\begin{aligned}
\frac{16x^5 - 8x^3 + 20x}{4x} &= \frac{16x^5}{4x} - \frac{8x^3}{4x} + \frac{20x}{4x} \\
&= 4x^4 - 2x^2 + 5
\end{aligned}
$$

7.
$$
\begin{aligned}
&-3y^2(-2y^2 + 3y - 6) \\
&= -3y^2(-2y^2) + (-3y^2)(3y) - (-3y^2)(6) \\
&= 6y^4 - 9y^3 + 18y^2
\end{aligned}
$$

8.
$$
\begin{aligned}
(2x - 5)^2 &= (2x - 5)(2x - 5) \\
&= 2x(2x) + (2x)(-5) + (-5)(2x) + (-5)(-5) \\
&= 4x^2 - 10x - 10x + 25 \\
&= 4x^2 - 20x + 25
\end{aligned}
$$

9. $(-3a^2b^{-3})^2 = (-3)^2 a^{2 \cdot 2} b^{-3 \cdot 2} = 9a^4b^{-6} = \dfrac{9a^4}{b^6}$

10. Move the decimal point 6 places to the right. The exponent on the factor of 10 will be -6:
$$
0.0000029 = 2.9 \times 10^{-6}
$$

11. $(4y - 3)(4y + 3)$
    $= (4y)(4y) + 3(4y) - 3(4y) - 3(3)$
    $= 16y^2 + 12y - 12y - 9$
    $= 16y^2 - 9$

12. $(2a - 7)(5a^2 - 2a + 3)$
    $= 2a(5a^2 - 2a + 3) - 7(5a^2 - 2a + 3)$
    $= 10a^3 - 4a^2 + 6a - 35a^2 + 14a - 21$
    $= 10a^3 - 39a^2 + 20a - 21$

13. $\dfrac{-2a^2b^3}{8a^4b^8} = -\dfrac{1a^2b^3}{4a^4b^8}$
    $= -\dfrac{1a^{2-4}b^{3-8}}{4}$
    $= -\dfrac{1a^{-2}b^{-5}}{4}$
    $= -\dfrac{1}{4a^2b^5}$

14.
$$(8x^2 + 4x - 3) \div (2x - 3)$$

$$
\begin{array}{r}
4x + 8 \\
2x - 3 \overline{\smash{)}8x^2 + 4x - 3} \\
\underline{8x^2 - 12x} \\
16x - 3 \\
\underline{16x - 24} \\
21
\end{array}
$$

$$(8x^2 + 4x - 3) \div (2x - 3) = 4x + 8 + \dfrac{21}{2x - 3}$$

15. Because the exponent on the factor of 10 is negative, move the decimal point to the left:
    $3.5 \times 10^{-8} = 0.000000035$

16. $(5x^2yz^4)(-2xy^3z^{-1})(7x^{-2}y^{-2}z^3)$
    $= (5)(-2)(7)(x^2xx^{-2})(yy^3y^{-2})(z^4z^{-1}z^3)$
    $= -70xy^2z^6$

17.
$$
\begin{array}{r|rrrr}
3 & 1 & -6 & 16 & -20 \\
  &   & 3 & -9 & 21 \\
\hline
  & 1 & -3 & 7 & 1
\end{array}
$$

$$(x^3 - 6x^2 + 16x - 20) \div (x - 3) = x^2 - 3x + 7 + \dfrac{1}{x - 3}$$

18. To find the area of a square, square the length of one side:
    $(2x + 3)^2 = (2x + 3)(2x + 3)$
    $ = 2x(2x) + 2x(3) + 3(2x) + 3(3)$
    $ = 4x^2 + 6x + 6x + 9$
    $ = 4x^2 + 12x + 9$

    The area of the square is $(4x^2 + 12x + 9)$ m^2.

19. 8.103×10^{19}
    $= 81,030,000,000,000,000,000$

20. $h(t) = -16t^2 + 60t$
    $h(2) = -16(2)^2 + 60(2)$
    $ = -64 + 120$
    $ = 56$

    The height of the ball after 2 s is 56 ft.

Chapter Test

1. $(12y^2 + 17y - 4) + (9y^2 - 13y + 3) = 21y^2 + 4y - 1$

2. $(6a^2b^5)(-3a^6b) = -18a^8b^6$

3. $4x^2(3x^3 + 2x - 7)$
   $= 4x^2(3x^3) + (4x^2)(2x) - (4x^2)(7)$
   $= 12x^5 + 8x^3 - 28x^2$

4. $\dfrac{-6x^{-2}y^4}{3xy} = -2x^{-2-1}y^{4-1} = \dfrac{-2y^3}{x^3}$

5. $(5a^{-1}b^{-4})(-2a^2b^3) = -10a^{-1+2}b^{-4+3}$
   $\phantom{(5a^{-1}b^{-4})(-2a^2b^3)} = -10a^1b^{-1}$
   $\phantom{(5a^{-1}b^{-4})(-2a^2b^3)} = \dfrac{-10a}{b}$

6. $\dfrac{12b^7 + 36b^5 - 3b^3}{3b^3} = \dfrac{12b^7}{3b^3} + \dfrac{36b^5}{3b^3} - \dfrac{3b^3}{3b^3}$
   $\phantom{\dfrac{12b^7 + 36b^5 - 3b^3}{3b^3}} = 4b^4 + 12b^2 - 1$

7. $(-2a^4b^{-5})^3 = (-2)^3a^{4\cdot3}b^{-5\cdot3} = -8a^{12}b^{-15} = \dfrac{-8a^{12}}{b^{15}}$

8. $78,000,000,000 = 7.8 \times 10^{10}$

9. $\dfrac{6^2}{6^{-2}} = 6^{2+2} = 6^4 = 1296$

10. $(6y - 5)(6y + 5) = 36y^2 - 25$

11. $(5.2 \times 10^{-3})(1.4 \times 10^7) = 7.28 \times 10^4$

12. $(2a + 3)(3a^2 + 4a - 7)$
    $= 2a(3a^2 + 4a - 7) + 3(3a^2 + 4a - 7)$
    $= 6a^3 + 8a^2 - 14a + 9a^2 + 12a - 21$
    $= 6a^3 + 17a^2 - 2a - 21$

13. $(6x^3 - 7x^2 + 6x - 7) - (4x^3 - 3x^2 + 7)$
    $= 6x^3 - 7x^2 + 6x - 7 - 4x^3 + 3x^2 - 7$
    $= 2x^3 - 4x^2 + 6x - 14$

14.
$$
\begin{array}{r|rrrr}
3 & 1 & -5 & 5 & 5 \\
  &   & 3 & -6 & -3 \\
\hline
  & 1 & -2 & -1 & 2
\end{array}
$$

$$(x^3 - 5x^2 + 5x + 5) \div (x - 3) = x^2 - 2x - 1 + \dfrac{2}{x - 3}$$

15. $2.971 \times 10^7 = 29,710,000$

16. $(-3x^{-2}y^{-3})^{-2} = (-3)^{-2}(x^4y^6) = \dfrac{x^4y^6}{9}$

17. $6x^2 - x + 1 - (12x^2 + 3x - 4)$
$= 6x^2 - x + 1 - 12x^2 - 3x + 4$
$= -6x^2 - 4x + 5$

18. To find the area of a rectangle, multiply the length times the width:
$(5x + 3)(2x - 7) = 10x^2 - 35x + 6x - 21$
$\qquad\qquad\qquad = 10x^2 - 29x - 21$
The area of the square is $(10x^2 - 29x - 21)$ cm^2.

19. $2.4 \times 10^{14} = 240{,}000{,}000{,}000{,}000$

20. Strategy
To find the length, substitute 30 for v in the equation and solve for L.

Solution
$L(v) = 0.6411v^2$
$L(30) = 0.6411(30)^2 = 0.6411(900) = 576.99$
The length of the wave is 576.99 m.

Cumulative Review Exercises

1. $5 \le a \le 10$
$20 \le b \le 30$
The maximum value of $\dfrac{a}{b} = \dfrac{10}{20} = \dfrac{1}{2}$.

2. $-2a^2 \div (2b) - c$
$-2(-4)^2 \div (2 \cdot 2) - (-1)$
$= -2(16) \div (4) + 1$
$= -32 \div 4 + 1$
$= -8 + 1$
$= -7$

3. The Associative Property of Addition

4. $-\dfrac{3}{4}(-24x^2) = 18x^2$

5. Domain: $\{-5, -3, -1, 1, 3\}$
Range: $\{-4, -2, 0, 2, 4\}$
Yes, the relation is a function.

6. $f(x) = \dfrac{4}{5}x - 3$

$f(-10) = \dfrac{4}{5}(-10) - 3 = -8 - 3 = -11$

$f(-5) = \dfrac{4}{5}(-5) - 3 = -4 - 3 = -7$

$f(0) = \dfrac{4}{5}(0) - 3 = -3$

$f(5) = \dfrac{4}{5}(5) - 3 = 4 - 3 = 1$

$f(10) = \dfrac{4}{5}(10) - 3 = 8 - 3 = 5$

The range is $\{-11, -7, -3, 1, 5\}$.

7. $4 + 3(x - 2) = 13$
$3x - 6 = 9$
$3x = 15$
$x = 5$

8. $-4x - 2 \ge 10$
$-4x \ge 12$
$x \le -3$
The solution is $(-\infty, -3]$.

9. x-intercept: $\qquad$ y-intercept:
$3x - 4y = 12 \qquad\qquad 3x - 4y = 12$
$3x - 4(0) = 12 \qquad\quad 3(0) - 4y = 12$
$3x = 12 \qquad\qquad\qquad -4y = 12$
$x = 4 \qquad\qquad\qquad\quad y = -3$
The x-intercept is $(4, 0)$.
The y-intercept is $(0, -3)$.

10. $f(x) = -3x - 3$

11. $-3x + 2y < 6$
$2y < 3x + 6$
$y < \dfrac{3}{2}x + 3$

12. $m = \dfrac{6 - 2}{5 - (-5)} = \dfrac{4}{10} = \dfrac{2}{5}$

Now use the point-slope formula to find the equation of the line.
$y - y_1 = m(x - x_1)$
$y - 2 = \dfrac{2}{5}[x - (-5)]$
$y - 2 = \dfrac{2}{5}(x + 5)$
$y - 2 = \dfrac{2}{5}x + 2$
$y = \dfrac{2}{5}x + 4$

13. (1) $2x - 3y = -4$
(2) $5x + y = 7$
Eliminate y.
$2x - 3y = -4$
$3(5x + y) = 3(7)$

$2x - 3y = -4$
$15x + 3y = 21$
Add the equations.
$17x = 17$
$x = 1$
Replace x in equation (2).
$5x + y = 7$
$5(1) + y = 7$
$5 + y = 7$
$y = 2$
The solution is $(1, 2)$.

14. $(-2x^{-4}y^2)^3 = (-2)^3(x^{-12}y^6)$
$= -\dfrac{8y^6}{x^{12}}$

15. $(3y^3 - 5y^2 - 6) - (2y^2 - 8y + 1)$
$= 3y^3 - 5y^2 - 6 - 2y^2 + 8y - 1$
$= 3y^3 - 7y^2 + 8y - 7$

16.
$$2x - 3 \overline{\smash{\big)}\, 8x^2 + 4x - 3} \quad\begin{array}{l}4x + 8\end{array}$$
$$\underline{8x^2 - 12x}$$
$$16x - 3$$
$$\underline{16x - 24}$$
$$21$$

$(8x^2 + 4x - 3) \div (2x - 3) = 4x + 8 + \dfrac{21}{2x - 3}$

17. Strategy
To find the rate of each train, let x represent the rate of one train and y represent the rate of the other train. Then
Rate of trains traveling toward each other: $x + y$
The distance traveled is 240 miles. Use the equation
$d = rt$ to express the distances traveled.
One train is twice as fast as the other train.

Solution
$2.5(x + y) = 240$
$x = 2y$

Use substitution to solve for y.
$2.5(2y + y) = 240$
$2.5(3y) = 240$
$7.5y = 240$
$y = 32$

$x = 2y$
$x = 2(32) = 64$
The rates of the trains are 32 mph and 64 mph.

18. Strategy
The number of ounces of pure gold: x
Value of pure gold: $360x$
Value of alloy: $80(120)$
Value of mixture: $200(x + 80)$
The sum of the values before mixing equals the value after mixing.
$360x + 80(120) = 200(x + 80)$

Solution
$360x + 80(120) = 200(x + 80)$
$360x + 9600 = 200x + 16{,}000$
$160x + 9600 = 16{,}000$
$160x = 6400$
$x = 40$
40 oz of pure gold must be mixed with the alloy.

19. Strategy
To find the rate of the plane in calm air and the rate of the wind, let x represent the rate of the plane in calm air and y represent the rate of the wind. Then
Rate of plane with wind: $x + y$
Rate of plane against wind: $x - y$
The distance traveled with the wind is 1000 miles. The time it takes to travel against the wind for the same distance is 5 h. Use the equation $d = rt$ to express the distances traveled with and against the wind as the two equations of a system.

Solution
$4(x + y) = 1000$
$5(x - y) = 1000$

$\dfrac{1}{4} \cdot 4(x + y) = \dfrac{1}{4} \cdot 1000$
$\dfrac{1}{5} \cdot 5(x - y) = \dfrac{1}{5} \cdot 1000$

$x + y = 250$
$x - y = 200$

$2x = 450$
$x = 225$

$x + y = 250$
$225 + y = 250$
$y = 25$

The rate of the plane in calm air is 225 mph. The rate of the wind is 25 mph.

20. $m = \dfrac{y_2 - y_1}{x_2 - x_1} = \dfrac{300 - 100}{6 - 2} = \dfrac{200}{4}$
$m = 50$
A slope of 50 means the average speed was 50 mph.

Exploring Introductory

and

A GRAPHING APPROACH

Intermediate Algebra

Student Activity Manual   Chapters 1–6

TABLE OF CONTENTS

PREFACE

Learning mathematics with understanding, and applying that understanding to new situations, is a goal for students in this course. Learning with understanding can be enhanced when you interact with other students, investigate new ideas, and evaluate your own thinking. In settings where student discourse is encouraged, connections are recognized and knowledge is formed. Using the *Student Activity Manual* will enhance your understanding of the mathematics being studied.

The *Student Activity Manual* contains both activities and investigations, each correlated to a lesson in the textbook. Activities provide an opportunity to practice, apply, or extend the learner's knowledge of a concept or skill. Investigations are designed to help the learner build conceptual understanding of a procedure or concept. Each is intended to actively engage the learner in thinking about, and discussing, mathematics.

Section 1.1   Problem Solving
Lesson Activity – Reviewing Problem-Solving Strategies

In your study of mathematics, you have been introduced to a variety of strategies that are useful in solving problems. The box below contains a list of the more common strategies that might be useful in solving the assortment of problems that follow. Polya's four-step process is provided as a reference.

Problem-Solving Strategies	**Polya's Four-Step Process**
• Draw a diagram. • Work backwards. • Guess and check. • Solve an easier problem. • Look for a pattern. • Make a table or a chart. • Write an equation. • Produce a graph.	• Understand the problem and state the goal. • Devise a strategy to solve the problem. • Solve the problem. • Review the solution and check your work.

Directions: Solve each problem and identify the strategy used.

1. Place the numbers 1-8 in the squares so that no consecutive numbers (like 5 and 6) are located in adjacent squares horizontally, vertically, or diagonally.

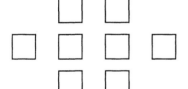

2. You need to schedule a video game contest among eight players. Each player must play each other player once. How many games must you schedule?

3. The first three figures of a sequence are shown. If each figure is made of unit squares, what will be the perimeter of figure 20?

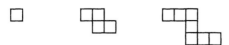

4. The organizers of an awards program wanted to have music during the social hour. Five musicians, Amy, Barb, Charles, David, and Eli, auditioned and each performed a different type of music (blues, classical, country, jazz, and rock and roll). From the following statements, determine which person played what type of music.

   a. Amy lives in the same town as both Barb and the country musician.
   b. The jazz musician auditioned before Eli, who auditioned second.
   c. The country musician auditioned last, after David.
   d. The rock and roll musician followed Barb, who was the first to audition.
   e. Amy left before David's audition because she doesn't like the classical music that he sings.

5. What is the sum of all the positive, proper fractions with denominators less than or equal to 10?

$$\frac{1}{2} + \frac{1}{3} + \frac{2}{3} + \frac{1}{4} + \frac{2}{4} + \frac{3}{4} + \frac{1}{5} + \dots + \frac{1}{10} + \frac{2}{10} + \dots + \frac{9}{10} = ?$$

Name _____ Date_____

Section 1.2   Sets
Lesson Activity – Are You All *Set* with *Technology*?

Part A: Sets of Numbers

1. Identify the sets of numbers which each of the following is a member of. If a number **IS** a member of the set, write an X. If a number **IS NOT** a member of the set, leave it blank. A number may belong to more than one set.

n	Natural Numbers	Whole Numbers	Integers	Rational Numbers	Irrational Numbers	Real Numbers
22.5						
$\sqrt{40}$						
0						
$\dfrac{3}{8}$						
-0.012						
-8						

2. Give examples of each of the following. If it is not possible, write NP.

a. an odd prime number _____

b. a negative integer greater than $-2\dfrac{3}{8}$ _____

c. a natural number less than 0 _____

d. an irrational number between -π and π _____

3. Use the roster method or set-builder notation to list the elements of each set.

a. {W, O, R, K} ∩ {H, A, R, D} = _____

b. {N, O, S, E} ∪ {E, A, R, S} = _____

c. $\{x \mid x \in$ rational numbers$\} \cap \{x \mid x \in$ irrational numbers$\}$ = _____

d. $\{x \mid x \in$ integers$\} \cup \{x \mid x \in$ natural numbers$\}$ = _____

Part B: Technology ∪ Graphing Inequalities

Your graphing calculator can be used to graph inequalities. Press 2nd MATH to view the equivalence and inequality tests available. Then press the right arrow key to view the logical operators.

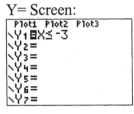

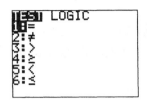

Example: Graph $\{x \mid x \le -3\}$.

Solution: Press the Y= button. Type the inequality $x \le -3$. To do this, press the following sequence of buttons: x,T,θ,n 2nd MATH 6 (-) 3. For the standard viewing rectangle, press ZOOM 6.

Y= Screen:

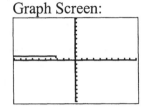

Graph Screen:

Displayed on the horizontal axis is a graph that appears from the left side of the screen and terminates at $x = -3$. It is raised off the axis. This is a Boolean graph, meaning any values of x that satisfy the inequality are graphed at a vertical value of 1 (true) and any values of x that do not satisfy the inequality are graphed at a vertical value of 0 (false). Press TRACE to verify. What cannot be determined from the graph screen is whether -3 is part of the solution set. Knowing the original problem confirms that -3 is part of the solution set.

Example: Graph a. $\{x \mid x \le -3\} \cup \{x \mid x \ge 2\}$
          b. $\{x \mid -2 < x \le 4\}$

Solution:

a. Enter both inequalities in Y = using the logical connector OR for union.

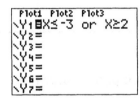

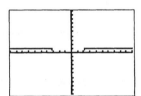

b. Enter this compound inequality as two inequalities joined by the logical connector AND for intersection.

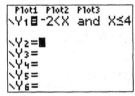

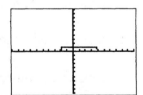

Directions: Use your calculator to graph the following. Make a sketch of each graph.

4. $\{x \mid x \ge -4.5\}$ 5. $\{x \mid -6 < x \le 8\}$ 6. $\{x \mid x \le -6\} \cup \{x \mid x \ge 2.5\}$

Directions: Use set builder notation to write an inequality for each graph. Assume endpoints are solutions.

7.
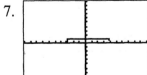

8.
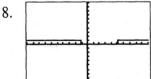

9.
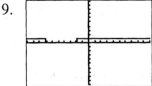

Name _____ Date_____

Section 1.3   Operations on Integers
Lesson Investigation – Using Technology to Operate on Integers

Part A: Looking for Patterns

Directions: Look for patterns as you answer the following problems.

1. Addition of Integers

3 + 3 = _____	-3 + (-4) = _____	3 + 6 = _____
3 + 2 = _____	-3 + (-3) = _____	3 + 4 = _____
3 + 1 = _____	-3 + (-2) = _____	3 + 2 = _____
3 + 0 = _____	-3 + (-1) = _____	3 + 0 = _____
3 + (-1) = _____	-3 + 0 = _____	3 + (-2) = _____
3 + (-2) = _____	-3 + 1 = _____	3 + (-4) = _____
3 + (-3) = _____	-3 + 2 = _____	3 + (-6) = _____

2. Describe the pattern in each column of problems in Exercise 1.

3. Subtraction of Integers

3 – 3 = _____	-3 – (-2) = _____	3 – 6 = _____
3 – 2 = _____	-3 – (-1) = _____	3 – 4 = _____
3 – 1 = _____	-3 – 0 = _____	3 – 2 = _____
3 – 0 = _____	-3 – 1 = _____	3 – 0 = _____
3 – (-1) = _____	-3 – 2 = _____	3 – (-2) = _____
3 – (-2) = _____	-3 – 3 = _____	3 – (-4) = _____
3 – (-3) = _____	-3 – 4 = _____	3 – (-6) = _____

4. Describe the pattern in each column of problems in Exercise 3.

5. Describe how the problems in each column of Exercise 1 are related to each column of problems in Exercise 3.

Part B: Hit the Target

You are given four integers and a target for each problem. Place the integers in the boxes and evaluate using the Order of Operations Agreement.

Example:
Integers = -4, 8, -6, 3
Target = maximum value

$$\square + \square \times \square - \square = \square$$

Solution: You might first try $-4 + 8 \times 3 - (-6) = 26$. However, the product of two negatives is positive so try $8 + (-4) \times (-6) - 3 = 29$, which is the maximum value.

Directions: Use the integers provided to hit the target. If the target is a number, try to get as close to the target without going over. Your answer may not be an integer.

6. Integers = 5, -9, -6, 7
   Target = maximum value

$$\square + \square \times \square - \square = \square$$

7. Integers = -8, -2, 5, 9
   Target = minimum value

$$\square - \square \times \square + \square = \square$$

8. Integers = 1, 8, -2, -4
   Target = 20

$$\square \times \square \div \square - \square = \square$$

9. Integers = 3, -5, 8, -9
   Target = 10

$$\square - \square + \square \div \square = \square$$

10. Integers = -6, 7, -1, 8
    Target = 100

$$\square^2 + \square \times \square - \square = \square$$

Section 1.4   Operations on Rational Numbers
Lesson Activity – Using Technology to Operate on Mixed Numbers

Part A: Fractions and Calculators

A mixed number, such as $2\frac{3}{5}$, is the sum of a whole

number and a fraction. Enter $2\frac{3}{5}$ on the home screen of

the calculator as shown.

```
2+3/5
            2.6
13/5
            2.6
```

When operating on mixed numbers, it is important to remember the order of operations! Study the examples below. Although parentheses are not needed in all cases, their use makes the problem easier to read. Note that it is possible to convert a decimal answer to an improper fraction by pressing the [MATH] button and then selecting [1]. The decimal answer is converted.

$$1\frac{1}{2}+3\frac{3}{4}=$$

$$3\frac{2}{5}-4\frac{1}{2}=$$

$$2\frac{3}{8}\times1\frac{3}{10}=$$

$$2\frac{5}{9}\div3\frac{1}{3}=$$

```
(1+1/2)+(3+3/4)
              5.25
5.25▶Frac
              21/4
■
```

```
(3+2/5)-(4+1/2)
              -1.1
Ans▶Frac
            -11/10
■
```

```
(2+3/8)*(1+3/10)
            3.0875
Ans▶Frac
           247/80
■
```

```
(2+5/9)/(3+1/3)
       .7666666667
Ans▶Frac
            23/30
```

$$1\frac{1}{2}+3\frac{3}{4}=5\frac{1}{4}$$

$$3\frac{2}{5}-4\frac{1}{2}=-1\frac{1}{10}$$

$$2\frac{3}{8}\times1\frac{3}{10}=3\frac{7}{80}$$

$$2\frac{5}{9}\div3\frac{1}{3}=\frac{23}{30}$$

Directions: Simplify. Write answers in simplest form.

1. $\dfrac{5}{8}+\left(-\dfrac{3}{4}\right)$

2. $3\dfrac{1}{2}-2\dfrac{3}{5}$

3. $-3\dfrac{5}{12}+2\dfrac{1}{4}$

4. $\dfrac{7}{9}\cdot\left(2\dfrac{1}{3}\right)$

5. $1\dfrac{5}{6}\div2\dfrac{2}{5}$

6. $\left(4\dfrac{1}{8}\right)\left(2\dfrac{1}{3}\right)$

7. $-4\dfrac{1}{6}-2\dfrac{2}{3}$

8. $4\dfrac{5}{9}\div1\dfrac{1}{6}$

9. $3\dfrac{2}{5}+6\dfrac{1}{3}-4\dfrac{1}{2}$

10. Write the answers for Exercises 1 to 9 in order from least to greatest.

11. What is the difference between the least and greatest answers for Exercises 1 to 9?

Part B: Rising Gasoline Prices

The table below shows the average cost per gallon of unleaded regular gasoline from 1976 to 2000. The real price reflects the price paid that year, unadjusted. Increases in price are shown as positive numbers; decreases in price are shown as negative numbers.

(*Source:* Energy Information Administration)

Year	Real Price	Change
1976	0.61	-
1977	0.66	0.05
1978	0.67	0.01
1979	0.90	0.23
1980	1.25	0.35
1981	1.38	0.13
1982	1.30	-0.08
1983	1.24	-0.06
1984	1.21	-0.03
1985	1.20	-0.01
1986	0.93	-0.27
1987	0.95	0.02
1988	0.95	0.00
1989	1.02	0.07
1990	1.16	0.14
1991	1.14	-0.02
1992	1.13	-0.01
1993	1.11	-0.02
1994	1.11	0.00
1995	1.15	0.04
1996	1.23	0.08
1997	1.23	0.00
1998	1.06	-0.17
1999	1.17	0.11
2000	1.51	0.34

12. During what year did the price of gasoline increase by the greatest amount?

13. During what year did the price of gasoline decrease by the greatest amount?

14. Calculate the difference in price per gallon
    a. from 1976 to 1986.
    b. from 1986 to 1996.

15. What was the average annual change in price during the 1980's, from 1980 to 1989?

16. If the trend during the 1980's had continued into the 1990's, what would be the approximate price per gallon in 1999? (Use your answer from Exercise 15.)

17. How much more money did it cost to fill a 15-gallon tank in 2000 than it did in 1976?

Name _____ Date_____

Section 1.5 Evaluating Variable Expressions
Lesson Activity – Using Technology to Evaluate Expressions

Part A: Knowing Your Calculator

Knowing how to use a graphing calculator to evaluate an expression correctly is important. The expressions below have been evaluated for $a = 2$, $b = -4$, and $c = 5$ but the $\boxed{\text{ENTER}}$ key has not been pressed. Decide which screen(s) will yield the correct answer.

1. $-3a^2$ A.
```
2→X
        2
-3XX■
```
B.  C.

2. $3(a-4)$ A. 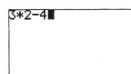 B. 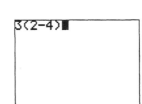 C.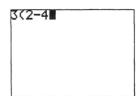

3. $\dfrac{3a}{4}$ A.  B. 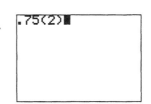 C.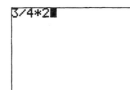

4. $\dfrac{a+2}{4}$ A.  B. 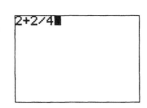 C.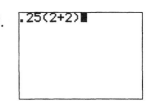

5. $b^2 - 4ac$ A. 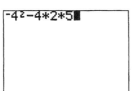 B. 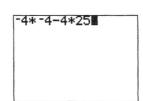 C.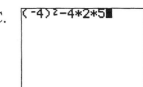

6. $a^2 + c^2$ A.  B.  C.
```
2→A
        2
5→C
        5
AA+CC■
```

Part B: The Problem Solving Plan

Example: The radius of an aluminum can is 5 centimeters and it has a height of 15 centimeters. Which will increase the surface area more, doubling the radius or doubling the height?

    Solution:

    State the goal. We need to compute the surface area of a cylinder several times. The formula for the surface area of a cylinder is $SA = 2\pi r^2 + 2\pi rh$ where r is the radius and h is the height.

    Devise a strategy. Use a calculator to evaluate the expression for the original cylinder and two new cylinders, one with the radius doubled and one with the height doubled.

    Solve the problem. Since the formula is evaluated three times and we want to make minor changes each time, use the recall feature that allows the previous expression to be edited. To recall the previous calculation, press $\boxed{2^{nd}}$ $\boxed{\text{ENTER}}$ (Fig. 1). To change the radius to 10, use the left arrow key to position the cursor over the 5. Press the $\boxed{2^{nd}}$ $\boxed{\text{INS}}$ keys and insert the number 10. Press $\boxed{\text{DEL}}$ to delete the 5. Right arrow over to the next occurrence of the radius and repeat the change (Fig. 2). Press $\boxed{\text{ENTER}}$ to find the new surface area when the radius has been doubled. Finally, to double the height, press $\boxed{2^{nd}}$ $\boxed{\text{ENTER}}$ again and edit the previous expression. The radius must be changed back to 5 and the new height is 30. Press $\boxed{\text{ENTER}}$ (Fig. 3).

Figure 1	Figure 2	Figure 3

2π5²+2π5*15
    628.3185307
2π5²+2π5*15■
	2π5²+2π5*15
	    628.3185307
	2π10²+2π■*15
		2π5²+2π5*15
		    628.3185307
		2π10²+2π10*15
		    1570.796327
		2π5²+2π5*30
		    1099.557429

Figure 1	Figure 2	Figure 3

    Check your work. The greatest surface area results when the radius is doubled. This makes sense since it is the variable that is being squared in the formula.

Directions: Evaluate the formulas below for the values of the variables stated. Practice using the $\boxed{2^{nd}}$ $\boxed{\text{ENTER}}$ feature of the calculator to edit your work.

7. If the radius of a sphere is doubled or tripled, what happens to the volume? To decide, evaluate the formula for the volume of a sphere, $V = \dfrac{4}{3}\pi r^3$, for $r = 2$, 4, and 6.

8. Should you shop around for lower interest rates when you take a loan? To decide, evaluate the simple interest formula $I = Prt$ for $r = 0.08$, 0.09, and 0.1 when $P = \$5000$ and $t = 5$ years.

9. When an object (with little air resistance) is dropped, its height h, in feet, is given by $h = -16t^2 + s$, where s is the initial height and t is the number of seconds it has fallen. Describe the height of an object dropped from 32 feet for $t = 0.5$, 1, and 1.2 seconds.

Name _____ Date_____

Section 1.6   Simplifying Variable Expressions
Lesson Investigation – Algebra Tiles

Part A: Modeling Expressions
Visual models can be used to represent terms in an expression. The models are based upon an area model for rectangles.

Name	Dimensions
unit-piece	1 by 1
x-piece	x by 1
y-piece	y by 1

$1\ \boxed{1}$ $1\ \boxed{x\text{-piece}}$ $\boxed{-1}$

$1\ \boxed{y\text{-piece}}$

Shade each piece to represent the opposite.

Directions: Write the problem suggested by each model. An example is done for you.

0. $\boxed{x}$ $\boxed{x}$ $\boxed{-x}$ $\boxed{x}$

$\blacksquare\ \blacksquare\ \blacksquare\ \blacksquare$ $+$ $\square\ \square\ \square$ $=$ $\blacksquare$

Solution: $\underline{(2x-4)+(-x+3)=x-1}$

1. $\boxed{x}\ \square$ $+$ $\boxed{y}\ \blacksquare$ $=$
     $\boxed{x}\ \square$ $\blacksquare\ \blacksquare\ \blacksquare\ \blacksquare$

Solution: _____

2. $\boxed{-y}\ \square$ $\boxed{y}$ $\boxed{y}$
     $\boxed{-y}\ \square$ $+$ $\boxed{y}$ $\boxed{y}$ $=$
     $\boxed{-y}$ $\blacksquare\ \blacksquare\ \blacksquare$

Solution: _____

3. $\boxed{-x}$ $+$ $\boxed{x}$ $\boxed{x}$ $=$
     $\boxed{y}$ $\boxed{x}$ $\blacksquare\ \blacksquare$

Solution: _____

Part B: Rectangular Models

Algebra tiles can be used to model different ways to group 3 x-tiles and 6 unit-pieces. When the pieces are grouped together, rectangles are formed.

	Two rectangles	One rectangle
Total Area = $3x + 6$	$3(x) + 3(2)$ 3 rows of x and 3 rows of 2	$3(x + 2)$ 3 rows of $(x + 2)$

Since the number of tiles did not change, all of the expressions must be equivalent.

$$3(x + 2) = 3(x) + 3(2) = 3x + 6$$

Directions: For each set of tiles, sketch two different groupings following the example above. Write the algebraic expression for each.

	Total Area	Rows of x and Rows of 1's	Rows of $(x + 1$'s$)$
4.			
5.			
6.			
7.			

8. Make a sketch of the expression $2(x + 5)$. How does the sketch relate to the Distributive Property?

Section 2.1   Rectangular Coordinates and Graphs
Lesson Investigation – Symmetry in the Coordinate Plane

Part A: Plotting in the Coordinate Plane

1. Plot the following ordered pairs.

(7, 3)	(7, -3)
(4, 6)	(4, -6)
(0, -5)	(0, 5)
(-3, -2)	(-3, 2)
(-5, 1)	(-5, -1)

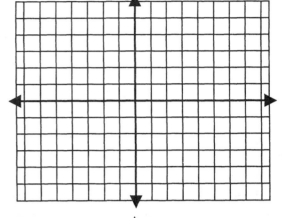

2. Describe the relationship between the ordered pairs (a, b) and $(a, -b)$.

3. Plot the following ordered pairs.

(-6, 2)	(6, 2)
(3, -5)	(-3, -5)
(-2, 0)	(2, 0)
(-1, 4)	(1, 4)
(5, -3)	(-5, -3)

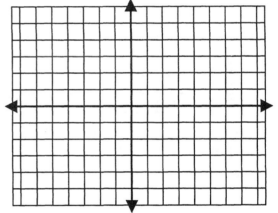

4. Describe the relationship between the ordered pairs (a, b) and $(-a, b)$.

5. Plot the following ordered pairs.

(5, 3)	(3, 5)
(-4, 2)	(2, -4)
(0, 1)	(1, 0)
(-2, -5)	(-5, -2)
(3, -4)	(-4, 3)

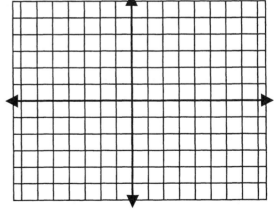

6. Describe the relationship between the ordered pairs (a, b) and (b, a).

7. Without plotting points, describe the relationship between the ordered pairs (a, b) and $(-a, -b)$.

8. Without plotting points, describe the relationship between the ordered pairs (a, b) and $(-b, -a)$.

Part B: Reflect on This!

Directions: Create a design that contains symmetry. To do this, plot a minimum of 15 ordered pairs (a, b) in the coordinate plane. Then, use the ideas investigated in Part A to create a variation of the ordered pairs (a, b). To finish your design you may wish to connect ordered pairs to form line segments. Add color to the design as desired.

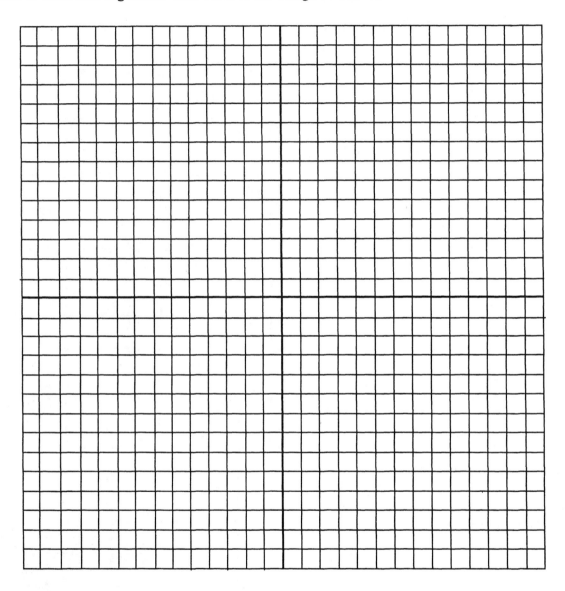

9. Describe the symmetry in your design.

Name _____ Date_____

Section 2.2   Relations and Functions
Lesson Activity – Graphs and Functions

Part A: A Picture is Worth a Thousand Words
Functions can be described in terms of words, ordered pairs, in a table, or by a graph. In the problems that follow, you will be asked to make connections between the words and a graph.
Directions: For each graph, make the best match for the words (stories) provided. Write the words (story) for the remaining graph.

1. a. I bought a plant that grew very slowly.

   b. My seed germinated and the plant was doing okay, but the fertilizer finally did the trick!

   c. My seed germinated. I left town for a few days and without water, my plant didn't survive.

(i)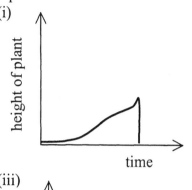

(ii)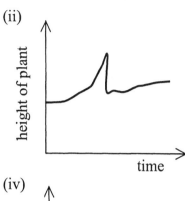

(iii)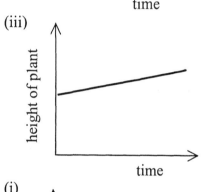

(iv)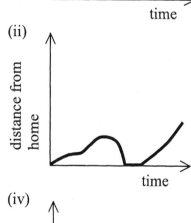

2. a. I left for work on time, but early slow traffic caused me to drive faster on the highway.

   b. There's a long stop light not too far from home.

   c. I left for class but had to go home to pick up my report due today.

(i)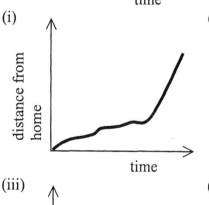

(ii)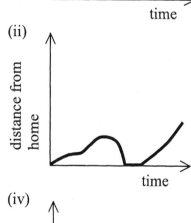

(iii)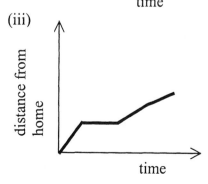

(iv)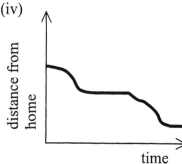

Part B: Matching

Directions: Each graph below is a visual representation of a relationship. Match each graph with the appropriate axes labeled A to F.

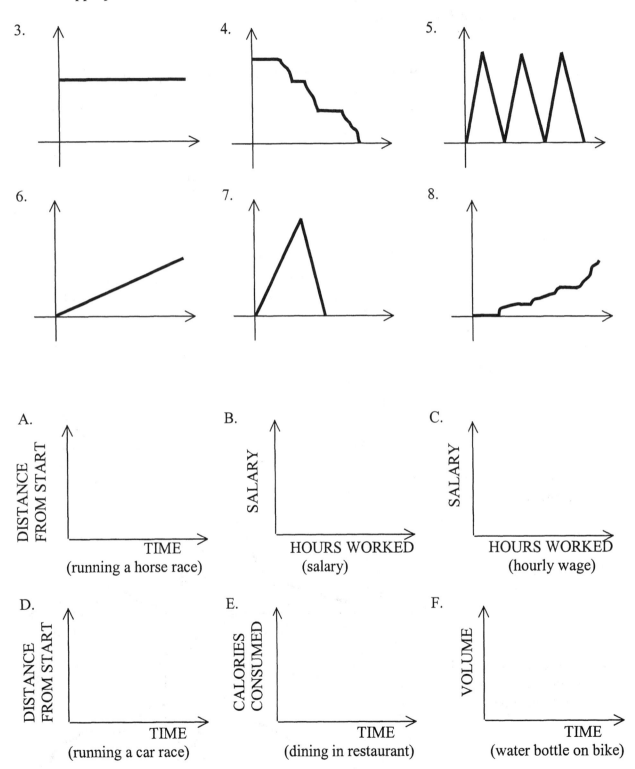

3.

4.

5.

6.

7.

8.

A.

DISTANCE FROM START

TIME

(running a horse race)

B.

SALARY

HOURS WORKED

(salary)

C.

SALARY

HOURS WORKED

(hourly wage)

D.

DISTANCE FROM START

TIME

(running a car race)

E.

CALORIES CONSUMED

TIME

(dining in restaurant)

F.

VOLUME

TIME

(water bottle on bike)

Name _____ **Date**_____

Section 2.3 Properties of Functions
Lesson Activity – Using Technology to Determine Intercepts

Part A: Determining Intercepts

The graph at the right shows a function that intersects both the x- and y-axes. These points of intersection are the x- and y-intercepts. A point on the x-axis has the form $(x, 0)$ and a point on the y-axis has the form $(0, y)$.

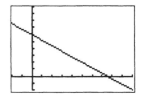

In this activity you will use a graphing calculator to determine the x- and y-intercepts.

$$f(x) = -0.75x + 6$$

Example: Determine the x- and y-intercepts for the function $f(x) = 1.2x - 4$.

Solution: There are several ways to determine the x-intercept using a graphing calculator. One method is to graph the function and a horizontal line at the x-axis, then use the intersect feature to find the point of intersection of the graph and the horizontal line. First enter Y2 = 0 in the editor.

Press $\boxed{\text{GRAPH}}$. Press $\boxed{2^{nd}}$ $\boxed{\text{CALC}}$ $\boxed{5}$ $\boxed{\text{ENTER}}$ $\boxed{\text{ENTER}}$ $\boxed{\text{ENTER}}$. The intersection point is the x-intercept $(3.\overline{3}, 0)$.

Y= Editor

2nd CALC Intersect

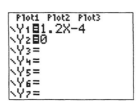

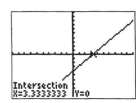

There are several ways to determine the y-intercept using a graphing calculator. One method is to graph the function and then evaluate it at $x = 0$ from the graphing screen. First enter the function in the Y= editor. Press $\boxed{\text{GRAPH}}$. Press $\boxed{\text{TRACE}}$ $\boxed{0}$ $\boxed{\text{ENTER}}$. The y-intercept $(0, -4)$ appears at the bottom of the graphing window. A second method is to use the Table feature.

TRACE and X = 0   TABLE

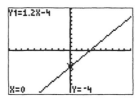

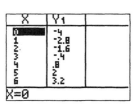

Directions: Use the methods described to find the x- and y-intercepts for the graph of each function.

1. $f(x) = 2x - 6$

2. $f(x) = 0.4x + 3.4$

3. $f(x) = -2.2x + 15$

4. $f(x) = x^2 - 5x + 4$

5. $f(x) = x^2 + 4x - 12$

6. $f(x) = 0.125x^2 - x - 6$

7. Sketch functions that have the following number of x-intercepts: 0, 1, 2, and 3.

Part B: What Does It Mean?

Example: A hotel receives income from guests who stay there. The income is used to pay the expenses of operating the hotel. The graph shows how the hotel's revenue is a function of the number of guests. Interpret the meaning of the *x*- and *y*-intercepts.

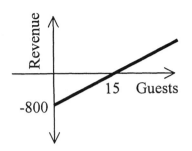

Solution: The *x*-intercept of 15 means that 15 guests must stay for the night in order for the hotel to meet its expenses. The *y*-intercept of -800 means that if no guests stay for the night, the hotel's expenses exceed its revenue by $800.

Directions: Interpret the meaning of the *x*- and *y*-intercepts for each problem.

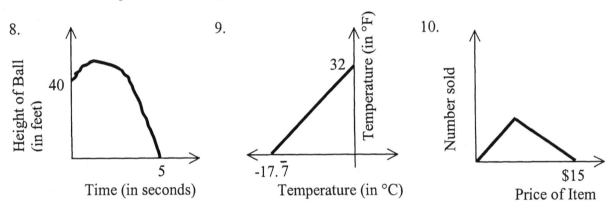

8.

9.

10.

11. Describe a context in which there would be no *x*-intercept.

12. Describe a context in which there would be no *y*-intercept.

Name _____ Date_____

Section 3.1   Solving First-Degree Equations
Lesson Activity – Using Tables to Solve First-Degree Equations

Part A: Make It Equal

The table feature of your graphing calculator can be used to find exact or approximate solutions to an equation. The approach is to find the value of x that makes the two sides of the equation equivalent.

Example: Solve $3x - 4 = -2x + 11$.

Solution:

$Y1 = 3x - 4$ and $Y2 = -2x + 11$

Treat each side of the equation as a function.

Y= Screen:

TblSet Screen:

Table Screen:

Enter each side of the equation as a function in Y= as shown. In the Table Setup, set a starting value of 0 and an increment (Δ Tbl) of 1. This setup means that each equation will be evaluated for a value of $x = 0$, $x = 1$, $x = 2$, and so on.

From the Table Screen, look for the value of x that makes the two equations equal. You may need to scroll with the up- and down-arrow keys to increase or decrease the value of x.

Directions: Solve using the table feature of your calculator.

1. $7x - 9 = -5x + 15$

    $x =$ _____

2. $-3x + 14 = 3x - 4$

    $x =$ _____

3. $10x - 6 = 6x + 14$

    $x =$ _____

4. $-2x - 19 = 4x + 5$

    $x =$ _____

5. $8x - 28 - 4x = 12x + 20$

    $x =$ _____

6. $-2(x + 8) = 7x + 11$

    $x =$ _____

7. $-6(x + 4) = 4 - 2(x + 4)$

    $x =$ _____

8. $3.2(x - 4) = 1.2(x - 4)$

    $x =$ _____

9. $-3(2x + 8) = -2(x - 18)$

    $x =$ _____

10. $\frac{1}{4}x - 14 = -\frac{3}{4}x + 6$

    $x =$ _____

11. $\frac{2}{3}x - 8 = -3x + 14$

    $x =$ _____

12. $\frac{4}{5}x - 7 = 11 - \frac{7}{10}x$

    $x =$ _____

Part B: Decimal Solutions

Example: Solve $3x - 7 = -2x + 4$.

Solution: Use the same technique for this problem.	Y= Screen:	TblSet Screen:	Table Screen:

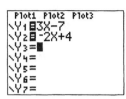

Scrolling through the table you will have difficulty finding the solution since it is not an integer. When the solution to the equation is not an integer value, set a smaller increment in order to zoom in on the solution. You might begin by setting the increment to 0.5. You may need to change the starting value and the increment several times. In the Table Screen shown, notice that the table starts at 2 and increments by 0.1. Observe how the values in Y1 and Y2 are changing.

Directions: Solve using the table feature of your calculator. State answers to the nearest tenth.

13. $4x + 1.5 = 6 - 5x$

$x =$ _____

14. $8 + 3x = -5x + 4$

$x =$ _____

15. $-0.5x + 5 = 2x - 3$

$x =$ _____

16. $7.8 - (x + 2.2) = 5(x - 2)$

$x =$ _____

17. $2.5x - 5.3 = 16.4 - 3.7x$

$x =$ _____

18. $-33.5 + 8x = 3.5(6x + 14.2)$

$x =$ _____

19. $-5(x + 3.2) = 2(7.5 + 2.5x)$

$x =$ _____

20. $8x + 4 = 3x - 2$

$x =$ _____

21. $0.4x - 6 = 3x + 0.5$

$x =$ _____

22. Use the table shown to approximate the solution. Explain your reasoning and describe how to get a more accurate answer.

X	Y1	Y2
-5	9	-10
-4.5	6.5	-7.5
-4	4	-5
-3.5	1.5	-2.5
-3	-1	0
-2.5	-3.5	2.5
-2	-6	5

X= -5

Section 3.2   Applications of First-Degree Equations
Lesson Investigation – The Trail Mix Problem

Part A: Value Mixture Problems

    Problem: The owners of Real Mountain Products are experimenting with different ingredients to combine for a new trail mix. To create a simple trail mix, they want to combine two ingredients that have different prices into a single blend.

    Technique: Use the formula $AC = V$, where A is the amount of the ingredient, C is the cost per unit of the ingredient, and V is the value of the ingredient.

Warm-up Problems

1. How many pounds of peanuts that cost $2.25 per pound must be mixed with 10 pounds of M&M's that cost $3.50 per pound to make a mixture that costs $3 per pound?

	AMOUNT (A)	UNIT COST (C)	VALUE (V)
Peanuts		$2.25	
M&M's	10	$3.50	
Mixture (trail mix)		$3.00	

Solution: Let x = the number of pounds of $2.25 peanuts that are needed. Fill in the chart. To solve, remember that the value of the peanuts and M&M's equals the value of the mixture.

  a. Equation: _____

  b. Solution: _____ pounds of peanuts

2. If Real Mountain Products sells 250 pounds of the mixture for $4.49 per pound, what is their profit? _____

Part B: Problem Set

3. In an attempt to reduce the unit cost of the trail mix, Real Mountain Products decides to add dried fruit to the mixture. It costs $1.80 per pound. Since the dried fruit has the lowest unit cost, the owners decide to use 10 pounds each of peanuts and M&M's. How many pounds of dried fruit should they use to achieve a trail mix that costs $2.50 per pound?

	AMOUNT (A)	UNIT COST (C)	VALUE (V)
Peanuts	10	$2.25	
M&M's	10	$3.50	
Dried Fruit		$1.80	
Mixture (trail mix)		$2.50	

4. In the last problem, if 10 pounds each of dried fruit and M&M's were used, how many pounds of peanuts would be needed to achieve the $2.50 per pound cost of the trail mix?

5. Finally, if 10 pounds each of dried fruit and peanuts were used, how many pounds of M&M's would be needed to achieve the $2.50 per pound cost of the trail mix?

6. If you used equal amounts of each ingredient, what would be a reasonable unit cost for the trail mix? Explain your reasoning.

Name _____ **Date** _____

Section 3.3   Applications to Geometry
Lesson Investigation – Using Technology to Investigate Angle Relationships

Directions: Investigate the graphical relationship between complementary angles using your calculator.

Step 1: In L1 of the stat list editor, enter angle measures from 0° to 90°, incrementing by 10°.

Step 2: In L2, enter the complement of each angle in L1. One way to do this is to position your cursor at the top of the L2 column and enter the equation 90 – L1. Press enter to display the results.

Step 3: Make a scatter plot of the ordered pairs (L1, L2). Set the viewing window. Sketch the plot below.

1. Use the trace key to complete.

   (20, _____)   (40, _____)   (_____, 40)

2. Describe the features of your scatter plot.

Directions: Investigate the graphical relationship between supplementary angles using your calculator.

Step 1: In L3 of the stat list editor, enter angle measures from 0° to 180°, incrementing by 10°.

Step 2: In L4, enter the supplement of each angle in L3. One way to do this is to position your cursor at the top of the L4 column and enter the equation 180 – L3. Press enter to display the results.

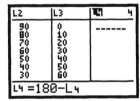

Step 3: Make a scatter plot of the ordered pairs (L3, L4). Set the viewing window. Sketch the plot below.

3. Use the trace key to complete.

   (20, _____)   (90, _____)   (_____, 40)

4. Describe the features of your scatter plot.

Summary

5. As the measure of an angle increases, the measure of its complement _____.

6. As the measure of an angle increases, the measure of its supplement _____.

7. Turn both scatter plots on and display using an appropriate viewing window. Describe how the scatter plots are alike and how they are different.

8. Does every angle have a complement and a supplement? Use your scatter plots to answer.

Section 3.4   Inequalities in One Variable
Lesson Activity – Matching Inequalities with Solutions and Graphs

Directions: Make a copy of the table below and cut on the dotted lines. Work with others in your group to match each inequality with its solution written in interval notation and set-builder notation, along with the graphic solution. There are four parts for each of the eight problems.

Inequality	Interval Notation Solution	Set-builder Notation Solution	Graph of Solution
$2x - 7 \geq 5$	$(-\infty, -1] \cup [2, \infty)$	$\{x \mid -1 \leq x \leq 2\}$	number line, points at -2, 0, 1
$4 - 3x \geq -8$	$[-2, 1]$	$\{x \mid -2 \leq x \leq 1\}$	number line, points at 0, 2
$9x - 4 \geq 3x + 20$	$(-\infty, 4]$	$\{x \mid x \geq 2\}$	number line, points at 0, 4
$3(x - 5) \geq -2(x + 1) - 3$	$[-1, 2]$	$\{x \mid x \geq 6\}$	number line, points at 0, 6
$5x - 7 \geq 3$ or $6 \geq 3x + 9$	$[2, \infty)$	$\{x \mid x \leq 4\}$	number line, points at -1, 0, 2
$5 \leq 3x + 8 \leq 14$	$[6, \infty)$	$\{x \mid x \geq 4\}$	number line, points at 4, 6
$1 \leq -4x + 5 \leq 13$	$(-\infty, 4] \cup [6, \infty)$	$\{x \mid x \leq 4$ or $x \geq 6\}$	number line, points at 0, 4
$2x + 6 \geq 2(2x - 1)$ or $-4x + 2 \geq 8 - 5x$	$[4, \infty)$	$\{x \mid x \leq -1$ or $x \geq 2\}$	number line, points at -1, 0, 2

Section 3.5   Absolute Value Equations and Inequalities
Lesson Activity – Exploring Inequalities and Absolute Values

Part A: Inequalities
Let x = your birth month. (1 = January, 2 = February, ... , 12 = December)
For each of the following phrases, record the months that satisfy the description. Then write an algebraic equation or inequality that describes the solution for each problem. It is understood that x will be a whole number from 1 to 12.

Example: Your birth month is greater than 7.

Solution: Months Satisfying: 8, 9, 10, 11, 12
Inequality: $x > 7$

	Months Satisfying	Equation or Inequality
1. Your birth month is less than 6.	_____	_____
2. Your birth month is less than or equal to 4.	_____	_____
3. Your birth month is greater than 9.	_____	_____
4. Twice your birth month is less than 10.	_____	_____
5. Your birth month is less than 2 or greater than 7.	_____	_____
6. Your birth month is within 2 months of September, inclusive.	_____	_____

Part B: Compound Inequalities

Let x = your birth month. For each of the following phrases, translate the phrase into an absolute value equation or inequality. Then write a compound algebraic equation or inequality that describes the solution for each problem. It is understood that x will be a whole number from 1 to 12.

Example: Your birth month is less than 2 months from March, inclusive.

Solution: Absolute Value Inequality: $|x - 3| \leq 2$
Compound Inequality: $1 \leq x \leq 5$

	Absolute Value Equation/Inequality	Compound Equation/Inequality
7. Your birth month is exactly 2 months from June.	_____	_____
8. Your birth month is exactly 4 months from August.	_____	_____
9. Your birth month is less than 1 month from July, inclusive.	_____	_____
10. Your birth month is more than 3 months from May, exclusive.	_____	_____
11. Your birth month is less than 3 months from September, exclusive.	_____	_____
12. Your birth month is more than 2 months from March, inclusive.	_____	_____

Name _____ Date_____

Section 4.1   Slopes and Graphs of Linear Functions
Lesson Investigation – Using Technology to Investigate $y = mx + b$

Part A: Investigating Changes in Slope

Step 1: In Y=, enter the expression $y = \{1, 2, 3, 6\}x$,
as shown at the right.

Step 2: Graph the equations in the square viewing
window. The calculator substitutes four
different values for m, the slope. The result
will be the graphs of $y = 1x$, $y = 2x$, $y = 3x$,
and $y = 6x$.

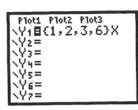 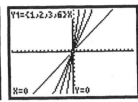

1. Compare the four graphs displayed.
    a. As the slope increases from 1 to 6, how do the graphs change?

    b. What point do all of the graphs have in common?

2. In Y=, enter the expression $y = \{1, 1/2, 1/3, 1/6\}x$. Graph. Compare the four graphs
displayed.
    a. As the slope decreases from 1 to 1/6, how do the graphs change?

    b. How are the four graphs similar to the four graphs in Exercise 1?

3. In Y=, enter the expression $y = \{-4, -2, -1, -1/2, -1/4\}x$. Graph. Compare the five graphs
displayed.
    a. How do the graphs change from a slope of -4 to $-1/4$?

    b. Describe the difference between graphs with positive slopes and graphs with negative
slopes.

4. When the slope of a line is 1 or -1, the line makes a 45° angle with the x-axis. Describe the
angles made by lines for which $|m| > 1$ and also for which $0 < |m| < 1$.

31

Part B: Investigating Changes in y-Intercepts

Step 1: In Y=, enter the expression $y = x + \{1, 2, 5, -3, -6\}$, as shown at the right.

Step 2: Press $\boxed{\text{GRAPH}}$. This will result in the calculator substituting six different values for b, the y-intercept. The result will be the graphs of $y = x + 1$, $y = x + 2$, $y = x + 5$, $y = x - 3$, and $y = x - 6$.

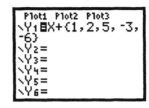
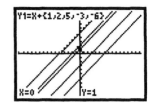

5. Compare the five graphs displayed.
    a. How are the five graphs the same?

    b. How are the five graphs different?

6. Describe what the graph of $y = 3x - 4$ looks like. Do not use your calculator.

Section 4.2   Finding Equations of Straight Lines
Lesson Activity – Investigating Parallel and Perpendicular Lines

Part A: Equations in Standard Form
Equations written in standard form, $Ax + By = C$, can be rewritten in slope-intercept form by solving the equation for y.

$$Ax + By = C \qquad \text{- Standard Form}$$
$$By = -Ax + C \qquad \text{- Subtract Ax from each side.}$$
$$y = -\frac{A}{B}x + \frac{C}{B} \qquad \text{- Divide each side by B.}$$

slope   y-intercept

For an equation written in standard form, $Ax + By = C$, the slope is $-\dfrac{A}{B}$ and the y-intercept is $\dfrac{C}{B}$.

Directions: By inspection, state the slope and y-intercept of each equation.

1. $3x + 5y = 6$

   slope = _____

   y-intercept = _____

2. $-2x + 3y = 1$

   slope = _____

   y-intercept = _____

3. $x - 4y = 8$

   slope = _____

   y-intercept = _____

4. $4x - y = -8$

   slope = _____

   y-intercept = _____

5. $-x + 5y = 1$

   slope = _____

   y-intercept = _____

6. $9x + 5y = -10$

   slope = _____

   y-intercept = _____

Directions: The following linear equations are not in standard form or slope-intercept form. By inspection, state the slope and y-intercept of each equation.

7. $4y - 2x = -4$

   slope = _____

   y-intercept = _____

8. $-6x = 5 + 3y$

   slope = _____

   y-intercept = _____

9. $2x - y + 8 = 0$

   slope = _____

   y-intercept = _____

Part B: Matching

Use the skill from Part A and your knowledge of the slopes of parallel and perpendicular lines to complete this matching activity. Match each equation in Column A with an equation in Column B to which it is parallel, and with an equation in Column C to which it is perpendicular.

	Column A	Column B	Column C
10.	$y = \dfrac{3}{2}x - 7$	A. $6x - 3y = 4$	S. $-4x - 2y = 5$
11.	$y = \dfrac{1}{2}x + 2$	B. $5x + 3y = 0$	T. $3x - 5y = -2$
12.	$y = -2x - 4$	C. $6x - 2y = 7$	U. $-10x + 4y = 5$
13.	$y = -3x - 1$	D. $9x + 3y = -4$	V. $2x - 4y = 5$
14.	$y = 3x + 3$	E. $3x - 6y = -8$	W. $2x - 3y = -2$
15.	$y = -\dfrac{2}{5}x + \dfrac{1}{2}$	F. $-2x - y = 5$	X. $2x + 6y = 5$
16.	$y = -\dfrac{5}{3}x + 6$	G. $6x - 4y = -3$	Y. $4x + 8y = -1$
17.	$y = 2x + \dfrac{1}{4}$	H. $2x + 5y = 10$	Z. $2x - 6y = 9$

Section 4.3   Linear Regression
Lesson Activity – Knot Enough Rope?

Materials Needed: rope (approximately 80 - 100 centimeters), meter stick, graphing calculator

Directions: Your group will gather data about the length of a rope as successive knots are tied. Be consistent and tie each knot to the same degree of tightness. Measure the length of the rope after each knot is tied, rounding all measurements to the nearest half-centimeter. Record your data in the chart.

Number of Knots	Length of Rope (in centimeters)
0	
1	
2	
3	
4	
5	
6	
7	
8	

Helpful Hints and Notes:
The placement of the knots does not matter, but you will need to leave some space between each knot. You may be expected to untie your knots at the conclusion of the activity, so don't make the knots extremely tight.

Quick Sketch:

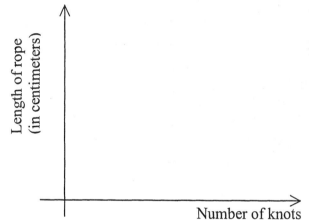

Length of rope (in centimeters)

Number of knots

Calculator Analysis:

Figure 1

Figure 2

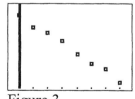

Figure 3

Figure 4

a. In the Stat List Editor enter the number of knots in L1 and the length of rope in L2 (Fig. 1).
b. In the Stat Plot Editor select Plot 1, turn it on, select scatter plot for L1 and L2, and select an icon to be plotted (Fig. 2).
c. Press ZOOM 9 for the calculator to select the appropriate viewing window and reveal the scatter plot (Fig. 3).

d. Perform a linear regression on the data in L1 and L2, and store the regression equation in Y1 (Fig. 4).

e. Press GRAPH again to show the graph of the regression line on the scatter plot.

Directions: Answer the following based upon the data collected.

1. What is the regression equation for the data? (Round values to 2 decimal places.)

2. State the slope and explain its meaning in the context of the problem.

3. State the y-intercept and explain its meaning in the context of the problem.

4. Compare your equation with other groups. If the slopes are different, explain why they might be.

5. Does the thickness of the rope itself have anything to do with the results?

6. Use your equation to predict the length of the rope with 10 knots.

Section 4.4   Linear Inequalities in Two Variables
Lesson Activity – Name That Inequality

Directions: Examine the graphs below. Use your knowledge of the slope and y-intercept of a linear equation to write a linear inequality for each graph. Assume that all inequalities are $\leq$ or $\geq$. All intercepts are integers and the viewing rectangle is $[-5, 5]$ for x and $[-4, 4]$ for y. Use your calculator to test your answer.

1.
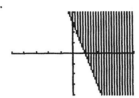

2.
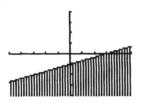

3.
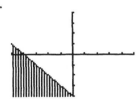

4.

5.
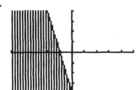

6.
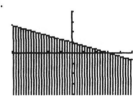

7.
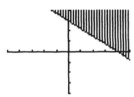

8.
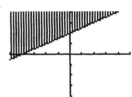

9.
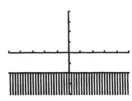

10.
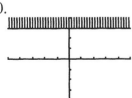

11.
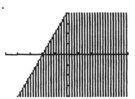

12.
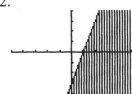

13. The graph shown at the right is a square with vertices at (4, 0), (0, 4), (-4, 0), and (0, -4). Write the four inequalities that have been graphed in order to form the square.

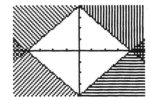